编写委员会

总　主　编：郁云峰

副总主编：于天琪　陈维昌

主　　编：张雅茹　王　乐

副　主　编：易紫婧

编　　者：孙国艳　孙雪娇　朱俊博　孙　柳　孟　皎　丁明辉　刘延利

编辑委员会

主　　任：陈维昌

副　主　任：付彦白

项目负责人：付彦白

项目秘书：武传霞

项目审定：王俊毅

项目成员：武传霞　王巧燕　方兴龙　赫　栗　张　彪

专家委员会（按音序排列）

陈曼倩　哈尔滨职业技术大学

梁赤民　中国–赞比亚职业技术学院

刘建国　哈尔滨职业技术大学

宋　凯　有色金属工业人才中心

赵丽霞　有色金属工业人才中心

崔永华　北京语言大学

梁　宇　北京语言大学

宋继华　北京师范大学

苏英霞　北京语言大学

职通中文
Access to Vocational Chinese

机械制造技术
Mechanical Manufacturing Technology

郁云峰　总主编
于天琪　陈维昌　副总主编
济南职业学院　编

初级篇
Elementary

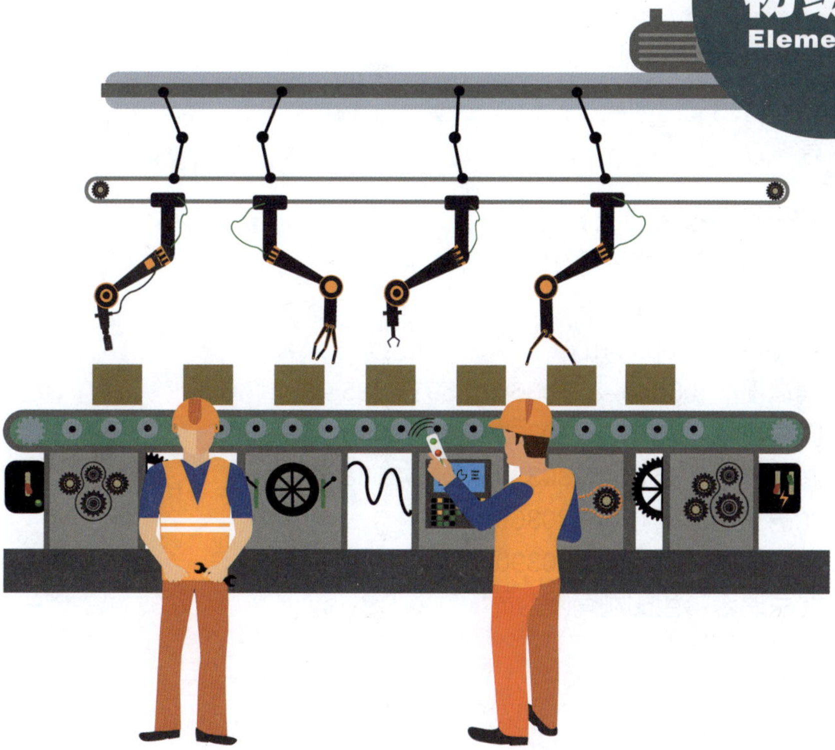

北京语言大学出版社
BEIJING LANGUAGE AND CULTURE UNIVERSITY PRESS

图书在版编目（CIP）数据

机械制造技术．初级篇 / 郁云峰总主编 ；济南职业学院编．-- 北京 ：北京语言大学出版社，2024．11．（“职通中文”系列教材）．-- ISBN 978-7-5619-6652-5

I. H195.4

中国国家版本馆 CIP 数据核字第 20248QX995 号

机械制造技术（初级篇）

JIXIE ZHIZAO JISHU (CHUJIPIAN)

责任编辑：付彦白　武传霞
英文编辑：侯晓娟
排版制作：北京青侣文化创意设计有限公司
责任印制：周　燚

出版发行：北京语言大学出版社
社　　址：北京市海淀区学院路 15 号，100083
网　　址：www.blcup.com
电子信箱：service@blcup.com
电　　话：编辑部　8610-82303647/3592/3395
国内发行　8610-82303650/3591/3648
海外发行　8610-82303365/3080/3668
北语书店　8610-82303653
网购咨询　8610-82303908
印　　刷：北京瑞禾彩色印刷有限公司

版　　次：2024 年 11 月第 1 版　　印　　次：2024 年 11 月第 1 次印刷
开　　本：787 毫米 × 1092 毫米　1/16　　印　　张：20.75
字　　数：248 千字
定　　价：115.00 元

PRINTED IN CHINA
凡有印装质量问题，本社负责调换。售后QQ号1367565611，电话010-82303590

前言

为进一步推动各国学习者中文语言能力和专业技能深度融合，提升学习者围绕特定行业场景、典型工作任务使用中文进行沟通和交流的能力，持续满足中文学习者的职业规划和个人发展需求，实现优质教育资源共享，促进多彩文明交流互鉴，教育部中外语言交流合作中心联合有色金属工业人才中心，根据各国“中文+职业技能”教学发展实际需求，以中国职业院校为依托，组织职业教育、国际中文教育、出版和相关企业等领域的专家，共同研发“职通中文”系列教材及配套教学资源。

“职通中文”系列教材参照《国际中文教育中文水平等级标准》和《职业中文能力等级标准》，分为初、中、高三个等级。各等级均遵循“语言和技能相融合”“好学、好教、好用”的编写理念，根据相关职业的典型工作场景、工作任务和高频用语，设计课文、会话、语言点和练习等板块，不断提升学习者在职业技术领域的中文应用水平和关键技术能力，为学习者尽快熟悉和适应工作环境提供帮助。本系列教材适用于在中国企业从事相关职业工作的各国员工，也适用于在华留学生或长短期培训人员，以及有意向了解中国语言文化和职业技能的学习者。

《机械制造技术（初级篇）》是“职通中文”系列教材之一，适用于中文和技能为零起点的海外中资企业机械制造相关岗位的本土员工。通过学习本教材，海外本土员工在从事机械制造工作时能够与中国技术人员进行简单的沟通交流，能够根据工作现场状况选用合适的工具和方法，能够对常用机械加工设备进行操作、检测和维修，掌握安全常识，识读中国设备上的标记符号，看懂简单的中文说明书，了解中国的相关生产技术标准。

本教材共计30课，分为三大模块，分别是钳工技能、机床加工和焊接操作，教授学习者在运用技能时必需的中文专业词汇和常用表达。在内容整体设计上，教材采取从宏观、中观到微观的三层结构：宏观结构是机械制造技术实际操作流程板块，中观结构是各流程板块包含的具体业务活动，微观结构是每种具体业务活动中机械制造操作的常用语句。

学习者学习本教材后应当可以达到：

1. 在实际工作中能进行钳工、车铣床加工和焊接操作；
2. 掌握机械制造工作中常用的基本词汇；
3. 将动词和名词组合成短语或短句；
4. 能够与中方员工进行简单的工作交流；
5. 在工作中具备初步的跨文化交际能力。

本教材围绕钳工技能、机床加工和焊接操作三大模块，以中方资深员工指导外方新员工的方式展开语言与技能融合教学，始终坚持“以机械制造汉语为主、急用先学、实用够用”的原则，但又兼顾通用中文，与通用中文大纲、标准等有效衔接，通过学习实际工作中的典型语言，实现中文和技能的融合，从而使语言教育与技能教育两方面协调推进。专业词汇坚持选用实际工作中常用的名词；动词则以实用、简洁、重复度高为选择标准，尽量贴合工作场景。句子以短句为主，符合交际性原则和口语语体特征。课文练习多样化，重在帮助学习者巩固对语言的理解和对技能点的掌握。汉字练习则以激发学习者兴趣为主，利用独体字加一笔可以构成新字的结构特点和偏旁构字法等，提升学习者对汉字学习的热情，并逐渐转换其中文学习思维，不过于依赖拼音。

本教材从开发之初就建立了一体化设计理念，将纸质教材、数字教材、电子课件、网络课程等进行整体规划，科学部署，有序推进。研发过程由不同专业背景的人员精细分工，紧密协作，充分磨合，反复试用，不断完善；语言与技能容量科学、平衡，协调了专业技能学习与语言习得之间的关系。

本教材由济南职业学院中德技术学院（现中德技术系）党总支书记、院长张雅茹教授及有多年海外教学经历的对外汉语教研室主任王乐担任主编，具有海外教学经验的国际焊接工程师易紫婧担任副主编，孙国艳、孙雪娇、朱俊博、孙柳、孟皎、丁明辉、刘延利等行企校三方人员参与编写。具体分工是：张雅茹、王乐负责项目顶层设计和统筹，张雅茹、王乐负责统稿工作，丁明辉、孙国艳、易紫婧、刘延利负责提取机械制造各个流程中的工作语言，王乐、易紫婧、孙雪娇负责根据国际中文教学标准和要求对语料进行加工，孟皎、张雅茹负责翻译，朱俊博、孙柳负责了解并反馈教材在海外应用的实际效果。

本教材得到了宋凯、赵丽霞、苏旭勇、尹元华、蒋雪艳等领导的关心和支持，崔永华、苏英霞、梁宇、宋继华、刘建国、梁赤民、陈曼倩等专家学者提出了许多宝贵建议，我们在此表示衷心感谢。本教材还得益于济南职业学院和北京语言大学出版社的鼎力支持和精心指导，在此一并表示感谢。

“职通中文”系列教材的出版和应用能够促进各国“中文＋职业技能”人才的培养，推动当地经济发展，从而为构建人类命运共同体做出积极贡献。由于项目团队学识和相关经验有限，加之时间紧迫，本教材肯定有许多疏漏、不足之处。恳请教材的使用者将发现的问题反馈给我们，以便再版和编写相关教材时改进。

编写团队

2024年11月

Preface

In order to further promote the deep integration of Chinese language proficiency and professional skills among learners from various countries and enhance their ability to communicate and interact in Chinese in specific industry scenarios and typical work tasks, the Center for Language Education and Cooperation under the Ministry of Education, in collaboration with China Nonferrous Metal Industry Talent Center, has organized experts from vocational education, international Chinese education, publishing, and related enterprises to jointly develop the "Access to Vocational Chinese" series of textbooks and supporting teaching resources. Based on the actual needs of "Chinese + Vocational Skills" teaching development in various countries and relying on Chinese vocational colleges, the series aims to continuously meet the career planning and personal development needs of Chinese learners, realize the sharing of high-quality educational resources, and promote exchanges and mutual learning among diverse civilizations.

In reference to *Chinese Proficiency Grading Standards for International Chinese Language Education* and *Chinese Proficiency Standards for Vocational Education*, the "Access to Vocational Chinese" series of textbooks is divided into three levels: elementary, intermediate, and advanced. All the levels follow the writing philosophy of "integrating language and skills" and "being easy to learn, teach, and use." The textbooks are designed around typical work scenarios, work tasks, and high-frequency terms of relevant professions, with sections on texts, conversations, language points, and exercises, continuously improving learners' Chinese application skills and key technical abilities in the vocational and technical fields, providing assistance for learners to quickly familiarize themselves with and adapt to the work environment. This series of textbooks is suitable for international employees engaged in relevant professions in Chinese companies, international students or trainees in China, as well as learners interested in Chinese language, culture, and vocational skills.

Mechanical Manufacturing Technology (Elementary) is one of the "Access to Vocational Chinese" series, suitable for local employees in mechanical manufacturing positions of overseas Chinese-funded enterprises with previous learning experience of Chinese language and working skills. By studying this textbook, local employees abroad can engage in simple communication with Chinese technicians when working in mechanical manufacturing. They can choose appropriate tools and methods according to the work site conditions, operate, inspect, and repair commonly used mechanical processing equipment, understand safety protocols, read markings on Chinese equipment, comprehend simple Chinese instruction manuals, and understand relevant Chinese production technical standards.

This textbook consists of 30 lessons, divided into three major modules: benchwork skills, machine tool processing, and welding operations. It teaches learners the Chinese professional vocabulary and common expressions in applying skills. The overall content design adopts a three-level structure from macro, meso to micro: the macro level is the actual operation section of mechanical manufacturing technology, the meso level refers to the specific business activities contained in each section, and the micro level is the commonly used expressions in the mechanical manufacturing operation in each specific business activity.

After learning this textbook, learners should be able to:

1. Perform benchwork, lathe and milling machining, and welding operations in practical work.

2. Master the basic vocabulary commonly used in mechanical manufacturing work.

3. Combine verbs and nouns into phrases or short sentences.

4. Engage in simple work communication with Chinese colleagues.

5. Possess preliminary cross-cultural communication skills in the workplace.

This textbook highlights three major modules: benchwork skills, machine tool processing, and welding operations. It implements integrated language and technical training through a mentorship program where Chinese senior employees coach new foreigh staff. It consistently adheres to the principle of "prioritizing mechanical manufacturing Chinese as the main focus, learning what's immediately necessary first, and ensuring practical sufficiency" while also considering general Chinese, ensuring effective integration with the general Chinese syllabus, standards, and more. By learning typical language used in actual work, the integration of Chinese language and skills can be achieved, thereby coordinating the advancement of language education and skill education. Specialized terminology is carefully selected based on its common use in practical work, with verbs chosen for their practicality, simplicity, and frequent usage, aiming to fit the work environment as closely as possible. Sentences are primarily short, following the principles of communicative competence and oral style. The exercises in the text are diverse, designed to help learners consolidate their understanding of language and mastery of key skills. Character exercises primarily aim to stimulate learners' interest, utilizing the structural characteristic that a single character can be transformed into a new one by adding a stroke, as well as the method of constructing characters with radicals. This approach enhances learners' enthusiasm for learning Chinese characters and gradually transforms their thinking toward Chinese language learning without overly relying on Pinyin.

From its inception, this textbook has embraced an integrated design concept, with a comprehensive plan that includes printed materials, digital resources, electronic courseware, online courses, and more, all coordinated and implemented in an orderly manner. The development process involves meticulous division of labor, close collaboration among individuals with diverse professional backgrounds, thorough testing, and continuous refinement. The design ensures a scientific balance and coordination between language learning and professional skill acquisition.

This textbook is edited by Professor Zhang Yaru, Party Secretary and Dean of Sino-German Technical School (now the Sino-German Technical Department) at Jinan Vocational College, and Wang Le, Director of the Teaching and Research Office of Chinese as a Foreign Language, who has many years of overseas teaching experience. International welding engineer Yi Zijing, who has extensive experience in overseas teaching, serves as the deputy chief editor. The contributors from industry, enterprises, and college, including Sun Guoyan, Sun Xuejiao, Zhu Junbo, Sun Liu, Meng Jiao, Ding Minghui, Liu Yanli, also participated in the writing process. Specific responsibilities include: Zhang Yaru and Wang Le are responsible for the top-level design and overall coordination of the project; Zhang Yaru and Wang Le are in charge of overall manuscript coordination; Ding Minghui, Sun Guoyan, Yi Zijing and Liu Yanli are responsible for extracting the working language from various processes of mechanical manufacturing; Wang Le, Yi Zijing, and Sun Xuejiao are responsible for processing the materials according to the standards and requirements of international Chinese language education; Meng Jiao and Zhang Yaru are responsible for translation, and Zhu Junbo and Sun Liu are responsible for providing feedback on the practical effects of the textbook's application overseas.

This textbook has received the care and support of leaders such as Song Kai, Zhao Lixia, Su Xuyong, Yin Yuanhua, and Jiang Xueyan. We are deeply grateful for the invaluable suggestions provided by esteemed experts and scholars, including Cui Yonghua, Su Yingxia, Liang Yu, Song Jihua, Liu Jianguo, Liang Chimin, and Chen Manqian. We would also like to extend our sincere thanks to Jinan Vocational College and Beijing Language and Culture University Press for their strong support and meticulous guidance, which greatly contributed to the success of this textbook.

The publication and application of the "Access to Vocational Chinese" series of textbooks aim to develop talents with "Chinese + Vocational Skills" across the globe, promote local economic development, and make positive contributions to building a community with a shared future for mankind. Due to limited knowledge and relevant experience of the project team, as well as time constraints, this textbook is inevitably subject to many deficiencies that need improvement. We kindly ask users of this textbook to provide feedback on any issues discovered, so that we can make improvements in future editions and related materials.

Compiling team
November 2024

词类简称表
List of Abbreviations of Parts of Speech

词性 Part of speech	英译 English	简称 Abbreviation
名词 míngcí	noun	*n.*
专有名词 zhuānyǒu míngcí	proper noun	*pn.*
代词 dàicí	pronoun	*pron.*
数词 shùcí	numeral	*num.*
量词 liàngcí	measure word	*m.*
数量词 shùliàngcí	quantifier	*q.*
动词 dòngcí	verb	*v.*
能愿动词 néngyuàn dòngcí	optative	*opt.*
形容词 xíngróngcí	adjective	*adj.*
副词 fùcí	adverb	*adv.*
介词 jiècí	preposition	*prep.*
连词 liáncí	conjunction	*conj.*
助词 zhùcí	particle	*part.*
叹词 tàncí	interjection	*int.*
前缀 qiánzhuì	prefix	*pref.*
后缀 hòuzhuì	suffix	*suf.*
短语 duǎnyǔ	phrase	*phr.*

目录 Contents

第 1 课 认识员工 Lesson 1 Meeting Employees ············ 1

第 2 课 钳工安全 Lesson 2 The Safety of Benchwork ····· 10

第 3 课 划线 Lesson 3 Scribing ························ 20

第 4 课 装夹工件 Lesson 4 Clamping Workpieces ········ 30

第 5 课 换锯条 Lesson 5 Replacing Saw Blades ········· 40

第 6 课 锯割工件 Lesson 6 Sawing Workpieces ··········· 51

第 7 课 选择锉刀 Lesson 7 Choosing a File ··············· 60

第 8 课 锉削平面 Lesson 8 Filing Flat Surfaces ············ 71

第 9 课 检测平面度 Lesson 9 Testing Planeness ············· 81

第 10 课 开关钻床 Lesson 10 Switching on/off Drilling Machines ····················· 91

第 11 课 打样冲眼 Lesson 11 Punching ······················ 102

第 12 课 加工通孔 Lesson 12 Processing Through Holes ···· 112

第 13 课 加工内螺纹 Lesson 13 Processing Internal Threads ···· 123

第 14 课 机床加工安全 Lesson 14 The Safety of Machine Tool Processing ·················· 133

第 15 课 开关车床 Lesson 15 Switching on/off Lathes ······ 143

第 16 课 装夹轴类毛坯件 Lesson 16 Clamping Shaft-Type Blanks ··· 153

第 17 课 安装车刀 Lesson 17 Installing Turning Tools ······ 164

第 18 课 加工轴类零件 Lesson 18 Processing Shaft-Type Parts························ 175

第 19 课	开关铣床	Lesson 19	Switching on/off Milling Machines ······ 185
第 20 课	装夹平面类毛坯件	Lesson 20	Clamping Flat-Type Blanks ······ 196
第 21 课	安装铣刀	Lesson 21	Installing Milling Tools ······ 207
第 22 课	加工平面类零件	Lesson 22	Processing Flat-Type Parts ······ 218
第 23 课	焊接安全	Lesson 23	The Safety of Welding ······ 229
第 24 课	准备电弧焊机	Lesson 24	Preparing Arc Welding Machines ······ 240
第 25 课	电弧焊的操作	Lesson 25	Operating Arc Welding ······ 252
第 26 课	清理焊缝	Lesson 26	Cleaning Welding Seams ······ 263
第 27 课	目测焊接结果	Lesson 27	Visually Inspecting Welding Results ······ 274
第 28 课	超声波检测	Lesson 28	Ultrasonic Testing ······ 285
第 29 课	准备二保焊	Lesson 29	Preparing for CO_2 Welding ······ 295
第 30 课	二保焊的操作	Lesson 30	Operating CO_2 Welding ······ 306

第1课 Lesson 1

Rènshi yuángōng
认识员工
Meeting Employees

热身 Warm-up

图文连线。**Match the pictures with the words.**

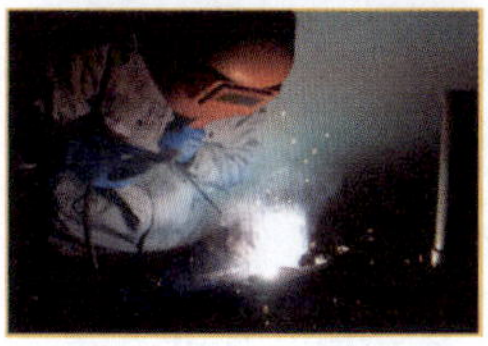

	chēgōng 车工	benchwork
	hàngōng 焊工	milling work
	qiángōng 钳工	lathe work
	xǐgōng 铣工	welding work

学习生词 Words and Expressions 01-01

1	认识	rènshi	*v.*	to meet
2	员工	yuángōng	*n.*	employee(s)
3	我	wǒ	*pron.*	I
4	叫	jiào	*v.*	to be named; to be called
5	是	shì	*v.*	to be (am / is / are)
6	会	huì	*opt.*	to be able to
7	干	gàn	*v.*	to do
8	钳工	qiángōng	*n.*	benchwork
9	车工	chēgōng	*n.*	lathe work
10	铣工	xǐgōng	*n.*	milling (work)
11	和	hé	*conj.*	and
12	焊工	hàngōng	*n.*	welding (work)
13	他	tā	*pron.*	he
14	新	xīn	*adj.*	new
15	想	xiǎng	*v.*	to want
16	学	xué	*v.*	to learn; to study

专有名词 Proper Nouns

1	马明	Mǎ Míng	*pn.*	Ma Ming
2	中方	Zhōngfāng	*pn.*	Chinese
3	杰克	Jiékè	*pn.*	Jack (an English name)

词语练习 Word Exercises

1. 认读词语。Recognize the words.

qiángōng
钳工

chēgōng
车工

xǐgōng
铣工

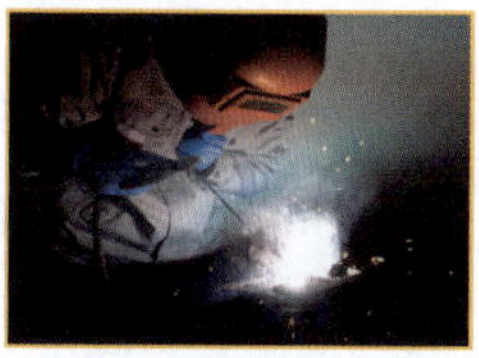

hàngōng
焊工

2. 根据拼音选择正确的词语。 Choose the correct words based on Pinyin.

❶	qiángōng	( )	A. 钳工	B. 车工
❷	xǐgōng	( )	A. 铣工	B. 焊工
❸	chēgōng	( )	A. 铣工	B. 车工
❹	hàngōng	( )	A. 车工	B. 焊工

学习课文 Text 01-02

Rènshi yuángōng
认识员工

Wǒ jiào Mǎ Míng. Wǒ shì Zhōngfāng yuángōng. Wǒ huì gàn qiángōng、
我叫马明。我是中方员工。我会干钳工、

chēgōng、xǐgōng hé hàngōng. Tā jiào Jiékè. Tā shì xīn yuángōng.
车工、铣工和焊工。他叫杰克。他是新员工。

Tā xiǎng xué qiángōng hé chēgōng.
他想学钳工和车工。

Meeting Employees

My name is Ma Ming. I am a Chinese employee. I can do benchwork, lathe work, milling, and welding. His name is Jack. He is a new employee. He wants to learn benchwork and lathe work.

课文练习 Text Exercises

1. 根据课文内容选择正确答案。Choose the correct answers according to the text.

1 马明是中方________。 A. 员工 B. 问题

2 杰克是________员工。 A. 学 B. 新

3 马明会干钳工、车工、铣工和________。 A. 焊工 B. 员工

4 ________想学钳工和车工。 A. 杰克 B. 马明

2. 选择合适的词语填空。Choose the appropriate words to fill in the blanks.

A. 干 B. 学 C. 会 D. 叫

1 他________杰克。

2 马明________干钳工。

3 杰克想________车工。

4 马明会________铣工。

学习语法 Grammar

语法点 1 Grammar Point 1

"是"字句 "是" Sentence

表示等同或类属。结构为"A是B"。否定式为"A不(bú, not)是B"。

The "是" sentence indicates equivalence or category. The structure is "A 是 B". The negative expression is "A 不是 B".

Wǒ shì xīn yuángōng.
1. 我是新员工。 I am a new employee.

Tā shì Zhōngfāng yuángōng.
2. 他是中方员工。 He is a Chinese employee.

Wǒ shì lǎoshī.
3. 我是老师。 I am a teacher.

语法点 1 练习 Exercise on Grammar Point 1

根据课文选择正确的词语。**Choose the correct words according to the text.**

Jiékè ______ xīn yuángōng.
1. 杰克________新员工。 A. 是 (shì) B. 不是 (bú shì)

Mǎ Míng ______ Zhōngfāng yuángōng.
2. 马明________中方员工。 A. 是 (shì) B. 不是 (bú shì)

Jiékè ______ chēgōng.
3. 杰克________车工。 A. 是 (shì) B. 不是 (bú shì)

Mǎ Míng ______ lǎoshī.
4. 马明________老师。 A. 是 (shì) B. 不是 (bú shì)

语法点 2　Grammar Point 2

能愿动词：会　The Optative: 会

表示有能力做某事，强调通过学习得到某种能力。否定形式是“不会”。

“会” means “to be able to”, emphasizing the ability acquired through learning. Its negative form is “不会”.

1. Wǒ huì gàn qiángōng.
   我 会 干 钳工。 I can do benchwork.
2. Mǎ Míng huì gàn chēgōng.
   马 明 会 干 车工。 Ma Ming can do lathe work.
3. Xīn yuángōng bú huì gàn hàngōng.
   新 员工 不 会 干 焊工。 New employees cannot do welding.

语法点 2 练习　Exercise on Grammar Point 2

连词成句。**Rearrange the following words to make sentences.**

例如：

huì　①会　gàn chēgōng　②干 车工　wǒ　③我

③①②

1. Mǎ Míng　①马 明　gàn qiángōng　②干 钳工　huì　③会

   ____

2. huì　①会　tā　②他　gàn xǐgōng　③干 铣工

   ____

3 ①干焊工（gàn hàngōng） ②我（wǒ） ③会（huì）

____

4 ①你（nǐ） ②会（huì） ③干车工（gàn chēgōng）

____

汉字书写 Writing Chinese Characters

yī 一
一 一 一 一 一

èr 二 二
二 二 二 二 二

sān 三 三 三
三 三 三 三 三

gōng 工 工 工
工 工 工 工 工

文化拓展 Culture Insight

中国概况

中国位于亚洲东部，人口超过14亿，是世界上人口最多的国家之一。中国面积广阔，是世界陆地面积第三大的国家。首都是北京，上海、广州等城市是重要的经济中心。中国的文化古老而深厚，56个民族在悠久的历史中创造出多元一体的中华文化。传统的书法、绘画、舞蹈，吸引着每一位来到中国的游客。中国菜也享有盛名，很多地区都有自己独特的美食。

Overview of China

China is located in the eastern part of Asia, with a population exceeding 1.4 billion, making it one of the most populous countries in the world. China has a vast area and is the third-largest country in the world by land area. The capital is Beijing, and cities like Shanghai and Guangzhou are important economic centers. China's culture is ancient and profound, with 56 ethnic groups creating a unified yet diverse Chinese culture over a long history. Traditional calligraphy, painting, and dance attract every visitor to China. Chinese cuisine is also famous, with many regions having their own unique dishes.

小结 Summary

词语 Words

朗读下列词语。Read the following words.

车工	钳工	铣工	焊工
会	干	想	学

语法 Grammar

熟读句子。Read the following sentences.

1. 我是中方员工。
2. 他是新员工。
3. 我会干钳工。
4. 马明会干车工。

课文理解 Text Comprehension

选择合适的词语填空。Choose the appropriate words to fill in the blanks.

A. 中方员工　B. 新员工　C. 钳工　D. 车工　E. 铣工　F. 焊工

1. 杰克是________。
2. 马明是________。
3. 马明会干________、________、________和________。
4. 杰克想学________和________。

第2课 Lesson 2

Qiángōng ānquán

钳工安全

The Safety of Benchwork

复习 Revision

根据词语选图片。**Choose the right pictures according to the words.**

A

B

C

D

❶ 车工（　　）

❷ 钳工（　　）

❸ 铣工（　　）

❹ 焊工（　　）

热身 Warm-up

选择正确的图片。Choose the right pictures.

A
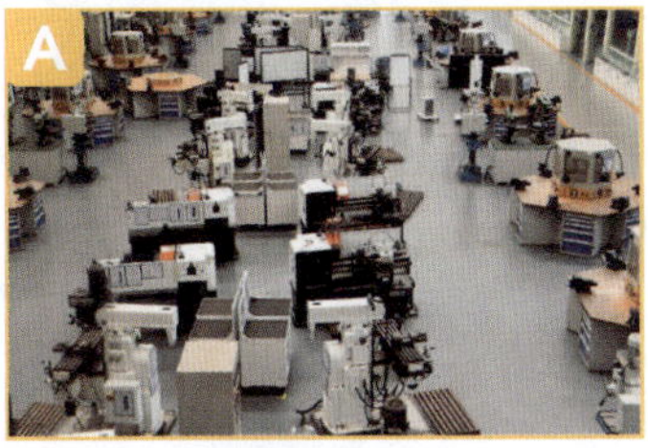
B

C
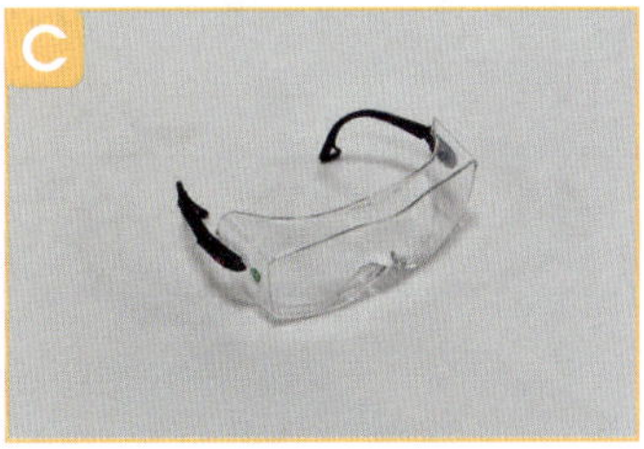
D

E

1. gōngzuòxié 工作鞋 work shoes (　　)
2. ānquánmào 安全帽 safety cap (　　)
3. gōngzuòfú 工作服 work clothes (　　)
4. fánghù yǎnjìng 防护眼镜 protective glasses (　　)
5. chējiān 车间 workshop (　　)

学习生词 Words and Expressions 02-01

1	安全	ānquán	*n.*	safety
2	在	zài	*prep.*	in or at

3	车间	chējiān	*n.*	workshop
4	工作	gōngzuò	*v.*	to work
5	要	yào	*opt.*	should
6	穿	chuān	*v.*	to wear; to put on
7	什么	shénme	*pron.*	what
8	工作服	gōngzuòfú	*n.*	work clothes
9	工作鞋	gōngzuòxié	*n.*	work shoes
10	戴	dài	*v.*	to wear; to put on
11	安全帽	ānquánmào	*n.*	safety cap
12	吗	ma	*part.*	*an interrogative modal particle*
13	防护眼镜	fánghù yǎnjìng	*phr.*	protective glasses
14	注意	zhùyì	*v.*	to pay attention to
15	用电安全	yòng diàn ānquán	*phr.*	electrical safety

词语练习 Word Exercises

1. 看图选词。Look at the pictures and choose the correct words.

❶ 

（　　）　A. 工作服　　B. 工作鞋

❷ 

（　　）　A. 车间　　B. 员工

3  (　　) A. 安全帽　B. 工作服

4 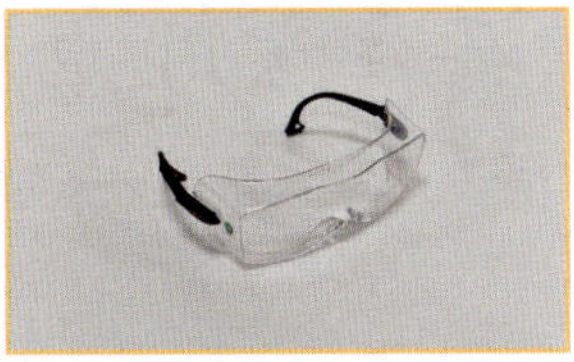 (　　) A. 防护眼镜　B. 工作鞋

2. 朗读词语搭配。Read the collocations.

1 chuān 穿	gōngzuòfú 工作服	2 dài 戴	ānquánmào 安全帽
	gōngzuòxié 工作鞋		fánghù yǎnjìng 防护眼镜

学习课文 Text 02-02

Qiángōng ānquán
钳工安全

Jiékè: Zài chējiān gōngzuò, qiángōng yào chuān shénme?
杰克：在车间工作，钳工要穿什么？

Mǎ Míng: Chuān gōngzuòfú hé gōngzuòxié.
马明：穿工作服和工作鞋。

Jiékè: Dài ānquánmào ma?
杰克：戴安全帽吗？

Mǎ Míng: Dài ānquánmào hé fánghù yǎnjìng. Yào zhùyì yòng diàn ānquán.
马明：戴安全帽和防护眼镜。要注意用电安全。

The Safety of Benchwork

Jack: What should be worn while doing benchwork in the workshop?

Ma Ming: We should wear work clothes and work shoes.

Jack: Should we wear a safety cap?

Ma Ming: Yes, we need to wear a safety cap and protective glasses and be aware of electrical safety.

课文练习 Text Exercises

1. 根据课文内容判断正误。True or False.

1. 在车间工作，要穿工作服。（　　）
2. 在车间工作，要戴安全帽。（　　）
3. 在车间工作，不要戴防护眼镜。（　　）
4. 要注意用电安全。（　　）

2. 选择合适的词语填空。**Choose the appropriate words to fill in the blanks.**

A. 防护眼镜　　B. 车间　　C. 用电安全　　D. 工作鞋

1. 钳工在________工作。
2. 在车间工作，钳工要穿工作服和________。
3. 在车间工作，要戴安全帽和________。
4. 要注意________。

学习语法 Grammar

语法点 1 Grammar Point 1

疑问代词：什么　The Interrogative Pronoun: 什么

"什么"用在疑问句中，对事物进行提问。

"什么" is used in interrogative sentences to inquire about things.

1. Zài chējiān gōngzuò, qiángōng yào chuān shénme?
   在车间工作，钳工要穿什么？
   What should be worn while doing benchwork in the workshop?
2. Yào zhùyì shénme?
   要注意什么？What should be paid attention to?
3. Mǎ Míng huì gàn shénme?
   马明会干什么？What can Ma Ming do?

语法点 1 练习　Exercise on Grammar Point 1

选择正确的答案。Choose the right answers.

Xīn yuángōng jiào shénme?
1 新 员工 叫 什么？（　　）

Jiékè
A. 杰克

gōngzuòfú
B. 工作服

Nǐ jiào shénme míngzi?
2 你 叫 什么 名字？（　　）

Mǎ Míng
A. 马 明

qiángōng
B. 钳工

Nǐ xiǎng xué shénme?
3 你 想 学 什么？（　　）

chēgōng
A. 车工

fánghù yǎnjìng
B. 防护 眼镜

Zài chējiān gōngzuò, qiángōng yào chuān shénme?
4 在 车间 工作， 钳工 要 穿 什么？（　　）

gōngzuòfú hé gōngzuòxié
A. 工作服 和 工作鞋

yòng diàn ānquán
B. 用 电 安全

语法点 2　Grammar Point 2

语气助词：吗　The Modal Particle: 吗

"吗"用在疑问句末，表示疑问的语气。

"吗" is used at the end of a question to indicate a questioning tone.

Zài chējiān gōngzuò yào dài ānquánmào ma?
1 在 车间 工 作 要 戴 安全帽 吗？
Should we wear a safety cap in the workshop?

Zài chējiān gōngzuò yào chuān gōngzuòfú ma?
2 在 车间 工 作 要 穿 工作服 吗？
Should we wear work clothes in the workshop?

Mǎ Míng huì gàn qiángōng ma?
3 马 明 会 干 钳工 吗？ Can Ma Ming do the benchwork?

语法点 2 练习 Exercise on Grammar Point 2

用"吗"字提问，并朗读出来。**Ask questions with "吗" and read them aloud.**

例如：

Zài chējiān gōngzuò yào dài ānquánmào.
在车间工作要戴安全帽。

Zài chējiān gōngzuò yào dài ānquánmào ma?
在车间工作要戴安全帽吗？

1. Tā shì chēgōng.
他是车工。

______________________________________?

2. Zài chējiān gōngzuò yào chuān gōngzuòxié.
在车间工作要穿工作鞋。

______________________________________?

3. Zài chējiān gōngzuò yào dài fánghù yǎnjìng.
在车间工作要戴防护眼镜。

______________________________________?

4. Zài chējiān gōngzuò yào chuān gōngzuòfú.
在车间工作要穿工作服。

______________________________________?

汉字书写 Writing Chinese Characters

shí 十 十
十 十 十 十 十

tǔ 土 土 土
土 土 土 土 土

gàn 干 干 干

干 干 干 干 干

wáng 王 王 王 王

王 王 王 王 王

职业拓展 Career Insight

钳工的分类

钳工分为普通钳工、机修钳工和工具钳工。其中，普通钳工主要负责零件的加工、修整和装配。机修钳工主要负责各种机械设备的维护和修理。工具钳工主要负责工具、模具、刀具的设计、制造和修理。钳工共设五个职业技能等级，分别为初级、中级、高级、技师、高级技师。

Classification of Benchwork

Benchwork is divided into ordinary benchwork, mechanical benchwork, and tool benchwork. Ordinary benchwork is mainly responsible for the processing, trimming and assembling of workpieces. Mechanical benchwork is mainly responsible for the maintenance and repair of various mechanical equipment. Tool benchwork is mainly responsible for the designing, manufacturing, and repairing of tools, molds, and cutting tools. There are five levels of benchwork: beginner, intermediate, senior, technician, and senior technician, respectively.

小结 Summary

词语 Words

朗读下列词语。Read the following words.

穿	工作鞋	工作服
戴	安全帽	防护眼镜

语法 Grammar

熟读句子。Read the following sentences.

1. 在车间工作，钳工要穿什么？
2. 你叫什么？
3. 在车间工作要戴安全帽吗？
4. 在车间工作要穿工作服吗？

课文理解 Text Comprehension

选择合适的词语填空。Choose the appropriate words to fill in the blanks.

A. 防护眼镜　B. 用电安全　C. 工作服　D. 工作鞋　E. 安全帽

1 在车间工作，钳工要穿________和________。

3 戴________吗？

4 戴安全帽和________。

4 注意________。

Huàxiàn

第3课 划线

Lesson 3 Scribing

复习 Revision

根据词语选图片。**Choose the right pictures according to the words.**

A

B

D

C

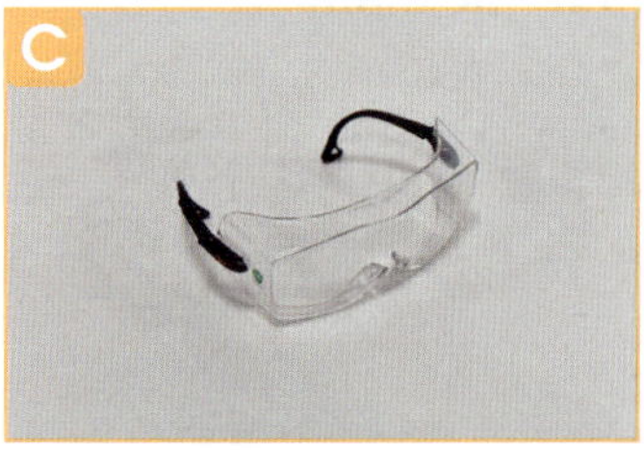

E

1. 工作鞋（　　）
2. 安全帽（　　）
3. 防护眼镜（　　）
4. 工作服（　　）
5. 车间（　　）

热身 Warm-up

选择正确的图片。**Choose the right pictures.**

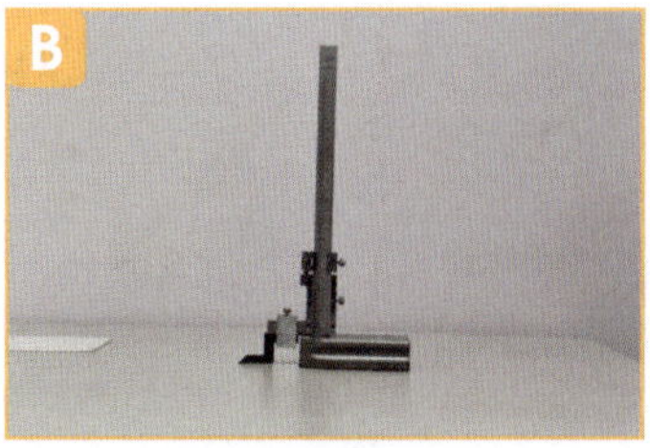

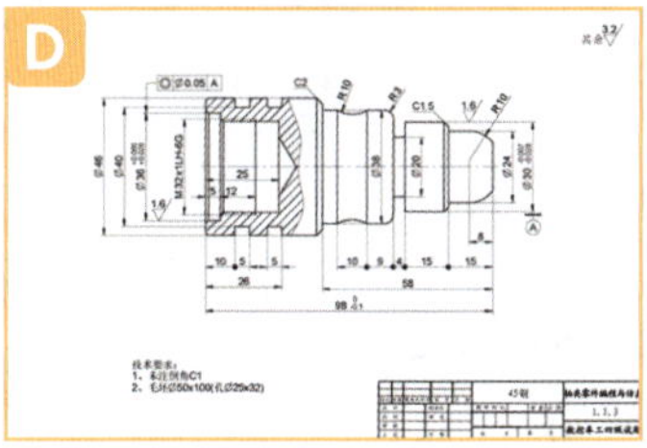

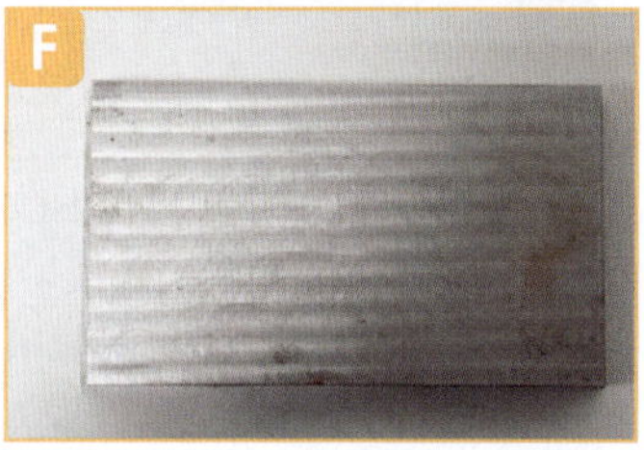

1. fāngxiāng 方箱 square box (　　)
2. huàxiàn píngtái 划线平台 scribing platform (　　)
3. gōngjiàn 工件 workpiece (　　)
4. túzhǐ 图纸 drawing (　　)
5. píngmiàn 平面 plane (　　)
6. gāodùchǐ 高度尺 height gauge (　　)

学习生词 Words and Expressions 03-01

1	划线	huàxiàn	*v.*	to scribe
2	平台	píngtái	*n.*	platform
3	上	shang	*n.*	above; upon; on

4	用	yòng	*prep.*	to use
5	高度尺	gāodùchǐ	*n.*	height gauge
6	工件	gōngjiàn	*n.*	workpiece
7	放在	fàng zài	*phr.*	to place; to put
8	贴紧	tiējǐn	*phr.*	to be tightly attached to
9	方箱	fāngxiāng	*n.*	square box
10	看	kàn	*v.*	to look at
11	图纸	túzhǐ	*n.*	drawing
12	调	tiáo	*v.*	to adjust
13	扶紧	fújǐn	*phr.*	to hold tightly
14	的	de	*part.*	*a particle meaning "of"*
15	平面	píngmiàn	*n.*	plane
16	清晰	qīngxī	*adj.*	clear, distinct

词语练习 Word Exercises

1. 看图选词。Look at the pictures and choose the correct words.

❶ 　(　　)　A. 工件　B. 工作鞋

❷ 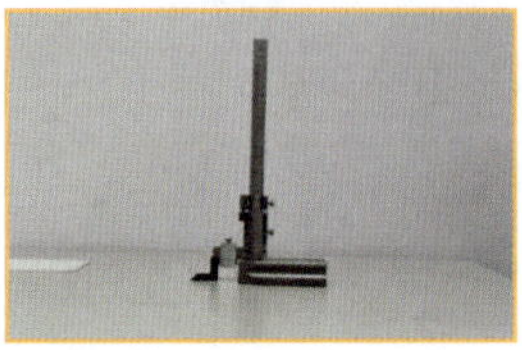　(　　)　A. 图纸　B. 高度尺

3 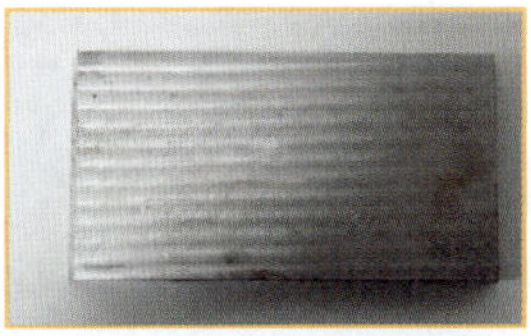 (　　) A. 平面　　B. 工作服

4  (　　) A. 划线平台　　B. 方箱

2. 选择正确的拼音。Choose the correct Pinyin.

A. gāodùchǐ　　B. fāngxiāng　　C. huàxiàn píngtái

D. gōngjiàn　　E. píngmiàn　　F. túzhǐ

1 图纸（　　）　2 高度尺（　　）　3 平面（　　）

4 划线平台（　　）　5 方箱（　　）　4 工件（　　）

学习课文 Text 03-02

Huàxiàn
划线

Zài huàxiàn píngtái shang, yòng gāodùchǐ huàxiàn. Gōngjiàn fàng zài
在划线平台上，用高度尺划线。工件放在

píngtái shang, tiējǐn fāngxiāng. Kàn túzhǐ, tiáo gāodùchǐ. Fújǐn
平台上，贴紧方箱。看图纸，调高度尺。扶紧

gōngjiàn, zài gōngjiàn de píngmiàn shang huàxiàn. Huàxiàn yào qīngxī.
工件，在工件的平面上划线。划线要清晰。

Scribing

On the scribing platform, a height gauge is used for scribing. The workpiece is placed on the platform and tightly attached to the square box. Read the drawings and then adjust the height gauge. Hold the workpiece tightly and scribe a line on the plane of the workpiece. The line must be clear.

课文练习 Text Exercises

1. 根据课文内容选择正确答案。Choose the correct answers according to the text.

1 在划线平台上，用________划线。　A. 工作鞋　B. 高度尺

2 ________放在平台上，贴紧方箱。　A. 图纸　B. 工件

3 看________，调高度尺。　A. 方箱　B. 图纸

4 扶紧工件，在工件的________上划线。　A. 平面　B. 图纸

2. 选择合适的词语填空。Choose the appropriate words to fill in the blanks.

A. 扶紧　B. 放在　C. 用　D. 看

1 ________高度尺划线。

2 工件________平台上，贴紧方箱。

3 ________图纸，调高度尺。

4 左手________工件，右手用高度尺在工件的平面上划线。

学习语法 Grammar

语法点1 Grammar Point 1

介词：在 The Preposition: 在

基本结构为“在 + 场所 + 动词 / 动词短语”，表示在某处做某事。

The basic structure is “在 + place + verb/verb phrase”, indicates doing something in a certain place.

1. Zài gōngjiàn de píngmiàn shang huàxiàn.
   在 工件 的 平面 上 划线。Scribe a line on the plane of the workpiece.
2. Zài fāngxiāng shang huàxiàn.
   在 方箱 上 划线。Scribe on the square box.
3. Zài chējiān chuān gōngzuòfú.
   在 车间 穿 工作服。Wear work clothes in the workshop.

语法点1练习 Exercise on Grammar Point 1

连词成句。**Rearrange the following words to make sentences.**

例如：

huàxiàn píngtái shang　huàxiàn　zài
①划线 平台 上　②划线　③在

③①②

1. zài　huàxiàn　gōngjiàn shang
   ①在　②划线　③工件 上

   ____

2. chuān gōngzuòxié　zài　chējiān
   ①穿 工作鞋　②在　③车间

   ____

3 ①在 zài ②平面 上 píngmiàn shang ③划线 huàxiàn

____

4 ①在 zài ②车间 chējiān ③戴 安全帽 dài ānquánmào

____

语法点 2 Grammar Point 2

能愿动词：要 The Optative: 要

用在动词前，表示应该（做什么），用于提出要求。否定式为“不要”。

It is used before a verb to indicate what should be done. It is used to make requests. The negative form is “不要”.

1. Huàxiàn yào qīngxī.
划线 要 清晰。The line should be clear.

2. Huàxiàn yào yòng gāodùchǐ.
划线 要 用 高度尺。Use a height gauge to scribe.

3. Zài chējiān gōngzuò yào chuān gōngzuòfú.
在 车间 工作 要 穿 工作服。
Wear work clothes when working in the workshop.

语法点 2 练习 Exercise on Grammar Point 2

根据课文选择正确的词语。Choose the correct words according to the text.

1. Zài chējiān shí, yào ________ gōngzuòfú hé gōngzuòxié.
在 车间 时，要________工作服 和 工作鞋。 A. 穿 chuān B. 戴 dài

2. Huàxiàn yào ________.
划线 要________。 A. 清晰 qīngxī B. 上 shang

3. Yào ________ yòng diàn ānquán.
要________用 电 安全。 A. 穿 chuān B. 注意 zhùyì

4. Huàxiàn yào ________ gāodùchǐ.
划线 要________高度尺。 A. 戴 dài B. 用 yòng

汉字书写 Writing Chinese Characters

rén 人

dà 大

gè 个

tiān 天

文化拓展 Culture Insight

指南针

指南针是中国古代“四大发明”之一。早在战国时期，中国的祖先就已发现了磁石吸铁和指向的特性。战国时期的《韩非子》一书中即提到了用磁石制成的司南，司南就是指南的意思。司南由“勺子”和“地盘”两部分组成。司南勺由整块磁石制成，磁石的指极性使勺子的长柄总是指向南方。

Compasses

The compass is one of the Four Great Inventions of ancient China. As early as the Warring States Period, Chinese ancestors had discovered the properties of magnets, including their ability to attract iron and indicate direction. In the book *Han Feizi* from the Warring States Period, *sinan* made of magnets is mentioned, meaning "to point south". *Sinan* consists of two parts: a spoon and a plate. The *sinan* spoon is made from a single piece of magnet, and the polarity of the magnet causes the long handle of the spoon to always point south.

小结 Summary

词语 Words

朗读下列词语。**Read the following words.**

看	调	图纸	清晰
划线平台	平面	高度尺	方箱

语法 Grammar

熟读句子。**Read the following sentences.**

1. 在划线平台上，用高度尺划线。
2. 工件放在平台上，贴紧方箱。

3 划线要清晰。

4 在车间工作要穿工作服。

课文理解 Text Comprehension

把下列句子按正确步骤排列。**Sort the following sentences according to the correct steps.**

1 贴紧方箱。

2 划线要清晰。

3 工件放在平台上。

4 看图纸，调高度尺。

5 在工件的平面上划线。

___③___ → ______ → ___④___ → ______ → ______

第4课 Lesson 4

Zhuāngjiā gōngjiàn

装夹工件

Clamping Workpieces

复习 Revision

根据图片，在正确的词语后面打“√”。Tick “√” after the correct words according to the pictures.

❶ 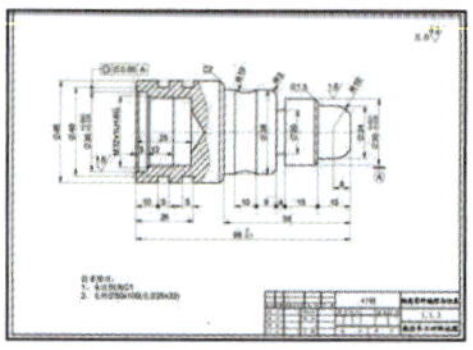

A. 图纸 (　　)

B. 平面 (　　)

❷ 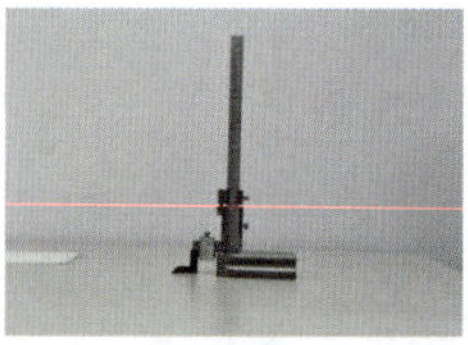

A. 高度尺 (　　)

B. 工件 (　　)

❸ 

A. 划线平台 (　　)

B. 车间 (　　)

❹ 

A. 工作鞋 (　　)

B. 方箱 (　　)

热身 Warm-up

选择正确的图片。**Choose the right pictures.**

1. nìshízhēn 逆时针 anticlockwise (　　)
2. shǒubǐng 手柄 handle (　　)
3. qiánkǒu 钳口 jaw (　　)
4. shùnshízhēn 顺时针 clockwise (　　)
5. qiángōngtái 钳工台 vice bench (　　)
6. táihǔqián 台虎钳 bench vice (　　)

学习生词 Words and Expressions 04-01

1	装夹	zhuāngjiā	*v.*	to clamp
2	台虎钳	táihǔqián	*n.*	bench vice
3	哪儿	nǎr	*pron.*	where
4	钳工台	qiángōngtái	*n.*	vice bench

5	有	yǒu	*v.*	there be; to have
6	几	jǐ	*num.*	how many
7	步	bù	*n.*	step
8	三	sān	*num.*	three
9	逆时针	nìshízhēn	*adj.*	anticlockwise; counterclockwise
10	转	zhuàn	*v.*	to turn
11	手柄	shǒubǐng	*n.*	handle
12	打开	dā//kāi	*v.*	to open
13	钳口	qiánkǒu	*n.*	jaw
14	放入	fàngrù	*phr.*	to put in
15	顺时针	shùnshízhēn	*adj.*	clockwise
16	闭合	bìhé	*v.*	to close
17	夹紧	jiājǐn	*phr.*	to clamp tightly

词语练习 Word Exercises

1. 看图选词。Look at the pictures and choose the correct words.

❶  （　　）　A. 钻床　　B. 钳工台

❷  （　　）　A. 台虎钳　　B. 高度尺

❸ 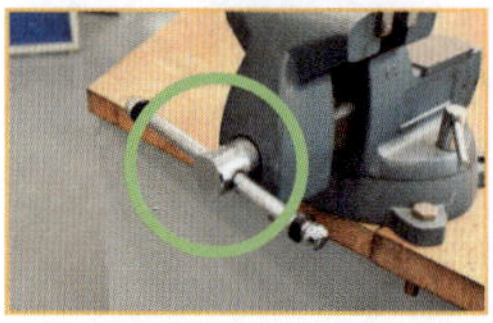 （　　）　A. 手柄　　B. 钳口

❹  （　　） A. 顺时针　B. 逆时针

2. 朗读词语搭配。Read the collocations.

❶	dǎkāi 打开	qiánkǒu 钳口	❸	zhuāngjiā 装夹	gōngjiàn 工件
	bìhé 闭合			fàngrù 放入	
❷	shùnshízhēn 顺时针	zhuàn shǒubǐng 转 手柄		jiājǐn 夹紧	
	nìshízhēn 逆时针				

学习课文 Text 04-02

Zhuāngjiā gōngjiàn
装夹 工件

Jiékè: Táihǔqián zài nǎr?
杰克：台虎钳在哪儿？

Mǎ Míng: Zài qiángōngtái shang.
马明：在钳工台上。

Jiékè: Zhuāngjiā gōngjiàn yǒu jǐ bù?
杰克：装夹 工件 有几步？

Mǎ Míng: Yǒu sān bù.
马明：有三步。

Nìshízhēn zhuàn shǒubǐng, dǎkāi qiánkǒu.
（1）逆时针转手柄，打开钳口。

Fàngrù gōngjiàn.
（2）放入工件。

Shùnshízhēn zhuàn shǒubǐng, bìhé qiánkǒu, jiājǐn gōngjiàn.
（3）顺时针转手柄，闭合钳口，夹紧工件。

Clamping Workpieces

Jack: Where is the bench vice?

Ma Ming: It is on the vice bench.

Jack: How many steps are there to clamp the workpiece?

Ma Ming: There are three steps.

(1) Turn the handle counterclockwise to open the jaws;

(2) Place in the workpiece;

(3) Turn the handle clockwise to close the jaws, and then clamp the workpiece tightly.

课文练习 Text Exercises

1. 根据课文内容选择正确答案。Choose the correct answers according to the text.

1. 台虎钳在________上。　A. 划线平台　B. 钳工台
2. ________转手柄，打开钳口。　A. 顺时针　B. 逆时针
3. ________转手柄，闭合钳口。　A. 顺时针　B. 逆时针
4. 装夹工件有________。　A. 一步　B. 三步

2. 选择合适的词语填空。Choose the appropriate words to fill in the blanks.

A. 有　B. 装夹　C. 转　D. 闭合

1. ________工件。
2. 顺时针转手柄，________钳口，夹紧工件。
3. 装夹工件________几步？
4. 逆时针________手柄，打开钳口。

学习语法 Grammar

语法点 1 Grammar Point 1

疑问代词：哪儿　The Interrogative Pronoun: 哪儿

"哪儿"用在疑问句中，用来询问地点或者处所。

"哪儿" is used in interrogative sentences to ask about the place or location.

Táihǔqián zài nǎr?
1 台虎钳 在 哪儿？ Where is the bench vice?

Gāodùchǐ hé fāngxiāng zài nǎr?
2 高度尺 和 方箱 在 哪儿？ Where are the height gauge and square box?

Túzhǐ zài nǎr?
3 图纸在哪儿？ Where are the drawings?

语法点 1 练习 Exercise on Grammar Point 1

选择合适的词语填空。**Choose the appropriate words to fill in the blanks.**

nǎr A. 哪儿　　　ma B. 吗

Táihǔqián zài　　　Táihǔqián zài qiángōngtái shang.
1 台虎钳 在________？ 台虎钳 在 钳工台 上。

Zài chējiān gōngzuò, yào chuān gōngzuòfú
2 在 车间 工作，要 穿 工作服________？

Gāodùchǐ zài　　　Gāodùchǐ zài huàxiàn píngtái shang.
3 高度尺 在________？ 高度尺 在 划线 平台 上。

Gōngjiàn zài　　　Gōngjiàn zài qiángōngtái shang.
4 工件 在________？ 工件 在 钳工台 上。

语法点 2 Grammar Point 2

动词：有 The Verb: 有

动词“有”表示领有，其否定形式是“没（méi）有”。

The verb “有” indicates possession. Its negative form is “没有”.

Zhuāngjiā gōngjiàn yǒu jǐ bù?
1 装夹 工件 有 几 步？ How many steps are there to clamp the workpiece?

Wǒ yǒu gōngzuòfú hé gōngzuòxié.
2 我 有 工作服 和 工作鞋。 I have work clothes and work shoes.

Xīn yuángōng yǒu fánghù yǎnjìng.
3 新 员工 有 防护 眼镜。 New employees have protective glasses.

语法点 2 练习 Exercise on Grammar Point 2

连词成句。**Rearrange the following words to make sentences.**

例如：
jǐ bù ①几步　yǒu ②有　zhuāngjiā gōngjiàn ③装夹 工件

③②①

1 gōngzuòfú ①工作服　wǒ ②我　yǒu ③有

______

2 fánghù yǎnjìng ①防护 眼镜　yǒu ②有　xīn yuángōng ③新 员工

______

3 gōngzuòxié ①工作鞋　yǒu ②有　Mǎ Míng ③马 明

______

4 ānquánmào ①安全帽　yǒu ②有　Jiékè ③杰克

______

汉字书写 Writing Chinese Characters

shàng 上 上 上

上 上 上 上 上

xià 下 下 下

下 下 下 下 下

shān 山 山 山

山	山	山	山	山						

chū 出 出 出 出 出

出	出	出	出	出						

职业拓展 Career Insight

木牛流马

木牛和流马是三国时期蜀汉丞相诸葛亮发明的两种运输工具。史载建兴九年至十二年（231—234）诸葛亮在北伐时使用木牛流马，其载重量大约在四百斤以上，每日行程为“特行者数十里，群行者二十里”，为蜀汉十万大军运输粮食。

Wooden Ox and Flowing Horse

The Wooden Ox and Flowing Horse were two transportation tools invented by Zhuge Liang, the Chancellor of Shu Han during the Three Kingdoms Period. According to historical records, Zhuge Liang employed the Wooden Ox and Flowing Horse during his northern expeditions from the ninth to the twelfth year of Jianxing (231–234). Each unit had a carrying capacity of over 400 *jin* (approximately 200 kilograms) and could cover a daily distance of “several dozen *li* for individual units, and 20 *li* (approximately 10 kilometers) for groups”, providing support for transporting grain to Shu Han’s army of 100,000 soldiers.

小结 Summary

词语 Words

朗读下列词语。Read the following words.

顺时针	钳工台	台虎钳	钳口
逆时针	手柄	打开	闭合

语法 Grammar

熟读句子。Read the following sentences.

1 台虎钳在哪儿?

2 高度尺和方箱在哪儿?

3 装夹工件有几步?

4 我有工作服和工作鞋。

课文理解 Text Comprehension

把下列句子按正确步骤排列。Sort the following sentences according to the correct steps.

1 打开钳口

2 顺时针转手柄

3 闭合钳口，夹紧工件

4 放入工件

5 逆时针转手柄

⑤ → ______ → ④ → ______ → ______

第5课 Lesson 5

Huàn jùtiáo

换锯条

Replacing Saw Blades

复习 Revision

根据图片，在正确的词语后面打“√”。Tick “√” after the correct words according to the pictures.

❶ 

A. 工件（　　）

B. 钳工台（　　）

❷ 

A. 顺时针（　　）

B. 逆时针（　　）

❸ 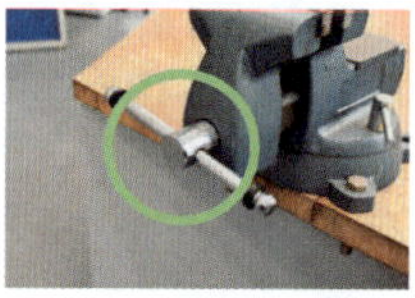

A. 图纸（　　）

B. 手柄（　　）

❹ 

A. 台虎钳（　　）

B. 手柄（　　）

❺ 

A. 钳口（　　）

B. 方箱（　　）

❻ 

A. 顺时针（　　）

B. 逆时针（　　）

热身 Warm-up

选择正确的图片。Choose the right pictures.

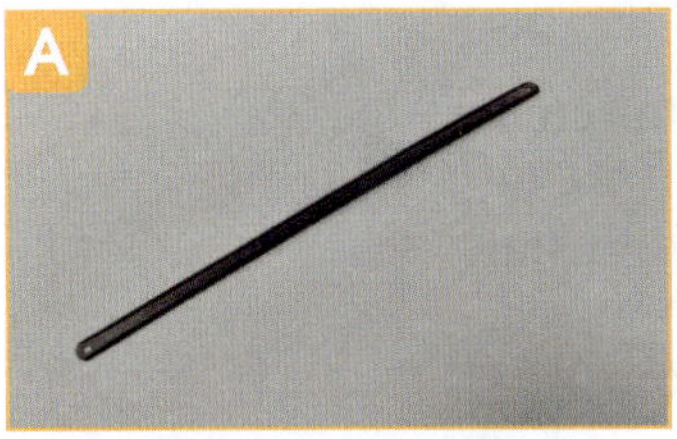

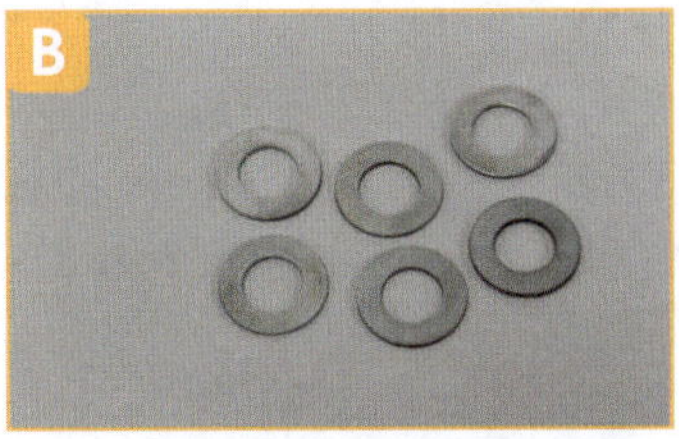

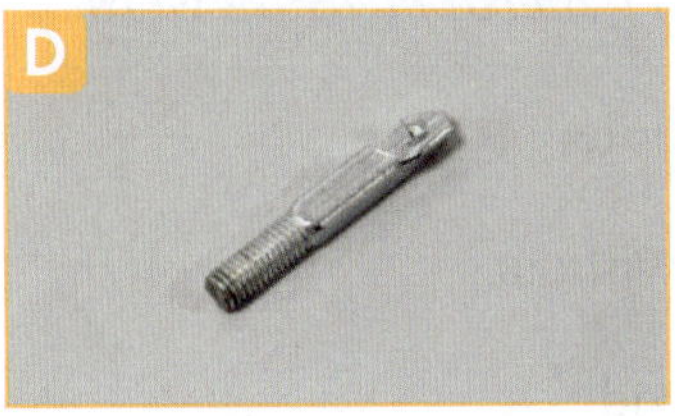

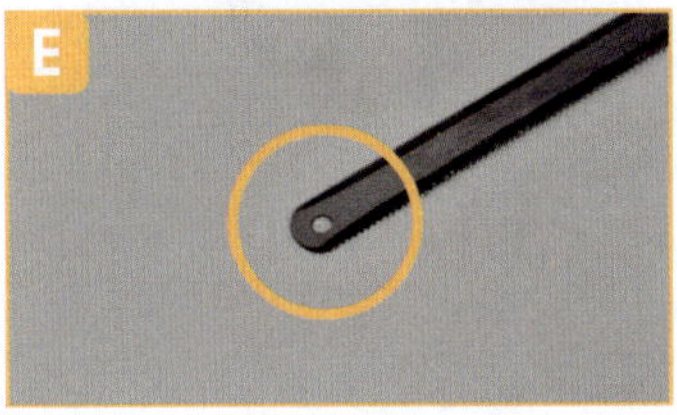

kǒng
❶ 孔 hole ( )

diànpiàn
❷ 垫片 gasket ( )

jùtiáo
❸ 锯条 saw blade ( )

V xíng luómǔ
❹ V 型 螺母 V-nut ( )

lāgǎn
❺ 拉杆 rod ( )

学习生词 Words and Expressions 05-01

1	换	huàn	*v.*	to replace
2	锯条	jùtiáo	*n.*	saw blade
3	怎么	zěnme	*pron.*	how
4	旧	jiù	*adj.*	used

5	松开	sōngkāi	*phr.*	to loosen
6	V型螺母	V xíng luómǔ	*phr.*	V-nut
	螺母	luómǔ	*n.*	nut
7	垫片	diànpiàn	*n.*	gasket
8	取下	qǔxia	*phr.*	to remove
9	装	zhuāng	*v.*	to install
10	一	yī	*num.*	one
11	个	gè	*m.*	*a general measure word*
12	孔	kǒng	*n.*	hole
13	没有	méiyǒu	*v.*	without
14	拉杆	lāgǎn	*n.*	rod
15	另	lìng	*pron.*	the other
16	拧紧	nǐngjǐn	*phr.*	to tighten

词语练习 Word Exercises

1. 看图选词。Look at the pictures and choose the correct words.

❶ 　（　　）　A. V 型螺母　B. 方箱

❷ 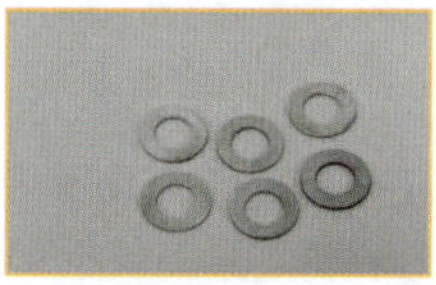　（　　）　A. 平面　B. 垫片

❸ 　（　　）　A. 锯弓　B. 锯条

❹ 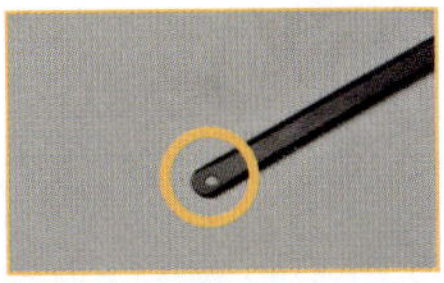 ( ) A. 孔 B. 拉杆

2. 选择正确的拼音。**Choose the correct Pinyin.**

A. kǒng B. diànpiàn C. V xíng luómǔ D. jùtiáo E. lāgǎn

❶ 垫片 ( ) ❷ 拉杆 ( ) ❸ 孔 ( )

❹ V 型螺母 ( ) ❺ 锯条 ( )

学习课文 Text 05-02

Huàn jùtiáo
换锯条

Jiékè: Zěnme huàn jiù jùtiáo?
杰克：怎么换旧锯条？

Mǎ Míng: Sōngkāi V xíng luómǔ hé diànpiàn, qǔxia jiù jùtiáo.
马明：松开 V 型螺母和垫片，取下旧锯条。

Jiékè: Zěnme zhuāng xīn jùtiáo?
杰克：怎么装新锯条？

Mǎ Míng: Yí gè kǒng zhuāng zài méiyǒu luómǔ de lāgǎn shang, lìng yí gè kǒng zhuāng zài yǒu luómǔ de lāgǎn shang. Nǐngjǐn V xíng luómǔ.
马明：一个孔装在没有螺母的拉杆上，另一个孔装在有螺母的拉杆上。拧紧 V 型螺母。

Replacing Saw Blades

Jack: How to replace the used saw blade?

Ma Ming: Loosen the V-nut and gasket , and remove the used saw blade.

Jack: How to install a new saw blade?

Ma Ming: One hole is installed on the rod without a nut, and the other hole is installed on the rod with a nut. And then tighten the V-nut.

课文练习 Text Exercises

1. 根据课文内容选择正确答案。Choose the correct answers according to the text.

1 换旧锯条时要松开________。

A. V 型螺母和垫片　　B. 方箱和高度尺

2 换锯条时要取下________。

A. 旧锯条　　B. 工件

3 一个孔装在没有螺母的________上。

A. 拉杆　　B. 垫片

4 另一个孔装在________螺母的拉杆上。

A. 有　　B. 没有

2. 选择合适的词语填空。**Choose the appropriate words to fill in the blanks.**

A. 松开　　B. 拧紧　　C. 换　　D. 装

1 ________V 型螺母和垫片。

2 一个孔________在没有螺母的拉杆上。

3 ________V 型螺母。

4 怎么________旧锯条？

学习语法 Grammar

语法点 1 Grammar Point 1

疑问代词：怎么　The Interrogative Pronoun: 怎么

用在疑问句中，用来询问动作行为的方式。

"怎么" is used in an interrogative sentence to inquire about the manner of actions.

1 Zěnme zhuāng xīn jùtiáo?
怎么 装 新 锯条？ How to install a new saw blade?

2 Zěnme zhuāngjiā gōngjiàn?
怎么 装夹 工件？ How to clamp the workpiece?

3 Zěnme huàxiàn?
怎么 划线？ How to scribe?

语法点 1 练习 Exercise on Grammar Point 1

选择合适的词语填空。**Choose the appropriate words to fill in the blanks.**

例如：

Yòng ___ zhuāngjiā gōngjiàn?
用___B___装夹 工件？

zěnme / shénme
A. 怎么　　B. 什么

1. huàn jiù jùtiáo?
___换 旧 锯条？
zěnme / shénme
A. 怎么　　B. 什么

2. Zài chējiān gōngzuò yào chuān ___?
在 车间 工作 要 穿___？
zěnme / shénme
A. 怎么　　B. 什么

3. huàxiàn?
___划线？
zěnme / shénme
A. 怎么　　B. 什么

4. dài ānquánmào?
___戴 安全帽？
zěnme / shénme
A. 怎么　　B. 什么

语法点 2 Grammar Point 2

一个……，另一个……

用于列举说明同一类别的两种不同情况。

"一个……, 另一个……" is used to illustrate two different situations within the same category.

1. Yí gè kǒng zhuāng zài méiyǒu luómǔ de lāgǎn shang, lìng yí gè kǒng zhuāng zài yǒu luómǔ de lāgǎn shang.
一个孔 装 在没有螺母的拉杆 上，另一个 孔 装 在有螺母的拉杆 上。
One hole is installed on the rod without a nut, and the other hole is installed on the rod with a nut.

Yí gè fàng zài qiángōngtái shang, lìng yí gè fàng zài huàxiàn píngtái shang.
2 一个放在钳工台上，另一个放在划线平台上。
One is placed on the vice bench, and the other is placed on the scribing platform.

Yí gè huì gàn chēgōng, lìng yí gè huì gàn qiángōng.
3 一个会干车工，另一个会干钳工。
One can do lathe work, and the other can do benchwork.

语法点 2 练习 Exercise on Grammar Point 2

选择正确的答案。Choose the right answers.

例如：

Yí gè kǒng zhuāng zài méiyǒu luómǔ de lāgǎn shang, lìng yí gè
一个孔装在没有螺母的拉杆上，另一个 __A__。

kǒng zhuāng zài yǒu luómǔ de lāgǎn shang
A. 孔装在有螺母的拉杆上

qǔxia jiù jùtiáo
B. 取下旧锯条

Yí gè fàng zài qiángōngtái shang, lìng yí gè
1 一个放在钳工台上，另一个 ________。

yòng fāngxiāng hé gāodùchǐ
A. 用方箱和高度尺

fàng zài huàxiàn píngtái shang
B. 放在划线平台上

Yí gè huì gàn chēgōng, lìng yí gè
2 一个会干车工，另一个 ________。

huì gàn qiángōng
A. 会干钳工

zhuāngjiā gōngjiàn
B. 装夹工件

Yí gè shì lǎoshī lìng yí gè
3 一个是老师，另一个 ________。

huì gàn chēgōng
A. 会干车工

shì Zhōngfāng yuángōng
B. 是中方员工

Yí gè shì Jiékè, lìng yí gè
4 一个是杰克，另一个 ________。

huì gàn hàngōng
A. 会干焊工

shì Mǎ Míng
B. 是马明

汉字书写 Writing Chinese Characters

kǒu 口 口 口

口 口 口 口 口

rì 日 日 日 日

日 日 日 日 日

zhōng 中 中 中 中

中 中 中 中 中

mù 目 目 目 目 目

目 目 目 目 目

文化拓展 Culture Insight

鲁班与锯

鲁班是春秋时期鲁国一位杰出的工匠，他的发明和创造使当时的土木工艺出现了崭新的面貌，为后世的建筑事业奠定了坚实的基础，鲁班也因此被后世尊称为“工匠之祖”。有一次，鲁班在山坡上被茅草割破了手。细看之下，鲁班发现这茅草的边缘是锯齿状的，非常尖锐。受此启发，鲁班发明了锯。

Lu Ban and Saws

Lu Ban was an outstanding craftsman from the State of Lu during the Spring and Autumn Period. His inventions and creations brought new developments to the civil engineering industry at that time, laying a solid foundation for the construction industry in later generations. He was revered as the "Ancestor of Craftsmen" by later generations. Once, while on a hillside, Lu Ban's hand was cut by thatch. Under closer inspection, Lu Ban noticed that the edges of the thatch were serrated and very sharp. Inspired by this, Lu Ban invented the saw successfully.

小结 Summary

词语 Words

朗读下列词语。Read the following words.

锯条	V 型螺母	垫片
取下	拧紧	拉杆

语法 Grammar

熟读句子。Read the following sentences.

1 怎么装新锯条？

2 怎么装夹工件？

3 一个孔装在没有螺母的拉杆上，另一个孔装在有螺母的拉杆上。

4 一个放在钳工台上，另一个放在划线平台上。

课文理解 Text Comprehension

把下列句子按正确步骤排列。Sort the following sentences according to the correct steps.

1 拧紧 V 型螺母。

2 一个孔装在没有螺母的拉杆上。

3 松开 V 型螺母和垫片，取下旧锯条。

4 另一个孔装在有螺母的拉杆上。

________→ ________→ ________→ ________

第6课 Lesson 6

Jùgē gōngjiàn

锯割工件 Sawing Workpieces

复习 Revision

根据词语选图片。**Choose the right pictures according to the words.**

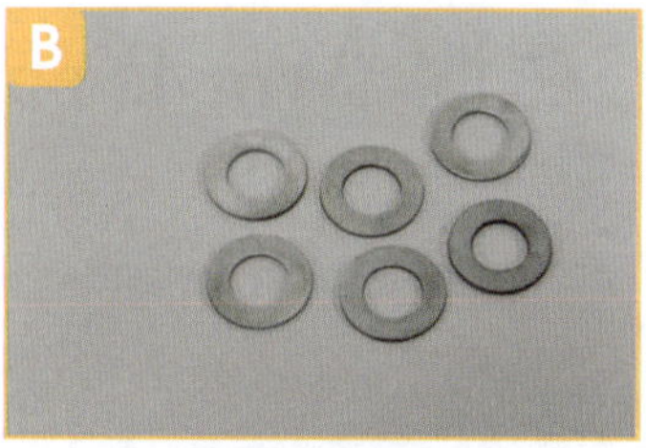

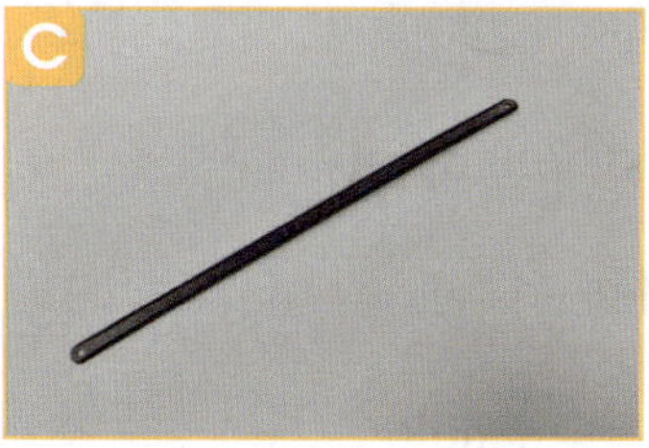

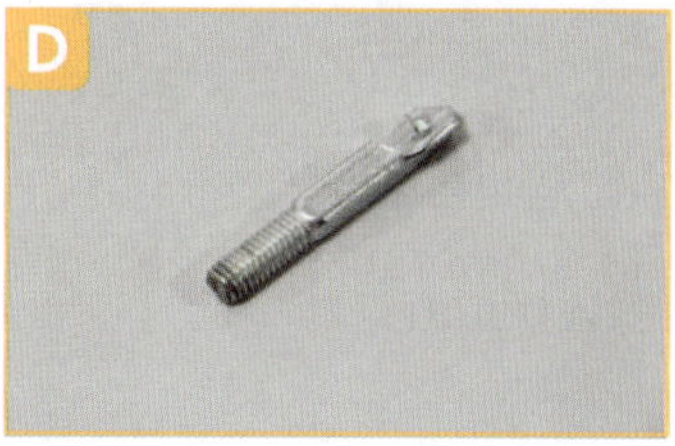

❶ 拉杆（　　）　　❷ V型螺母（　　）

❸ 锯条（　　）　　❹ 垫片（　　）

热身 Warm-up

选择正确的图片。**Choose the right pictures.**

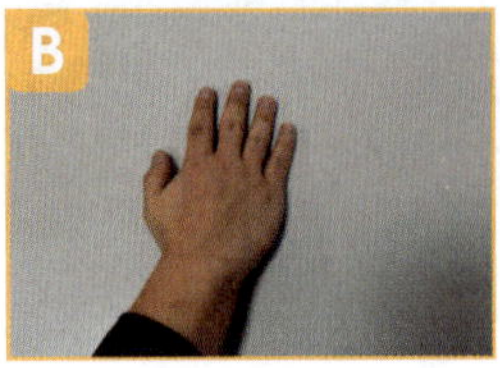

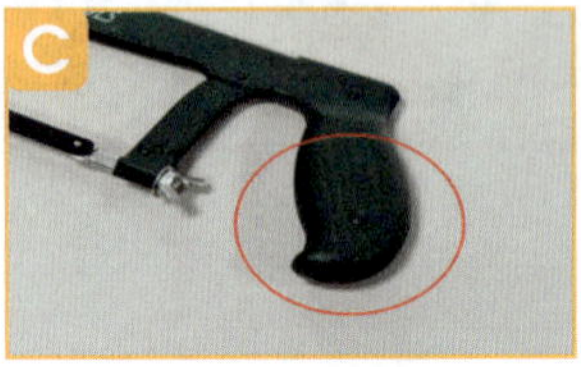

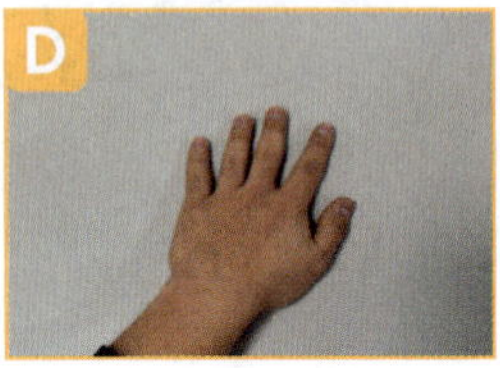

1. 左手 (zuǒshǒu) the left hand （ ）
2. 手锯 (shǒujù) hand saw （ ）
3. 锯柄 (jùbǐng) saw holder （ ）
4. 右手 (yòushǒu) the right hand （ ）

学习生词 Words and Expressions 06-01

1	锯割	jùgē	*v.*	to saw
2	右手	yòushǒu	*n.*	the right hand
3	握紧	wòjǐn	*phr.*	to hold tightly
4	手锯	shǒujù	*n.*	hand saw
5	锯柄	jùbǐng	*n.*	saw handle
6	左手	zuǒshǒu	*n.*	the left hand
7	前端	qiánduān	*n.*	the front end

8	双手	shuāngshǒu	*n.*	two hands
9	下压	xiàyā	*v.*	to press
10	向	xiàng	*prep.*	towards
11	前	qián	*n.*	front
11	推	tuī	*v.*	to push
12	然后	ránhòu	*conj.*	then
13	呢	ne	*part.*	*a question particle*
14	拉回	lāhuí	*phr.*	to pull back

词语练习 Word Exercises

1. 看图选词。Look at the pictures and choose the correct words.

❶ 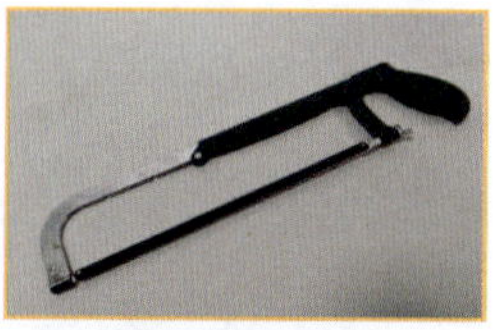 (　　) A. 手锯　B. 工件

❷ 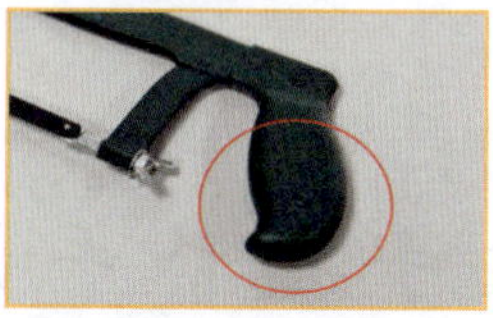 (　　) A. 锯柄　B. 锯条

❸ 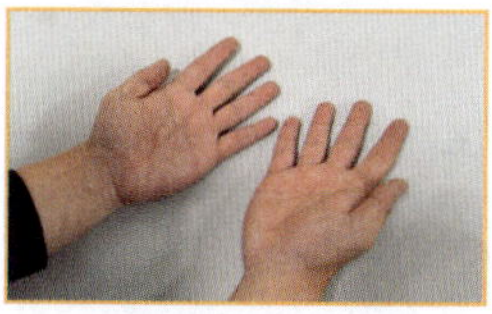 (　　) A. 双手　B. 右手

❹ 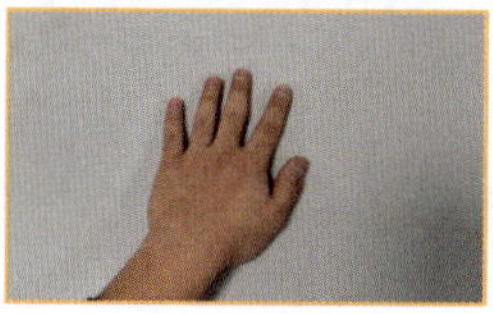 (　　) A. 左手　B. 右手

2. 词语连线。**Words Matching.**

❶ 锯割	A. 锯柄
❷ 握紧	B. 手锯
❸ 拉回	C. 锯
❹ 推	D. 工件

学习课文 Text 06-02

Jùgē gōngjiàn
锯割工件

Jiékè: Zěnme jùgē gōngjiàn?
杰克：怎么锯割工件？

Mǎ Míng: Yòushǒu wòjǐn shǒujù jùbǐng, zuǒshǒu fújǐn shǒujù qiánduān. Shuāngshǒu xiàyā, xiàng qián tuī jù.
马明：右手握紧手锯锯柄，左手扶紧手锯前端。双手下压，向前推锯。

Jiékè: Ránhòu ne?
杰克：然后呢？

Mǎ Míng: Lāhuí shǒujù, zài xiàng qián tuī jù.
马明：拉回手锯，再向前推锯。

Sawing Workpieces

Jack: How to saw the workpiece?

Ma Ming: Hold the saw handle tightly with the right hand and hold the front end of the saw tightly with the left hand. Press down the saw with both hands and push the saw forward.

Jack: And then?

Ma Ming: Pull back the saw and push the saw forward again.

课文练习 Text Exercises

1. 根据课文内容选择正确答案。Choose the correct answers according to the text.

1. ________握紧手锯锯柄。　A. 右手　B. 左手
2. ________扶紧手锯前端。　A. 左手　B. 右手
3. ________下压，向前推锯。　A. 双手　B. 锯柄
4. 拉回________，再向前推锯。　A. 锯柄　B. 手锯

2. 选择合适的词语填空。Choose the appropriate words to fill in the blanks.

A. 扶紧　B. 握紧　C. 拉回　D. 推

1. 左手________手锯前端。
2. 右手________手锯锯柄。
3. ________手锯，再向前推锯。
4. 双手下压，向前________锯。

学习语法 Grammar

语法点 1 Grammar Point 1

动词 + 紧 Verb + 紧

表示动作使物体变得固定或牢固。

"Verb + 紧" indicates that the action makes an object firm or secure.

1. Wòjǐn shǒujù jùbǐng.
   握紧 手锯 锯柄。 Hold the saw handle tightly.
2. Fújǐn shǒujù qiánduān.
   扶紧 手锯 前端。 Hold the front end of the saw tightly.
3. Nǐngjǐn V xíng luómǔ.
   拧紧 V 型 螺母。 Screw the V-nut tightly.

语法点 1 练习 Exercise on Grammar Point 1

选择合适的词语填空。**Choose the appropriate words to fill in the blanks.**

wòjǐn A. 握紧	fújǐn B. 扶紧	jiājǐn C. 夹紧	nǐngjǐn D. 拧紧

1. shǒujù jùbǐng.
   ________手锯锯柄。
2. shǒujù qiánduān.
   ________手锯 前端。
3. Bìhé qiánkǒu, gōngjiàn.
   闭合 钳口，________工件。
4. V xíng luómǔ.
   ________V 型 螺母。

语法点 2 Grammar Point 2

语气助词：呢 The Modal Particle: 呢

用于构成省略式疑问句，结构为“名词 / 代词 + 呢”。

The modal particle “呢” is used to form elliptical questions. The structure is “noun / pronoun + 呢”.

1. Zuǒshǒu fújǐn shǒujù qiánduān, ránhòu ne?
   左手扶紧手锯前端，然后呢？
   Hold the front end of the hand saw tightly with your left hand, and then?
2. Jiékè shì xīn yuángōng. Mǎ Míng ne?
   杰克是新员工。马明呢？
   Jack is a new employee. What about Ma Ming?
3. Mǎ Míng shì qiángōng. Nǐ ne?
   马明是钳工。你呢？ Ma Ming is a bench worer. And you?

语法点 2 练习 Exercise on Grammar Point 2

选择合适的句子填空。**Choose the appropriate sentences to fill in the blanks.**

1. Jiékè shì xīn yuángōng.
   杰克是新员工。________ 　A. Jiékè ne? 杰克呢？　B. Mǎ Míng ne? 马明呢？
2. Mǎ Míng shì qiángōng.
   马明是钳工。________ 　A. Nǐ ne? 你呢？　B. Gōngjiàn ne? 工件呢？
3. Wǒ huì gàn hàngōng.
   我会干焊工。________ 　A. Nǐ ne 你呢？　B. Jùbǐng ne? 锯柄呢？
4. Yí gè huì zhuāngjiā gōngjiàn,
   一个会装夹工件，________ 　A. lìng yí gè ne? 另一个呢？　B. shǒujù ne? 手锯呢？

汉字书写 Writing Characters

bā
丿 八

八 八 八 八 八

xiǎo　小 小 小

小	小	小	小	小						

bù　不 不 不 不

不	不	不	不	不						

shǎo　少 少 少 少

少	少	少	少	少						

职业拓展 Career Insight

锯割

当前，虽然各种自动化、机械化的切割设备已广泛使用，但手锯切割仍然有其不可替代的地位。手锯切割具有方便、简单和灵活的特点，在单件小批量生产、切割异形工件、开槽、修整等场合应用广泛。因此，手工锯割是钳工需要掌握的基本操作之一。

Sawing

Currently, although various automated and mechanized cutting equipment has been widely used, hand saw cutting still has an irreplaceable position. Hand saw cutting, with the characteristics of convenience, simplicity, and flexibility, is widely used in single piece and small batch production, cutting irregular workpieces, slotting, trimming, and other occasions. Therefore, hand sawing is one of the basic operations that fitters need to master.

小结 Summary

词语 Words

朗读下列词语。Read the following words.

手锯	锯柄	锯割
前端	拉回	下压

语法 Grammar

熟读句子。Read the following sentences.

1 握紧手锯锯柄。

2 扶紧手锯前端。

3 马明是钳工。你呢？

4 杰克是新员工。马明呢？

课文理解 Text Comprehension

把下列句子按正确步骤排列。Sort the following sentences according to the correct steps.

1 双手下压。

2 左手扶紧手锯前端。

3 右手握紧手锯锯柄。

4 向前推锯。

5 拉回手锯，再向前推锯。

___③___ → ______ → ___④___ → ______ → ______

第7课 Lesson 7

Xuǎnzé cuòdāo
选择锉刀
Choosing a File

复习 Revision

根据词语选图片。**Choose the right pictures according to the words.**

A

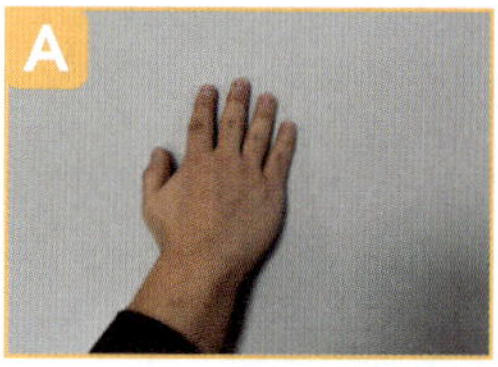

B

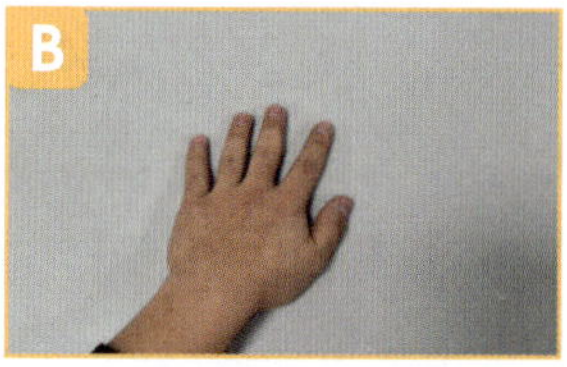

C

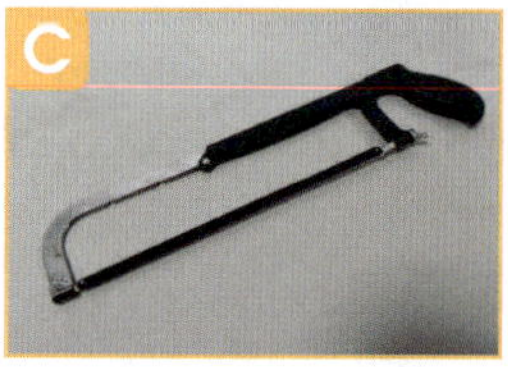

D

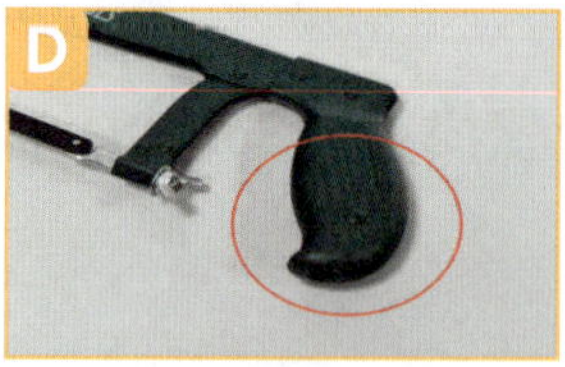

❶ 锯柄（　　）　❷ 手锯（　　）

❸ 左手（　　）　❹ 右手（　　）

热身 Warm-up

选择正确的图片。**Choose the right pictures.**

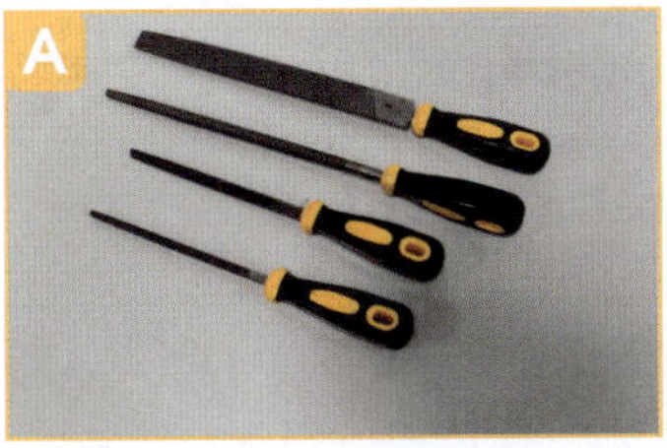

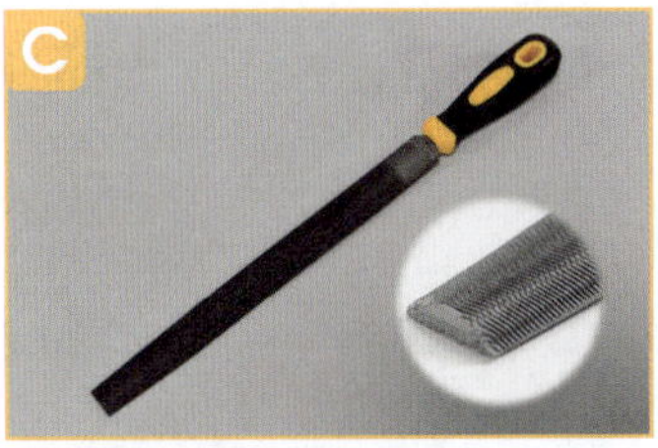

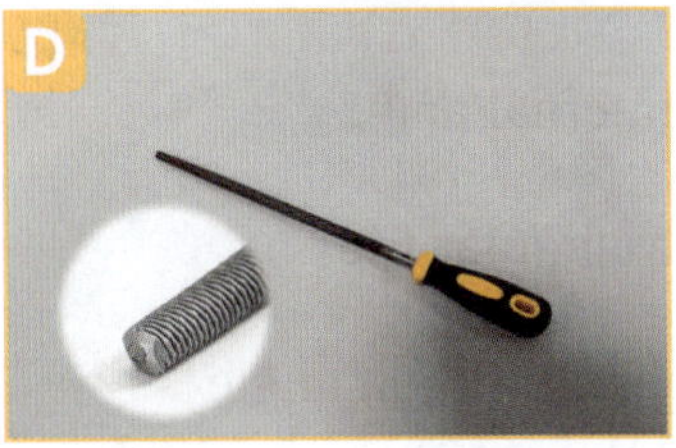

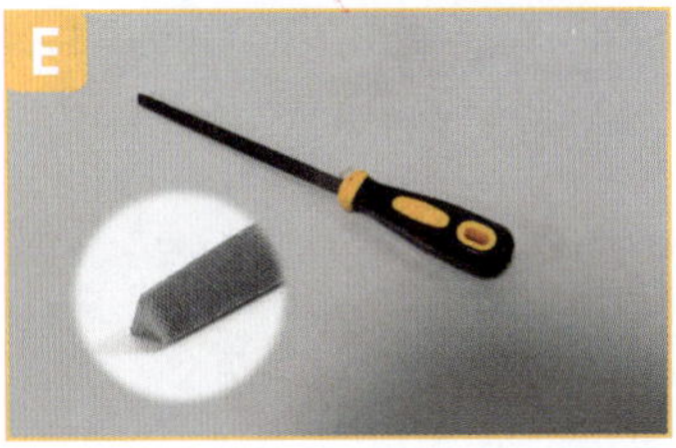

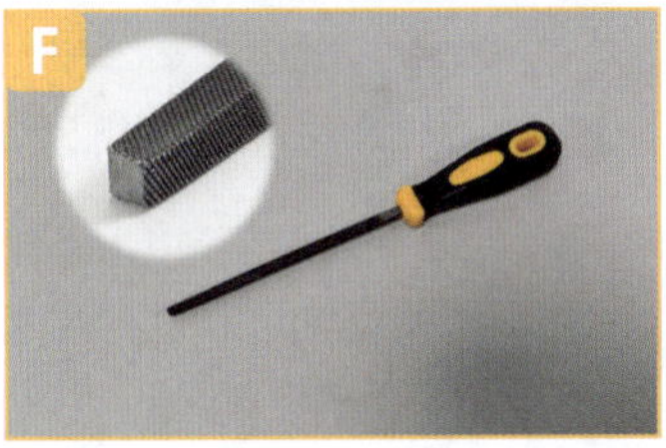

1. 方锉 (fāngcuò) square file (   )
2. 三角锉 (sānjiǎocuò) triangular file (   )
3. 圆锉 (yuáncuò) round file (   )
4. 锉刀 (cuòdāo) file (   )
5. 扁锉 (biǎncuò) flat file (   )
6. 半圆锉 (bànyuáncuò) half round file (   )

学习生词 Words and Expressions 07-01

1	选择	xuǎnzé	*v.*	to choose; to select
2	锉刀	cuòdāo	*n.*	file
3	根据	gēnjù	*prep.*	according to

4	形状	xíngzhuàng	*n.*	shape
5	锉削	cuòxiāo	*v.*	to file
6	时	shí	*n.*	when
7	扁锉	biǎncuò	*n.*	flat file
8	内圆弧面	nèiyuánhúmiàn	*n.*	inner arc surface
9	半圆锉	bànyuáncuò	*n.*	half round file
10	或者	huòzhě	*conj.*	or
11	圆锉	yuáncuò	*n.*	round file
12	内角	nèijiǎo	*n.*	internal angle
13	三角锉	sānjiǎocuò	*n.*	triangular file
14	内直角	nèizhíjiǎo	*n.*	internal right angle
15	或	huò	*conj.*	or
15	方锉	fāngcuò	*n.*	square file

词语练习 Word Exercises

1. 看图选词。Look at the pictures and choose the correct words.

❶ 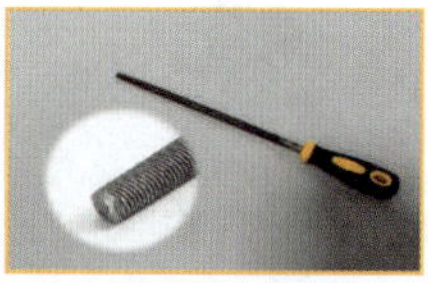 (　　) A. 圆锉　　B. 三角锉

❷ 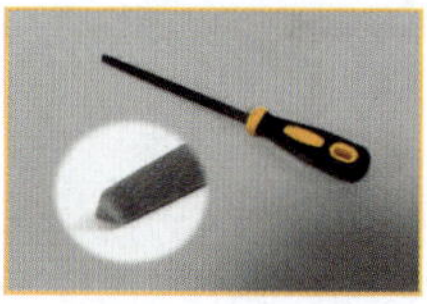 (　　) A. 圆锉　　B. 三角锉

❸ 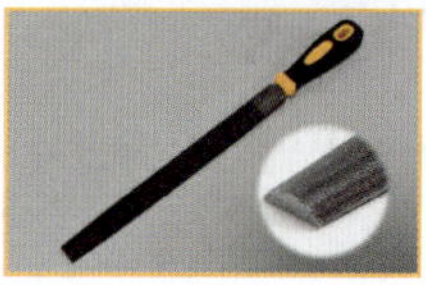 (　　) A. 圆锉　　B. 半圆锉

4  (　　) A. 扁锉　　B. 圆锉

5 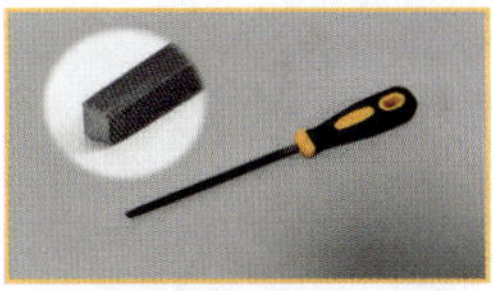 (　　) A. 扁锉　　B. 方锉

6 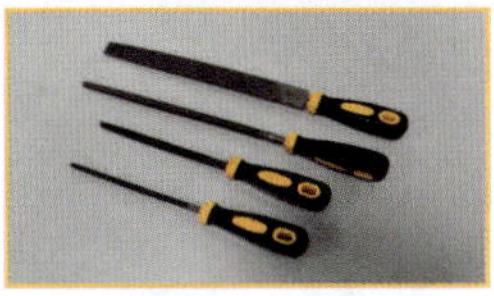 (　　) A. 锉刀　　B. 圆锉

2. 按照属性给下列词语归类。**Classify the following words according to their attributes.**

A. 工件形状类　　B. 锉刀类

1 圆锉 (　　)　　2 半圆锉 (　　)　　3 扁锉 (　　)

4 方锉 (　　)　　5 三角锉 (　　)　　6 内角 (　　)

7 内圆弧面 (　　)　　8 内直角 (　　)

学习课文 Text 07-02

Xuǎnzé cuòdāo
选择锉刀

Gēnjù gōngjiàn de xíngzhuàng xuǎnzé cuòdāo.
根据 工件 的 形状 选择 锉刀。

Cuòxiāo píngmiàn shí, xuǎnzé biǎncuò.
锉削 平面 时，选择扁锉。

Cuòxiāo nèiyuánhúmiàn shí, xuǎnzé bànyuáncuò huòzhě yuáncuò.
锉削内圆弧面时，选择半圆锉或者圆锉。

Cuòxiāo nèijiǎo shí, xuǎnzé sānjiǎocuò.
锉削内角时，选择三角锉。

Cuòxiāo nèizhíjiǎo shí, xuǎnzé biǎncuò huò fāngcuò.
锉削内直角时，选择扁锉或方锉。

Choosing a File

A file is chosen based on the shape of the workpiece.

A flat file is chosen when filing flat surfaces.

A half round file or a round file is chosen when filing inner arc surfaces.

A triangular file is chosen when filing internal angles.

A flat or square file is chosen when filing internal right angles.

课文练习 Text Exercises

1. 根据课文内容选择正确答案。Choose the correct answers according to the text.

1 根据工件的________选择锉刀。 A. 形状 B. 平面

2 锉削平面时，选择________。 A. 左手 B. 扁锉

3 锉削内圆弧面时，选择半圆锉或者________。 A. 锯割 B. 圆锉

4 锉削内角时，选择________。 A. 锯条 B. 三角锉

2. 根据工件的形状选择合适的锉刀。 **Choose the appropriate file according to the shape of each workpiece.**

A. 扁锉　　B. 圆锉　　C. 三角锉　　D. 方锉　　E. 半圆锉

1. 锉削平面时，选择________。
2. 锉削内圆弧面时，选择________或者________。
3. 锉削内角时，选择________。
4. 锉削内直角时，选择________或________。

学习语法 Grammar

语法点 1 Grammar Point 1

名词：时　The Noun: 时

表示在某一特定时点或在某一特定时段内。

"时" means at a specific time point or period.

---

1. Cuòxiāo píngmiàn shí, xuǎnzé biǎncuò.
   锉削 平面 时，选择 扁锉。A flat file is chosen when filing flat surfaces.
2. Cuòxiāo nèijiǎo shí, xuǎnzé sānjiǎocuò.
   锉削 内角 时，选择 三角锉。
   A triangular file is chosen when filing internal angles.
3. Cuòxiāo nèizhíjiǎo shí, xuǎnzé biǎncuò huò fāngcuò.
   锉削 内直角 时，选择 扁锉 或 方锉。
   A flat or square file is chosen when filing internal right angles.

语法点 1 练习　Exercise on Grammar Point 1

连词成句。**Rearrange the following words to make sentences.**

例如：

xuǎnzé biǎncuò	shí	cuòxiāo píngmiàn
①选择 扁锉	②时	③锉削 平面

③②①

1

xuǎnzé sānjiǎocuò	shí	cuòxiāo nèijiǎo
①选择 三角锉	② 时	③锉削 内角

____

2

shí	cuòxiāo nèizhíjiǎo	xuǎnzé biǎncuò huò fāngcuò
①时	②锉削 内直角	③选择 扁锉 或 方锉

____

3

zài chējiān gōngzuò	shí	chuān gōngzuòfú
①在 车间 工作	②时	③ 穿 工作服

____

4

shí	yòng táihǔqián	zhuāngjiā gōngjiàn
①时	② 用 台虎钳	③ 装夹 工件

____

语法点 2 Grammar Point 2

连词：或、或者 The Conjunctions: 或 and 或者

表示选择关系，多连接词或短语。

"或" and "或者" indicate a relationship of choice, commonly connecting words or phrases.

Cuòxiāo nèiyuánhúmiàn shí, xuǎnzé bànyuáncuò huòzhě yuáncuò.
1 锉削 内圆弧面 时，选择 半圆锉 或者 圆锉。
A half round file or a round file is chosen when filing inner arc surfaces.

Cuòxiāo nèizhíjiǎo shí, xuǎnzé biǎncuò huò fāngcuò.
2 锉削 内直角 时，选择 扁锉 或 方锉。
A flat or square file is chosen when filing internal right angles.

Huàxiàn yòng gāodùchǐ huò huàzhēn.
3 划线 用 高度尺 或 划针（huàzhēn; scribing needle）。
The height gauge or scribing needle can be used for scribing.

语法点 2 练习 Exercise on Grammar Point 2

选择正确的答案。**Choose the right answers.**

Cuòxiāo nèiyuánhúmiàn shí, xuǎnzé bànyuáncuò huò
1 锉削 内圆弧面 时，选择 半圆锉 或______。 A. 圆锉 (yuáncuò) B. 锉刀 (cuòdāo)

Cuòxiāo nèizhíjiǎo shí, xuǎnzé biǎncuò huò
2 锉削 内直角 时，选择 扁锉 或______。 A. 方锉 (fāngcuò) B. 形状 (xíngzhuàng)

Huàxiàn yòng huàzhēn huòzhě
3 划线 用 划针 或者______。 A. 高度尺 (gāodùchǐ) B. 手锯 (shǒujù)

Xuǎnzé Mǎ Míng huò zhuāngjiā gōngjiàn.
4 选择 马 明 或______装夹 工件。 A. 杰克 (Jiékè) B. 高度尺 (gāodùchǐ)

汉字书写 Writing Chinese Characters

mù
木 木 木 木

木 木 木 木 木

běn
本 本 本 本 本

本 本 本 本 本

shù
术 术 术 术 术

术 术 术 术 术

hé
禾 禾 禾 禾 禾

禾 禾 禾 禾 禾

文化拓展 Culture Insight

剪纸

剪纸是中国最为流行的民间艺术之一，起源于汉代，精熟于南北朝时期，然而真正繁盛却是在清朝中期以后。剪纸常用于宗教仪式、装饰和造型艺术等方面。剪纸又叫“窗花”，因人们把它作为年节装饰贴在纸窗上，故而得名。它由手工制作，再配以明快鲜艳的色彩，所以独具特色，令人爱不释手。

Paper Cutting

Paper cutting is one of the most popular folk arts in China. It originated in the Han Dynasty and became quite sophisticated in the Northern and Southern Dynasties, but it really flourished after the middle of the Qing Dynasty. Paper cutting is often used in religious ceremonies, decoration and plastic arts. It is also called "window flower", because people often paste it on paper windows as a New Year decoration. It is handmade and paired with bright and vibrant colors, making it unique and irresistible.

小结 Summary

词语 Words

朗读下列词语。**Read the following words.**

内圆弧面	内角	内直角	方锉
扁锉	半圆锉	圆锉	三角锉

语法 Grammar

熟读句子。**Read the following sentences.**

1. 锉削平面时，选择扁锉。
2. 锉削内角时，选择三角锉。

3 锉削内圆弧面时，选择半圆锉或圆锉。

4 锉削内直角时，选择扁锉或方锉。

课文理解 Text Comprehension

选择合适的词语填空。Choose the appropriate words to fill in the blanks.

A. 扁锉　B. 半圆锉　C. 圆锉　D. 三角锉　E. 方锉

1 锉削平面时，选择________。

2 锉削内圆弧面时，选择________或者________。

3 锉削内角时，选择________。

4 锉削内直角时，选择________或________。

Cuòxiāo píngmiàn

第8课 Lesson 8

锉削平面

Filing Flat Surfaces

复习 Revision

图文连线。**Match the pictures with the words.**

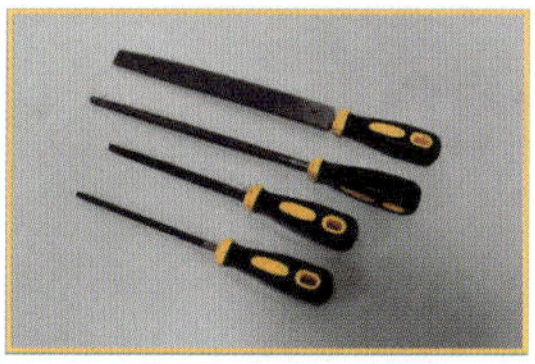

三角锉

半圆锉

锉刀

扁锉

方锉

圆锉

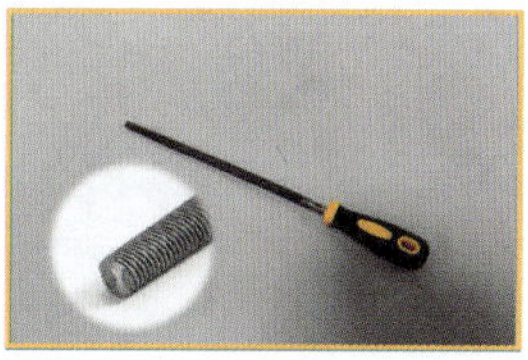

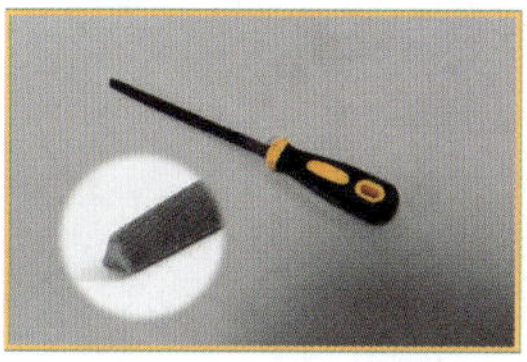

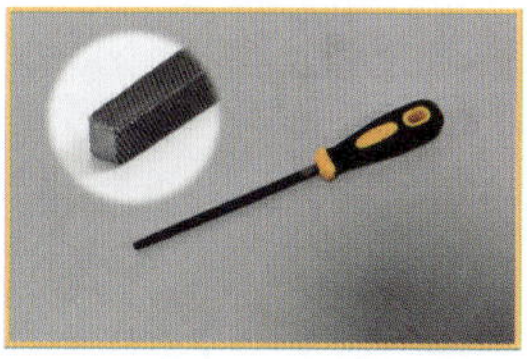

热身 Warm-up

选择正确的图片。**Choose the right pictures.**

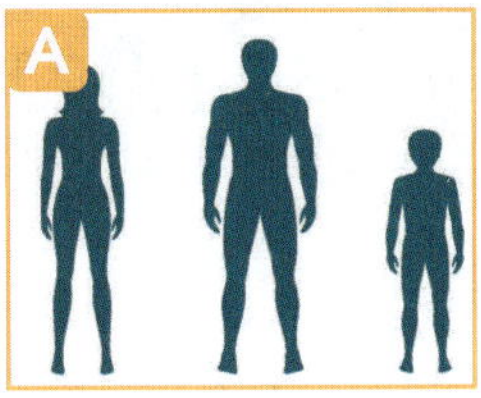

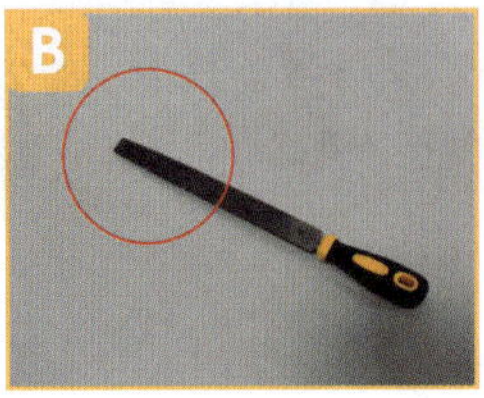

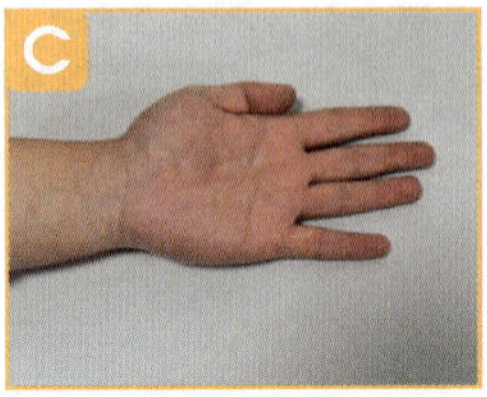

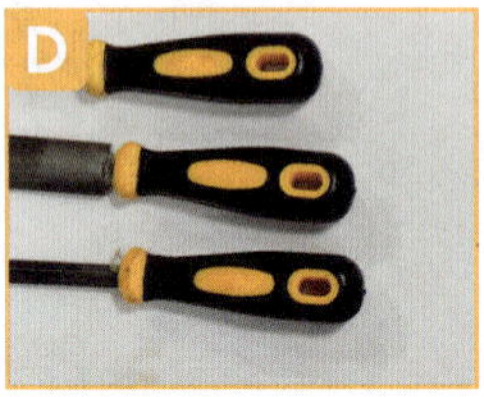

❶ 身体（shēntǐ） body （　　）

❷ 手掌（shǒuzhǎng） palm （　　）

❸ 刀柄（dāobǐng） tool handle （　　）

❹ 另一端（lìng yì duān） the other end （　　）

学习生词 Words and Expressions 08-01

1	哪些	nǎxiē	*pron.*	which
2	步骤	bùzhòu	*n.*	step
3	刀柄	dāobǐng	*n.*	tool handle
4	手掌	shǒuzhǎng	*n.*	palm
5	压	yā	*v.*	to press
6	另一端	lìng yì duān	*phr.*	the other end
7	身体	shēntǐ	*n.*	body
8	前倾	qián qīng	*phr.*	to lean forward
9	推动	tuīdòng	*v.*	to push
10	抬起	táiqǐ	*phr.*	to lift

词语练习 Word Exercises

1. 看图选词。Look at the pictures and choose the correct words.

❶ 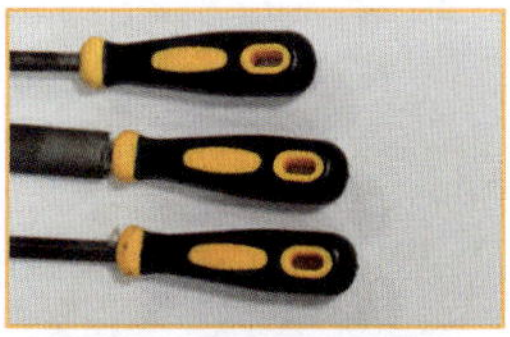 (　　) A. 锉刀　B. 刀柄

❷ 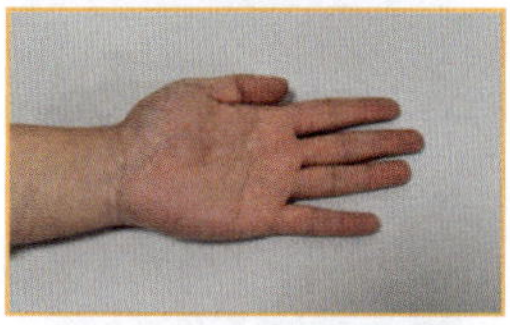 (　　) A. 手掌　B. 双手

❸ 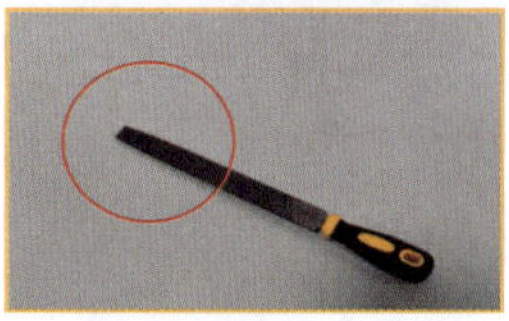 (　　) A. 另一端　B. 刀柄

❹ 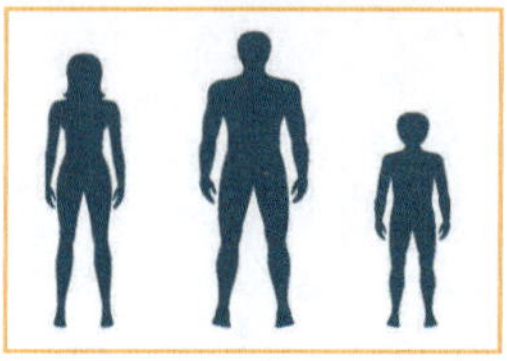 (　　) A. 手掌　B. 身体

2. 词语连线。Word Matching.

❶ 扶紧	A. 前倾
❷ 身体	B. 锉刀
❸ 抬起	C. 哪些步骤
❹ 有	D. 刀柄

学习课文 Text 08-02

Cuòxiāo píngmiàn
锉削 平面

Jiékè: Cuòxiāo píngmiàn yǒu nǎxiē bùzhòu?
杰克：锉削平面有哪些步骤？

Mǎ Míng: Yòushǒu wòjǐn cuòdāo dāobǐng, zuǒshǒu shǒuzhǎng yā zài cuòdāo lìng yì duān.
马明：右手握紧锉刀刀柄，左手手掌压在锉刀另一端。

Jiékè: Ránhòu ne?
杰克：然后呢？

Mǎ Míng: Shēntǐ qián qīng, shuāngshǒu xià yā, yòushǒu tuīdòng cuòdāo xiàng qián cuòxiāo. Táiqǐ、lāhuí cuòdāo.
马明：身体前倾，双手下压，右手推动锉刀向前锉削。抬起、拉回锉刀。

Filing Flat Surfaces

Jack: What are the steps for filing a flat surface?

Ma Ming: Hold the saw handle tightly with the right hand, and press the other end of the file with the left palm.

Jack: And then?

Ma Ming: The body should lean forward and both hands should press down. Push the file forward and cut with the right hand. Lift and pull the file back.

课文练习 Text Exercises

1. 根据课文内容选择正确答案。Choose the correct answers according to the text.

1. ________握紧锉刀刀柄。 A. 右手 B. 身体
2. ________手掌压在锉刀另一端。 A. 左手 B. 双手
3. 身体前倾，________下压。 A. 双手 B. 身体
4. 抬起、拉回________。 A. 锉刀 B. 双手

2. 选择合适的词语填空。Choose the appropriate words to fill in the blanks.

A. 拉回　　B. 压　　C. 握紧　　D. 锉削

1. ________平面有哪些步骤？
2. 抬起、________锉刀。
3. 左手手掌________在锉刀的另一端。
4. 右手________锉刀刀柄。

学习语法 Grammar

语法点 1 Grammar Point 1

疑问代词：哪些　The Interrogative Pronoun: 哪些

用在疑问句中，用来对众多人或者事物进行提问。

"哪些" is used in a question to inquire about multiple people or things.

Cuòxiāo píngmiàn yǒu nǎxiē bùzhòu?
1 锉削 平面 有 哪些 步骤？ What are the steps for filing a flat surface?

Cuòxiāo gōngjiàn yòng nǎxiē gōngjù?
2 锉削 工件 用 哪些 工具？ What tools are used to file workpieces?

Huàxiàn yòng nǎxiē gōngjù?
3 划线 用 哪些 工具？ What tools are used for scribing?

语法点 1 练习 Exercise on Grammar Point 1

连词成句。**Rearrange the following words to make sentences.**

例如：
nǎxiē ①哪些　bùzhòu ②步骤　yǒu ③有　cuòxiāo píngmiàn ④锉削 平面

④③①②

1 nǎxiē ①哪些　gōngjù ② 工具　yòng ③用　cuòxiāo nèizhíjiǎo ④锉削 内直角

______

2 nǎxiē ①哪些　yǒu ②有　chējiān ③ 车间　tóngxué ④同学

______

3 ①钳工台 上(qiángōngtái shang) ②锉刀(cuòdāo) ③有(yǒu) ④哪些(nǎxiē)

____

4 ①哪些(nǎxiē) ②装夹 工件(zhuāngjiā gōngjiàn) ③图纸(túzhǐ) ④看(kàn)

____

语法点 2 Grammar Point 2

动词 + 起 / 回　Verb + 起 / 回

"起"用在动词后，表示通过动作使人或物离开某个水平面，由低的位置向高的位置移动。"回"用在动词后，表示通过动作使人或者物回到原来的位置。

"起" is used after a verb to indicate moving a person or object away from a certain horizontal plane through an action, from a lower position to a higher one. "回" is used after a verb to indicate returning a person or object to the original position.

1 Táiqǐ cuòdāo.
抬起 锉刀。Lift the file.

2 Lāhuí cuòdāo.
拉回 锉刀。Pull the file back.

3 Lāhuí shǒujù.
拉回 手锯。Pull the hand saw back.

语法点 2 练习 Exercise on Grammar Point 2

选择合适的词语填空。**Choose the appropriate words to fill in the blanks.**

táiqǐ A. 抬起	lāhuí B. 拉回	nǐngjǐn C. 拧紧	jiājǐn D. 夹紧

1 ________锉刀。(cuòdāo.)　　2 ________手锯。(shǒujù.)

3 ________V 型 螺母。(V xíng luómǔ.)　　4 ________工件。(gōngjiàn.)

汉字书写 Writing Chinese Characters

dàn 旦 旦 旦 旦 旦

旦 旦 旦 旦 旦

zǎo 早 早 早 早 早 早

早 早 早 早 早

hàn 旱 旱 旱 旱 旱 旱 旱

旱 旱 旱 旱 旱

xīng 星 星 星 星 星 星 星 星 星

星 星 星 星 星

文化拓展 Culture Insight

北京烤鸭

提起北京的美食，人们脱口而出的就是北京烤鸭。北京烤鸭选用优质肉食鸭，采用果木炭火烤制而成，外皮酥脆，色泽金黄，肉质鲜嫩多汁。将酱料、葱、黄瓜和鸭肉卷入小饼里一起食用，人们可以获得视觉和味觉的双重享受。北京烤鸭分为“挂炉烤鸭”与“焖炉烤鸭”两大流派。其中，以全聚德的挂炉烤鸭和便宜坊的焖炉烤鸭最为出名。

Beijing Roast Duck

When it comes to Beijing cuisine, people will immediately mention Beijing Roast Duck. Beijing Roast Duck uses high-quality ducks raised for meat and is roasted over fruit wood charcoal fire. The skin is crispy and golden brown, and the meat is fresh, tender, and juicy. The sauce, scallions, cucumbers, and duck meat are wrapped and eaten together in small pancakes, providing both visual and taste enjoyment. Beijing Roast Duck is divided into two main schools: "hanging oven roast duck" and "stewed oven roast duck", of which Quanjude's Hanging Oven Roasted Duck and Bianyifang's Braised Oven Roasted Duck are the most famous.

小结 Summary

词语 Words

朗读下列词语。**Read the following words.**

步骤	手掌	刀柄
抬起	拉回	推动

语法 Grammar

熟读句子。Read the following sentences.

1. 锉削平面有哪些步骤?
2. 锉削工件用哪些工具?
3. 抬起锉刀。
4. 拉回锉刀。

课文理解 Text Comprehension

把下列句子按正确步骤排列。Sort the following sentences according to the correct steps.

1. 左手手掌压在锉刀另一端。
2. 抬起、拉回锉刀。
3. 右手握紧锉刀刀柄。
4. 身体前倾，双手下压。
5. 右手推动锉刀向前锉削。

___③___ → ______ → ___④___ → ______ → ______

第9课 Lesson 9

Jiǎncè píngmiàndù

检测平面度

Testing Planeness

复习 Revision

根据词语选图片。**Choose the right pictures according to the words.**

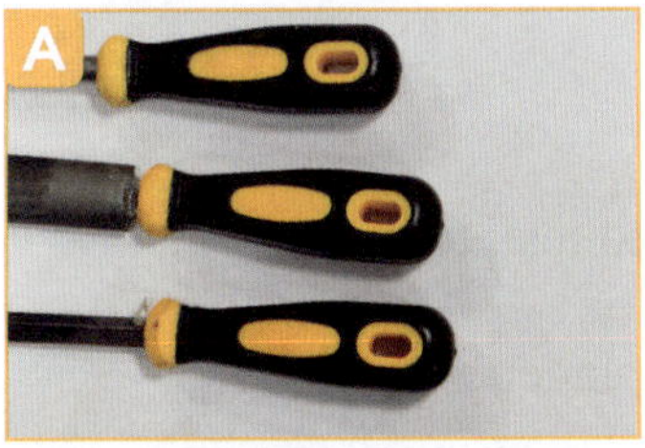

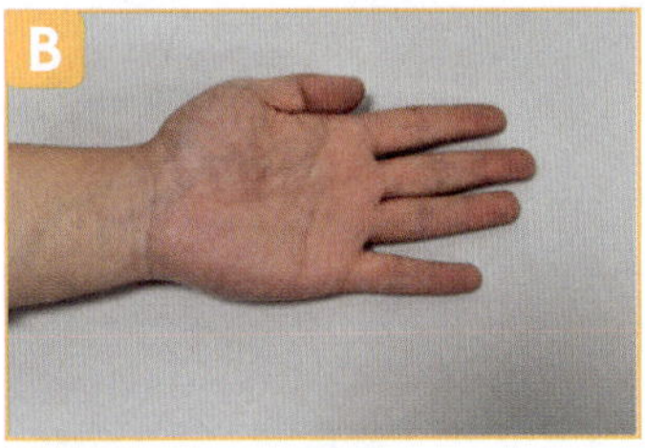

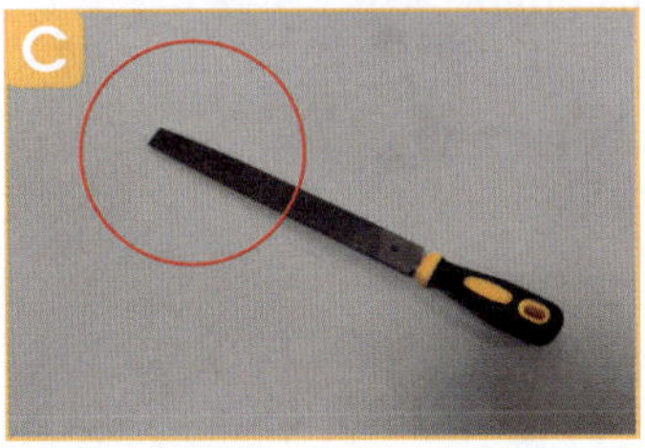

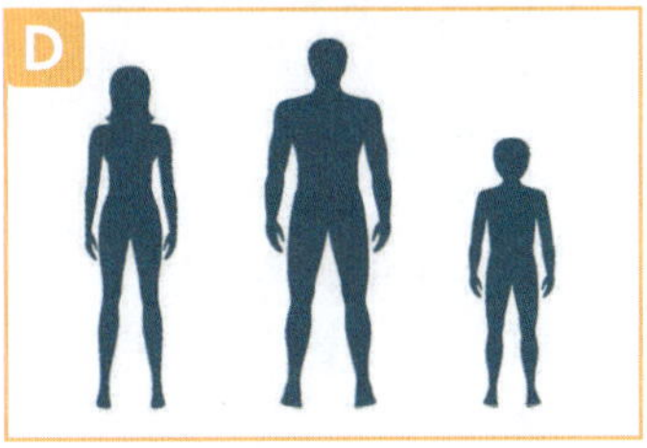

1. 身体（　　）
2. 另一端（　　）
3. 刀柄（　　）
4. 手掌（　　）

热身　Warm-up

选择正确的图片。**Choose the right pictures.**

A

B

C

D

❶ 塞尺 (sāichǐ) feeler gauge (　　)　　❷ 被测面 (bèicèmiàn) the measured surface (　　)

❸ 间隙 (jiànxì) gap (　　)　　❹ 规格数值 (guīgé shùzhí) specification value (　　)

学习生词　Words and Expressions　09-01

1	检测	jiǎncè	*v.*	to test; to check
2	平面度	píngmiàndù	*n.*	planeness
3	清理	qīnglǐ	*v.*	to clear
4	塞尺	sāichǐ	*n.*	feeler gauge
5	表面	biǎomiàn	*n.*	surface
6	把	bǎ	*prep.*	*a preposition indicating the object as the recipient of the action*
7	被测面	bèicèmiàn	*n.*	the measured surface
8	合适	héshì	*adj.*	suitable

9	塞入	sāirù	*phr.*	to insert
10	间隙	jiànxì	*n.*	gap
11	读取	dúqǔ	*v.*	to read
12	规格数值	guīgé shùzhí	*phr.*	specification value

词语练习 Word Exercises

1. 看图选词。Look at the pictures and choose the correct words.

❶  (　　) A. 高度尺　B. 塞尺

❷  (　　) A. 高度尺　B. 被测面

❸  (　　) A. 表面　B. 间隙

❹  (　　) A. 规格数值　B. 手锯

2. 词语连线。Word Matching.

❶ 检测	A. 间隙
❷ 清理	B. 平面度
❸ 塞入	C. 规格数值
❹ 读取	D. 塞尺

学习课文 Text 09-02

Jiǎncè píngmiàndù
检测平面度

Jiǎncè píngmiàndù yǒu 4 bù:
检测平面度有 4 步：

Qīnglǐ sāichǐ hé gōngjiàn de biǎomiàn.
（1）清理塞尺和工件的表面。

Bǎ gōngjiàn fàng zài huàxiàn píngtái shang, bèicèmiàn tiējǐn píngtái biǎomiàn.
（2）把工件放在划线平台上，被测面贴紧平台表面。

Xuǎnzé héshì de sāichǐ, sāirù jiànxì.
（3）选择合适的塞尺，塞入间隙。

Dúqǔ sāichǐ de guīgé shùzhí.
（4）读取塞尺的规格数值。

Testing Planeness

There are four steps to test the planeness:

First, clean the surface of the feeler gauge and workpiece.

Second, place the workpiece on the scribing platform and the measured surface is tightly attached to the platform surface.

Third, select a suitable feeler gauge and insert it into the gap.

Fourth, read the specification value of the feeler gauge.

课文练习 Text Exercises

1. 根据课文内容选择正确答案。Choose the correct answers according to the text.

1 清理________和工件的表面。

A. 右手　　　　B. 塞尺

2 把工件放在划线平台上，________贴紧平台表面。

A. 被测面　　　　B. 高度尺

3 选择合适的________，塞入间隙。

A. 塞尺　　　　B. 锯条

4 读取塞尺的________。

A. 规格数值　　　　B. 划线平台

2. 选择合适的词语填空。Choose the appropriate words to fill in the blanks.

A. 读取　　B. 塞入　　C. 清理　　D. 贴紧

1 ________塞尺和工件的表面。

2 ________塞尺的规格数值。

3 把工件放在划线平台上，被测面________平台表面。

4 选择合适的塞尺，________间隙。

学习语法 Grammar

语法点 1 Grammar Point 1

"把"字句 "把" Sentence

表示通过主语的动作行为，"把"后宾语所表示的人或事物的位置或状态发生了改变。基本结构为"（主语＋）把＋宾语＋动词短语"。

The "把" sentence indicates that the position or state of somebody or something is changed through the action or behavior of the subject. The basic structure is "(subject +) 把 + object + verb phrase".

1. Bǎ gōngjiàn fàng zài huàxiàn píngtái shang.
   把工件放在划线平台上。
   Place the workpiece on the scribing platform.
2. Bǎ lìng yí gè kǒng zhuāng zài yǒu luómǔ de lāgǎn shang.
   把另一个孔装在有螺母的拉杆上。
   The other hole is installed on the rod with a nut.
3. Bǎ fāngxiāng fàng zài huàxiàn píngtái shang.
   把方箱放在划线平台上。
   Place the square box on the scribing platform.

语法点 1 练习 Exercise on Grammar Point 1

连词成句。**Rearrange the following words to make sentences.**

例如：
gōngjiàn ①工件　fàng ②放　bǎ ③把　zài huàxiàn píngtái shang ④在划线平台上

③①②④

1. lìng yí gè kǒng ①另一个孔　bǎ ②把　zhuāng ③装　zài yǒu luómǔ de lāgǎn shang ④在有螺母的拉杆上

____

2 ①方箱（fāngxiāng） ②把（bǎ） ③在划线平台上（zài huàxiàn píngtái shang） ④放（fàng）

____

3 ①把（bǎ） ②图纸（túzhǐ） ③在钳工台上（zài qiángōngtái shang） ④放（fàng）

____

4 ①锯条的一个孔（jùtiáo de yí gè kǒng） ②把（bǎ） ③装（zhuāng） ④在没有螺母的拉杆上（zài méiyǒu luómǔ de lāgǎn shang）

____

语法点 2 Grammar Point 2

方位词：上 The Directional Word: 上

用在名词后，表示在某个物体的表面。

The directional word "上" is used after a noun to indicate being on the surface of something.

1 把工件放在划线平台上。（Bǎ gōngjiàn fàng zài huàxiàn píngtái shang.） Place the workpiece on the scribing platform.

2 钳工台上有台虎钳。（Qiángōngtái shang yǒu táihǔqián.） There are bench vices on the vice bench.

3 划线平台上有方箱。（Huàxiàn píngtái shang yǒu fāngxiāng.） There are square boxes on the scribing platform.

语法点 2 练习 Exercise on Grammar Point 2

为"上"选择适当的位置。**Fill "上" in the appropriate positions.**

1 ________ 把（bǎ）（A）工件（gōngjiàn）（B）放在（fàng zài）（C）划线平台（huàxiàn píngtái）（D）。

2 ________ （A）钳工台（qiángōngtái）（B）有（yǒu）（C）台虎钳（táihǔqián）（D）。

3 ________　（A）划线 平台（B）有（C）方箱（D）。
huàxiàn píngtái　yǒu　fāngxiāng

4 ________　把（A）图纸（B）放 在（C）钳工台（D）。
bǎ　túzhǐ　fàng zài　qiángōngtái

汉字书写 Writing Chinese Characters

wǔ　午 午 午 午

午 午 午 午 午

niú　牛 牛 牛 牛

牛 牛 牛 牛 牛

shēng　生 生 生 生 生

生 生 生 生 生

zhū　朱 朱 朱 朱 朱 朱

朱 朱 朱 朱 朱

职业拓展 Career Insight

三坐标测量仪

三坐标测量仪是能够检测平面度的设备之一，是近 50 年发展起来的一种高效率的新型精密测量仪器，广泛用于机械制造业、汽车工业、电子工业、航空航天工业和国防工业等领域，成为现代工业检测和质量控制不可缺少的万能测量设备。

Coordinate Measuring Machines (CMM)

The coordinate measuring machine is one of the devices capable of detecting flatness. It is a new type of high-efficiency precision measuring instrument developed over the past 50 years, widely used in machinery manufacturing, automobile industry, electronics industry, aerospace industry, national defense industry and other fields. It has become an indispensable universal measuring instrument for modern industrial detection and quality control.

小结 Summary

词语 Words

朗读下列词语。Read the following words.

塞尺	被测面	规格数值	间隙
读取	清理	塞入	贴紧

语法 Grammar

熟读句子。Read the following sentences.

1 把工件放在划线平台上。

2 把另一个孔装在有螺母的拉杆上。

3 钳工台上有台虎钳。

4 划线平台上有方箱。

课文理解 Text Comprehension

把下列句子按正确步骤排列。Sort the following sentences according to the correct steps.

1 把工件放在划线平台上，被测面贴紧平台表面。

2 选择合适的塞尺，塞入间隙。

3 清理塞尺和工件的表面。

4 读取塞尺的规格数值。

________ → ________ → ________ → ________

第10课 Lesson 10

Kāi guān zuànchuáng

开关钻床

Switching on/off Drilling Machines

复习 Revision

根据词语选图片。**Choose the right pictures according to the words.**

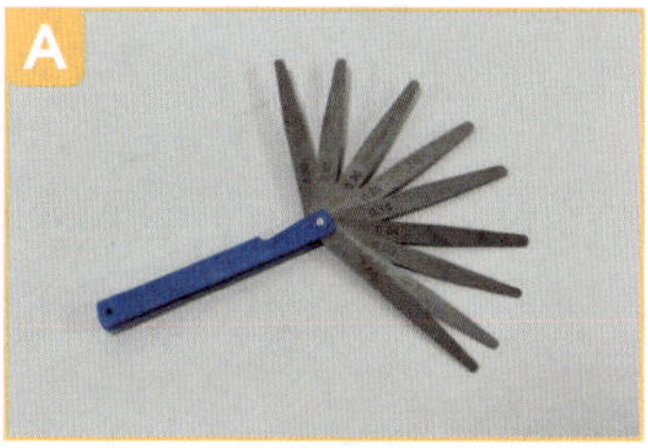

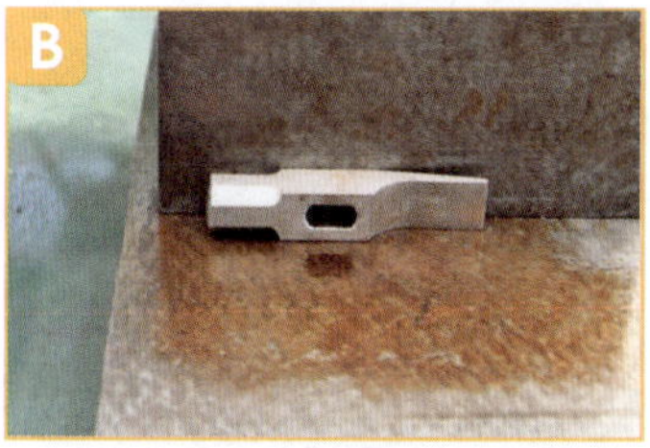

❶ 被测面（　　）　　❷ 规格数值（　　）

❸ 塞尺（　　）　　❹ 间隙（　　）

热身 Warm-up

选择正确的图片。Choose the right pictures.

A

B

C

D

❶	jítíng ànniǔ 急停按钮	emergency stop button	(　　)
❷	zǒngdiànyuán 总电源	main power	(　　)
❸	qǐdòng ànniǔ 启动 按钮	start button	(　　)
❹	zuànchuáng 钻床	drilling machine	(　　)

学习生词 Words and Expressions 10-01

1	开	kāi	*v.*	to switch on
2	关	guān	*v.*	to switch off
3	钻床	zuànchuáng	*n.*	drilling machine
4	先……，再……	xiān…, zài…		first...and then…
5	总电源	zǒngdiànyuán	*n.*	main power
	电源	diànyuán	*n.*	power
6	扳动	bāndòng	*v.*	to pull

7	启动手柄	qǐdòng shǒubǐng	*phr.*	start handle
8	拔出	báchū	*phr.*	to pull out
9	急停按钮	jítíng ànniǔ	*phr.*	emergency stop button
10	按下	ànxia	*phr.*	to press
11	启动按钮	qǐdòng ànniǔ	*phr.*	start button
12	右	yòu	*n.*	right
13	至	zhì	*v.*	to
14	空挡	kōngdǎng	*n.*	the neutral position
15	位置	wèizhì	*n.*	position

词语练习 Word Exercises

1. 看图选词。Look at the pictures and choose the correct words.

❶  (　　) A. 钳工台　B. 钻床

❷ 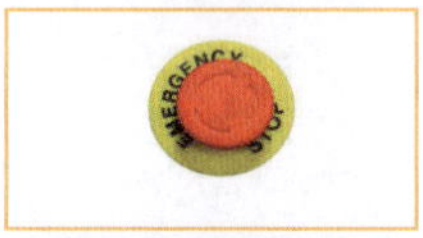

(　　) A. 急停按钮　B. 启动按钮

❸  (　　) A. 总电源　B. 启动手柄

❹  (　　) A. 急停按钮　B. 启动按钮

2. 词语连线。**Words Matching.**

❶ 打开	A. 启动手柄
❷ 扳动	B. 急停按钮
❸ 按下	C. 启动按钮
❹ 拔出	D. 总电源

学习课文 Text 10-02

Kāi guān zuànchuáng
开 关 钻 床

Kāi zuànchuáng:
（1）开 钻床：

Xiān dǎkāi zǒngdiànyuán, zài dǎkāi zuànchuáng diànyuán.
先打开总电源，再打开钻床电源。

Bāndòng qǐdòng shǒubǐng, báchū jítíng ànniǔ, ànxia zuànchuáng qǐdòng ànniǔ.
扳动启动手柄，拔出急停按钮，按下钻床启动按钮。

Guān zuànchuáng:
（2）关 钻床：

Xiàng yòu bāndòng qǐdòng shǒubǐng zhì kōngdǎng wèizhì, ànxia jítíng ànniǔ.
向右扳动启动手柄至空挡位置，按下急停按钮。

Xiān guānshang zuànchuáng diànyuán, zài guānshang zǒngdiànyuán.
先关上钻床电源，再关上总电源。

Switching on/off Drilling Machines

I. Switching on the drilling machine:

First, switch on the main power, and then switch on the power of the drilling machine.

Pull the start handle, pull out the emergency stop button, and press the start button of the drilling machine.

II. Switching off the drilling machine:

Pull the start handle to the right to the neutral position and press the emergency stop button.

First, switch off the power of the drilling machine, and then switch off the main power.

课文练习 Text Exercises

1. 根据课文内容选择正确答案。Choose the correct answers according to the text.

1 先打开________，再打开钻床电源。

A. 总电源　　　　B. 手柄

2 扳动________，拔出急停按钮，按下钻床启动按钮。

A. 启动手柄　　　　B. 电源开关

3 向右扳动启动手柄至空挡位置，按下________。

A. 急停按钮　　　　B. 钻床电源

4 先关上________，再关上总电源。

A. 钻床电源　　　　B. 空挡

2. 根据课文内容判断正误。True or False.

1 开钻床先打开总电源和钻床电源。（　　）

2 关钻床先打开总电源和钻床电源。（　　）

3 开钻床向左扳动启动手柄。（　　）

4 关钻床向右扳动启动手柄。（　　）

学习语法 Grammar

语法点 1 Grammar Point 1

先……，再……

“先”表示某个动作发生在前，“再”表示动作发生在前一个动作之后。

“先” indicates that an action occurs first, and “再” indicates that an action occurs after the previous action.

1. Xiān dǎkāi zǒngdiànyuán, zài dǎkāi zuànchuáng diànyuán.
先打开总电源，再打开钻床电源。
First switch on the main power, and then switch on the power of the drilling machine.

2. Xiān guānshang zuànchuáng diànyuán, zài guānshang zǒngdiànyuán.
先关上钻床电源，再关上总电源。
First switch off the power of the drilling machine, and then switch off the main power.

3. Xiān qǔxia jiù jùtiáo, zài zhuāngshang xīn jùtiáo.
先取下旧锯条，再装上新锯条。
First remove the used saw blade, and then install the new saw blade.

语法点 1 练习 Exercise on Grammar Point 1

连词成句。**Rearrange the following words to make sentences.**

例如：
dǎkāi zǒngdiànyuán　zài　xiān　dǎkāi zuànchuáng diànyuán
①打开 总电源　②再　③先　④打开 钻床 电源

③①②④

1. guānshang zuànchuáng diànyuán　zài　xiān　guānshang zǒngdiànyuán
①关上 钻床 电源　②再　③先　④关上 总电源

____

2 ①先（xiān） ②取下旧锯条（qǔxia jiù jùtiáo） ③再（zài） ④装上 新锯条（zhuāngshang xīn jùtiáo）

____

3 ①看图纸（kàn túzhǐ） ②先（xiān） ③再（zài） ④调 高度尺（tiáo gāodùchǐ）

____

4 ①再（zài） ②先（xiān） ③清理塞尺和 工件 的 表面（qīnglǐ sāichǐ hé gōngjiàn de biǎomiàn）
④把 工件 放 在 划线 平台 上（bǎ gōngjiàn fàng zài huàxiàn píngtái shang）

____

语法点 2 Grammar Point 2

介词：向 The Preposition: 向

引出动作的方向。

"向" introduces the direction of the action.

1 Xiàng yòu bāndòng qǐdòng shǒubǐng zhì kōngdǎng wèizhì.
向 右 扳动 启动 手柄 至 空挡 位置。
Pull the start handle to the right to the neutral position.

2 Xiàng qián tuī jù.
向 前 推 锯。 Push the saw forward.

3 Yòushǒu tuīdòng cuòdāo xiàng qián cuòxiāo.
右手 推动 锉刀 向 前 锉削。 Push the file forward with your right hand to file.

语法点 2 练习 Exercise on Grammar Point 2

为"向"选择适当的位置。**Fill "向" in the appropriate positions.**

1 ________ （A）右（B）扳动 启动 手柄（C）至 空挡 位置（D）。
（yòu bāndòng qǐdòng shǒubǐng zhì kōngdǎng wèizhì）

2 ________ （A）右手（B）前（C）推锯（D）。
（yòushǒu qián tuī jù）

3 ________ （A）右手（B）推动 锉刀（C）前 锉削（D）。

（yòushǒu / tuīdòng cuòdāo / qián cuòxiāo）

4 ________ （A）双手（B）下（C）压（D）。

（shuāngshǒu / xià / yā）

汉字书写 Writing Chinese Characters

yǐ 乙

乙	乙	乙	乙	乙						

jiǔ 九 九

九	九	九	九	九						

ér 儿 儿

儿	儿	儿	儿	儿						

jǐ 几 几

几	几	几	几	几						

职业拓展 Career Insight

钻床

钻床指主要用钻头在工件上加工孔的机床，是机械制造和维修必不可少的设备之一，分为台式钻床、立式钻床、摇臂钻床和多轴钻床等类型。

钻床结构简单，加工精度相对较低，适用于金属、木材等材料的钻孔、扩孔、铰孔、锪孔和攻螺纹等加工。加工过程中，工件固定不动，刀具做旋转运动。

Drilling Machines

A drilling machine refers to a machine tool that mainly uses drill bits to process holes on workpieces. It is one of the essential equipment for mechanical manufacturing and maintenance, and is divided into bench drilling machines, vertical drilling machines, radial drilling machines, and multi-axis drilling machines. The drilling machine has a simple structure and relatively low processing accuracy, and is suitable for drilling, expanding, reaming, countersinking, and threading of materials such as metal and wood. During the machining process, the workpiece remains stationary while the tool rotates.

小结 Summary

词语 Words

朗读下列词语。**Read the following words.**

钻床	总电源	启动手柄	拔出
扳动	按下	空挡	急停按钮

语法 Grammar

熟读句子。Read the following sentences.

1. 先打开总电源，再打开钻床电源。
2. 先关上钻床电源，再关上总电源。
3. 向右扳动启动手柄至空挡位置。
4. 向前推锯。

课文理解 Text Comprehension

把下列句子按正确步骤排列。Sort the following sentences according to the correct steps.

1. 扳动启动手柄，拔出急停按钮，按下钻床启动按钮。
2. 先关上钻床电源，再关上总电源。
3. 先打开总电源，再打开钻床电源。
4. 向右扳动启动手柄至空挡位置，按下急停按钮。

___③___ → ______ → ___④___ → ______

第11课 Lesson 11

Dǎ yàngchòngyǎn
打样冲眼
Punching

复习 Revision

根据所给词语描述开钻床的步骤。**Describe the steps of switching on a drilling machine based on the given vocabulary.**

总电源　　钻床电源　　启动手柄　　急停按钮　　启动按钮

热身 Warm-up

看图认读词语。**Recognize the words according to the pictures.**

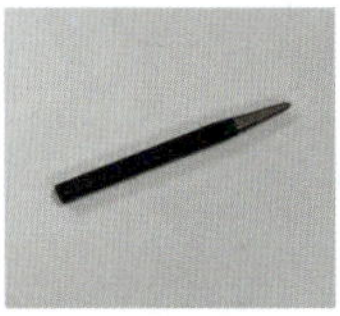

yàngchòng
样冲
punching

chuízhí
垂直
vertical

shǒuchuí
手锤
hand hammer

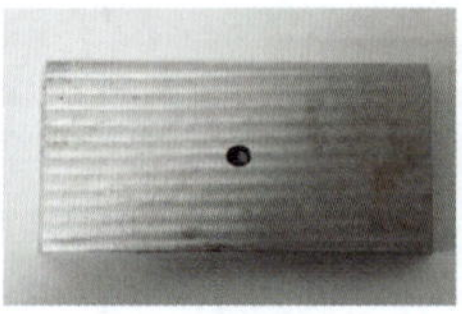

kǒng
孔
hole

qīngxié
倾斜
tilt

学习生词 Words and Expressions 11-01

1	打	dǎ	*v.*	to knock
2	样冲眼	yàngchòngyǎn	*n.*	punching hole
3	第	dì	*pref.*	*a prefix for ordinal numbers*
4	工具	gōngjù	*n.*	tool
5	划出	huàchū	*phr.*	to mark
6	中心点	zhōngxīndiǎn	*n.*	center point
7	样冲	yàngchòng	*n.*	punching
8	倾斜	qīngxié	*v.*	to tilt
9	尖	jiān	*n.*	tip
10	对准	duìzhǔn	*phr.*	to align
11	扶正	fúzhèng	*phr.*	to straighten
12	与	yǔ	*prep.*	with
13	垂直	chuízhí	*v.*	to be vertical to
14	手锤	shǒuchuí	*n.*	hammer
15	敲击	qiāojī	*v.*	to strike

词语练习 Word Exercises

1. 看图选词。Look at the pictures and choose the correct words.

❶ 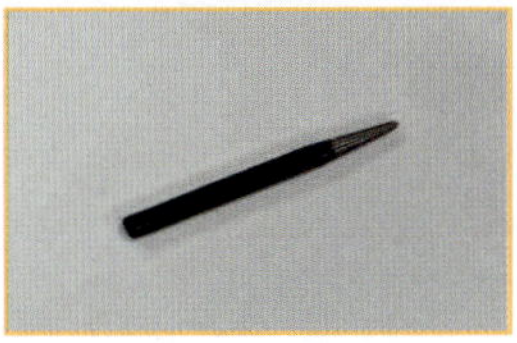

(　　) A. 样冲　　B. 手锤

❷  （　　）A. 样冲　　B. 手锤

❸  （　　）A. 垂直　　B. 倾斜

❹  （　　）A. 垂直　　B. 倾斜

❺ 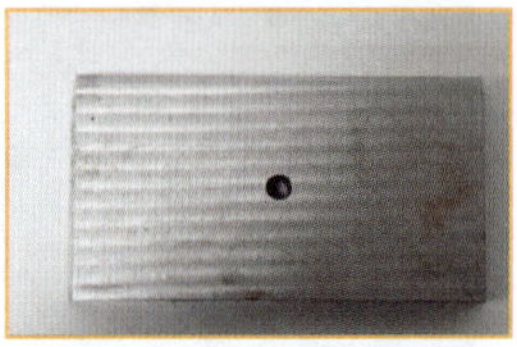 （　　）A. 孔　　B. 平面

❻ 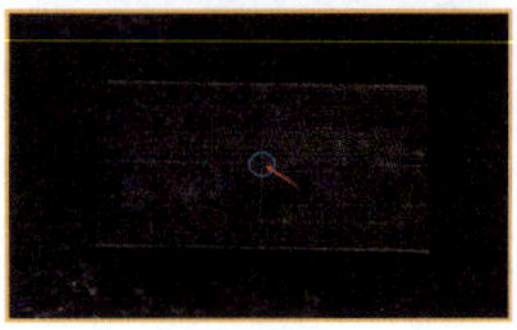 （　　）A. 倾斜　　B. 中心点

2. 词语连线。**Word Matching.**

❶ 划出	A. 样冲
❷ 握紧	B. 孔的中心点
❸ 用	C. 手锤敲击
❹ 倾斜	D. 60°

学习课文 Text 11-02

Dǎ yàngchòngyǎn
打样冲眼

Dǎ yàngchòngyǎn yǒu 4 gè bùzhòu:
打样冲眼有 4 个步骤：

Dì-yī bù, yòng huàxiàn gōngjù huàchū kǒng de zhōngxīndiǎn.
第一步，用划线工具划出孔的中心点。

Dì-èr bù, yòng zuǒshǒu wòjǐn yàngchòng, qīngxié 60°, yàngchòngjiān duìzhǔn zhōngxīndiǎn.
第二步，用左手握紧样冲，倾斜 60°，样冲尖对准中心点。

Dì-sān bù, fúzhèng yàngchòng, yǔ gōngjiàn biǎomiàn chuízhí.
第三步，扶正样冲，与工件表面垂直。

Dì-sì bù, yòng shǒuchuí qiāojī yàngchòng.
第四步，用手锤敲击样冲。

Punching

There are four steps of punching:

First, use a scribing tool to mark the center point of the hole.

Second, hold the punch tightly with the left hand, tilt it with an angle of 60 degrees, and align the punch tip with the center point.

Third, straighten the punch so that it is vertical to the surface of the workpiece.

Fourth, use a hammer to strike the punch.

课文练习 Text Exercises

1. 根据课文内容选择正确答案。Choose the correct answers according to the text.

1 第一步，用划线工具划出孔的________。 A. 中心点 B. 手柄

2 第二步，用左手握紧________。 A. 样冲 B. 电源开关

3 第三步，扶正样冲，与________垂直。 A. 急停按钮 B. 工件表面

4 第四步，用________敲击样冲。 A. 开关 B. 手锤

2. 根据课文内容判断正误。True or False.

1 打样冲眼有 3 步。 (　　)

2 用划线工具划出孔的中心点。 (　　)

3 用左手握紧样冲，倾斜 10°。 (　　)

4 用手锤敲击样冲。 (　　)

学习语法 Grammar

语法点 1 Grammar Point 1

用 + 名词 + 动词短语　用 + Noun + Verb Phrase

表示使用某种工具、方法、手段或材料等。

"用 + Noun + Verb Phrase" indicates using tools, methods, means or materials.

1. Yòng huàxiàn gōngjù huàchū kǒng de zhōngxīndiǎn.
   用 划线 工具 划出 孔 的 中心点。
   Use a scribing tool to mark the center point of the hole.
2. Yòng táihǔqián zhuāngjiā gōngjiàn.
   用 台虎钳 装夹 工件。Use a bench vice to clamp the workpiece.
3. Yòng cuòdāo cuòxiāo píngmiàn.
   用 锉刀 锉削 平面。File a flat surface with a file.

语法点 1 练习 Exercise on Grammar Point 1

连词成句。**Rearrange the following words to make sentences.**

例如： ①划线 工具 (huàxiàn gōngjù)　②划出 孔 的 中心点 (huàchū kǒng de zhōngxīndiǎn)　③用 (yòng)

③①②

1. ①用 (yòng)　②台虎钳 (táihǔqián)　③装夹 工件 (zhuāngjiā gōngjiàn)

   ____

2. ①锉削 平面 (cuòxiāo píngmiàn)　②锉刀 (cuòdāo)　③用 (yòng)

   ____

3 ①敲击（qiāojī） 样冲（yàngchòng） ②用（yòng） ③手锤（shǒuchuí）

____

4 ①用（yòng） ②左手（zuǒshǒu） ③握紧（wòjǐn） 样冲（yàngchòng）

____

语法点 2 Grammar Point 2

介词：与 The Preposition: 与

引出动作的对象或比较的对象。

"与" introduces the object of an action or comparison.

1 Fúzhèng yàngchòng, yǔ gōngjiàn biǎomiàn chuízhí.
扶正 样冲，与 工件 表面 垂直。
Straighten the punch so that it is vertical to the surface of the workpiece.

2 Bèicèmiàn yǔ píngtái biǎomiàn tiējǐn.
被测面 与 平台 表面 贴紧。
The measured surface is tightly attached to the platform surface.

3 Yàngchòngjiān yǔ zhōngxīndiǎn chónghé.
样冲尖 与 中心点 重合（chónghé; align with）。
The punch tip aligns with the center point.

语法点 2 练习 Exercise on Grammar Point 2

为"与"选择适当的位置。**Fill "与" in the appropriate positions.**

1 ________ 扶正（fúzhèng）（A）样冲（yàngchòng）（B），（C）工件表面（gōngjiàn biǎomiàn）（D）垂直（chuízhí）。

2 ________ （A）被测面（bèicèmiàn）（B）平台表面（píngtái biǎomiàn）（C）贴紧（tiējǐn）（D）。

3 ________　（A）样冲尖（yàngchòngjiān）（B）中心点（zhōngxīndiǎn）（C）重合（chónghé）（D）。

4 ________　（A）工件（gōngjiàn）（B）方箱（fāngxiāng）（C）贴紧（tiējǐn）（D）。

汉字书写 Writing Chinese Characters

nǚ　女

女	女	女	女	女						

hǎo　好

好	好	好	好	好						

rú　如

如	如	如	如	如						

miào　妙

妙	妙	妙	妙	妙						

文化拓展 Culture Insight

万里长城

长城是由城墙、敌楼、关城、墩堡、营城、卫所、镇城烽火台等多种防御工事所组成的完整防御工程体系，是中国古代人民创造的世界奇迹之一，具有极高的旅游观光价值和重要的历史文化意义。历史上，周朝的多个诸侯国和此后的很多王朝都修筑过长城。若把各个朝代修筑的长城连接起来，长度已经超过了 2 万公里，因此，长城被称为“万里长城”。

The Ten Thousand *Li* Great Wall

The Great Wall is a comprehensive defensive engineering system composed of various structures such as city walls, watchtowers, gates, fortresses, barracks, guard posts, and beacon towers. It is one of the wonders of the world created by ancient Chinese people and holds great tourism value as well as historical and cultural significance. Throughout history, multiple vassal states during Zhou Dynasty and many subsequent dynasties constructed sections of the Great Wall. If the sections of the Great Wall built by various dynasties were connected, its length would exceed 20,000 kilometers, which is why it is called “the Ten Thousand *Li* Great Wall”.

小结 Summary

词语 Words

朗读下列词语。**Read the following words.**

样冲	中心点	垂直
敲击	倾斜	手锤

语法 Grammar

把“用”或“与”填入适当的位置。Fill “用” or “与” in the appropriate positions.

1. ________划线工具划出孔的中心点。
2. ________台虎钳装夹工件。
3. 扶正样冲，________工件表面垂直。
4. 被测面________平台表面贴紧。

课文理解 Text Comprehension

把下列句子按正确步骤排列。Sort the following sentences according to the correct steps.

1. 用左手握紧样冲，倾斜 60°，样冲尖对准中心点。
2. 用手锤敲击样冲。
3. 用划线工具划出孔的中心点。
4. 扶正样冲，与工件表面垂直。

___③___ → ________ → ___④___ → ________

第12课 Lesson 12

Jiāgōng tōngkǒng 加工通孔 Processing Through Holes

复习 Revision

根据所给词语描述打样冲眼的步骤。**Describe the steps for punching based on the given vocabulary.**

划线工具　　孔的中心点　　样冲　　倾斜　　垂直　　手锤

热身 Warm-up

看图认读词语。**Recognize the words according to the pictures.**

		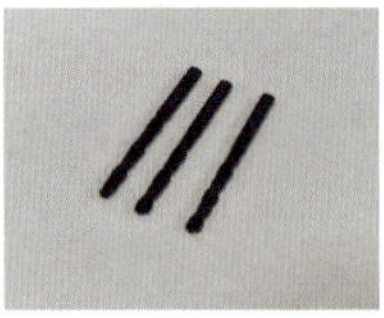	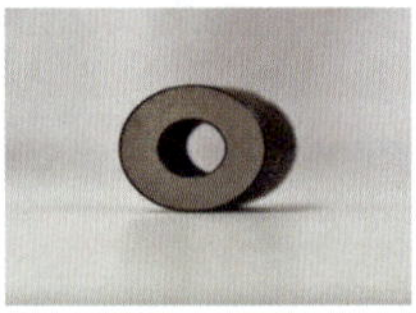	
bǎshou 把手 handle	píngkǒuqián 平口钳 flat-nose pliers	zuàntóu 钻头 drill	tōngkǒng 通孔 through hole	shuāzi 刷子 brush

学习生词 Words and Expressions 12-01

1	加工	jiāgōng	*v.*	to process
2	通孔	tōngkǒng	*n.*	through hole
3	平口钳	píngkǒuqián	*n.*	flat-nose pliers
4	钻头	zuàntóu	*n.*	drill bit
5	慢慢	mànmàn		slowly
6	地	de	*part.*	*a particle used after adverbs*
7	不断	búduàn	*adv.*	continuously
8	进给	jìnjǐ	*v.*	feed
9	把手	bǎshou	*n.*	handle; knob
10	钻	zuàn	*v.*	to drill
11	一边……，一边……	yìbiān…，yìbiān…		simultaneously
12	排屑	páixiè	*v.*	to remove chips
13	刷子	shuāzi	*n.*	brush
14	切屑	qiēxiè	*n.*	chip

词语练习 Word Exercises

1. 看图选词。Look at the pictures and choose the correct words.

❶  (　　) A. 台虎钳　B. 平口钳

②  (   ) A. 把手 B. 按钮

③ 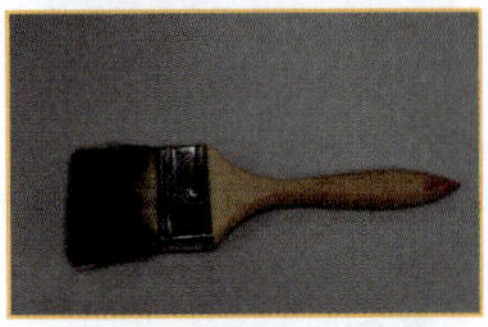 (   ) A. 刷子 B. 样冲

④ 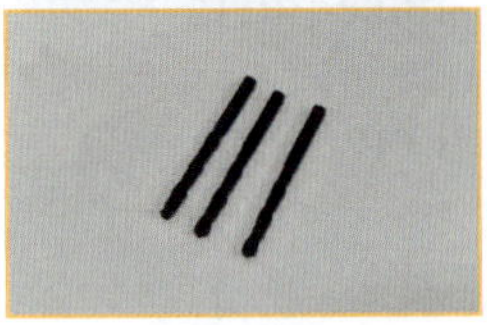 (   ) A. 锉刀 B. 钻头

⑤ 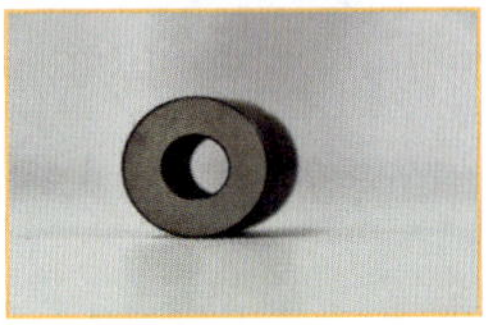 (   ) A. 平面 B. 通孔

⑥  (   ) A. 刷子 B. 切屑

2. 搭配练习。Matching.

① 夹紧	A. 切屑
② 选择	B. 工件
③ 扳动	C. 钻头
④ 清理	D. 进给把手

学习课文 Text 12-02

Jiāgōng tōngkǒng
加工 通孔

Xiān zài gōngjiàn biǎomiàn huàxiàn, dǎ yàngchòngyǎn, zài yòng píngkǒuqián jiājǐn gōngjiàn.
先在工件表面划线，打样冲眼，再用平口钳夹紧工件。

Xuǎnzé héshì de zuàntóu, zuàntóu duìzhǔn yàngchòngyǎn, mànmàn de、búduàn de xiàng xià bāndòng jìnjǐ bǎshou, zuànkǒng.
选择合适的钻头，钻头对准样冲眼，慢慢地、不断地向下扳动进给把手，钻孔。

Zuànkǒng shí, yìbiān zuàn, yìbiān páixiè, yòng shuāzi qīnglǐ qiēxiè.
钻孔时，一边钻，一边排屑，用刷子清理切屑。

Processing Through Holes

Firstly, scribe on the surface of the workpiece, punch a hole on it and clamp the workpiece tightly with flat-nose pliers.

Select the appropriate drill bit, align it with the punch hole, and pull the feed handle downwards slowly and continuously to drill the hole.

While drilling, simultaneously remove the chips and clean them with a brush.

课文练习 Text Exercises

1. 根据课文内容选择正确答案。Choose the correct answers according to the text.

1. 在工件表面正确划线，打________。　A. 中心点　B. 样冲眼
2. 用________夹紧工件。　A. 样冲　B. 平口钳
3. 选择合适的________。　A. 钻头　B. 工件
4. 钻头对准样冲眼，慢慢地、不断地向下扳动________，钻孔。　A. 进给把手　B. 手锤

2. 根据课文内容判断正误。True or False.

1. 加工通孔时先在工件表面上划线。（　　）
2. 用样冲夹紧工件。（　　）
3. 钻头对准样冲眼。（　　）
4. 一边钻，一边排屑。（　　）

学习语法 Grammar

语法点 1 Grammar Point 1

结构助词：地 The Structural Particle: 地

一般用在状语后、动词或形容词前，是状语的标志。单音节形容词做状语时，一般需要采用重叠的方式，比如“慢慢地”。

“地” is generally used after an adverb or before a verb or adjective, serving as a marker for the adverbial. When a monosyllabic adjective is used as the adverbial, it typically needs to be in reduplicated form, such as “慢慢地”.

1. Mànmàn de xiàng xià bāndòng jìnjǐ bǎshou.
   慢慢地向下扳动进给把手。Pull the feed handle downwards slowly.
2. Búduàn de xiàng xià bāndòng jìnjǐ bǎshou.
   不断地向下扳动进给把手。Pull the feed handle downwards continuously.
3. Qīngxī de huàxiàn.
   清晰地划线。Scribe a line clearly.

语法点 1 练习 Exercise on Grammar Point 1

连词成句。**Rearrange the following words to make sentences.**

例如：
bāndòng ①扳动 jìnjǐ bǎshou ②进给把手 mànmàn de ③慢慢地

③①②

1. huàxiàn ①划线 yào ②要 qīngxī de ③清晰地

____

2 ①样冲眼(yàngchòngyǎn) ②打(dǎ) ③准确地(zhǔnquè de)

____

3 ①急停按钮(jítíng ànniǔ) ②慢慢地(mànmàn de) ③拔出(báchū)

____

4 ①学习(xuéxí) ②不断地(búduàn de) ③中文(Zhōngwén)

____

语法点 2 Grammar Point 2

并列复句：一边……，一边……

Parallel Compound Sentence: 一边……，一边……

“一边……，一边……”连接两个分句，表示两种同时存在的状态或动作。

“一边……，一边……” connects two clauses and indicates the simultaneous existence of two states or actions.

1 Yìbiān zuàn, yìbiān páixiè.
一边钻，一边排屑。When drilling, remove chips simultaneously.

2 Jùgē shí, shuāngshǒu yìbiān xiàyā, yìbiān xiàng qián tuī shǒujù.
锯割时，双手一边下压，一边向前推手锯。
When sawing, press down with both hands while pushing the hand saw forward.

3 Cuòxiāo shí, shuāngshǒu yìbiān xiàyā, yìbiān xiàng qián tuī cuòdāo.
锉削时，双手一边下压，一边向前推锉刀。
When filing, press down with both hands while pushing the file forward.

语法点 2 练习 Exercise on Grammar Point 2

选择正确的答案。Choose the right answers.

1. Zhuāngjiā gōngjiàn shí, yìbiān ______, yìbiān shùnshízhēn xuánzhuǎn shǒubǐng.
装夹 工件 时，一边________，一边 顺时针 旋转 手柄。

A. fàngrù gōngjiàn 放入 工件　　B. huàn jùtiáo 换 锯条

2. Dǎ yàngchòngyǎn shí, yìbiān ______ yàngchòng, yìbiān shǐ yàngchòng yǔ gōngjiàn biǎomiàn chuízhí.
打 样冲眼 时，一边________样冲，一边 使 样冲 与 工件 表面 垂直。

A. zhuāngjiā 装夹　　B. fúzhèng 扶正

3. Cuòxiāo shí, shuāngshǒu yìbiān xiàng shàng yònglì, yìbiān ______ cuòdāo.
锉削 时，双手 一边 向 上 用力，一边________锉刀。

A. lāhuí 拉回　　B. zuàn 钻

4. Jùgē shí, shuāngshǒu yìbiān xiàyā, yìbiān xiàng qián ______ shǒujù.
锯割 时，双手 一边 下压，一边 向 前________手锯。

A. tuī 推　　B. lā 拉

汉字书写 Writing Chinese Characters

fēng 丰 丰 丰 丰

丰	丰	丰	丰	丰						

máo 毛 毛 毛 毛

毛 毛 毛 毛 毛

shǒu 手 手 手 手

手 手 手 手 手

diū 丢 丢 丢 丢 丢 丢

丢 丢 丢 丢 丢

职业拓展 Career Insight

麻花钻

麻花钻是一种形状较复杂的双刃钻孔或扩孔的标准刀具，因其容屑槽呈螺旋状、形似麻花而得名。麻花钻由尾部、颈部和工作部分组成。其中，工作部分是钻头的主要部分。前端为切削部分，承担主要的切削工作；后端为导向部分，起引导钻头的作用，也是切削部分的后备部分。

Twist Drills

A twist drill is a standard tool for drilling or reaming holes, characterized by its complex shape and dual cutting edges. It is named after its helical chip flutes, which resemble the shape of twisted dough. The twist drill consists of the shank, neck, and working part. Among the working part is the main section of the drill, with the front end serving as the cutting portion, responsible for the primary cutting tasks, while the rear end functions as the guiding portion, helping to direct the drill and acting as the backup for the cutting part.

小结 Summary

词语 Words

朗读下列词语。Read the following words.

通孔	平口钳	钻头	把手
钻孔	刷子	切屑	排屑

语法 Grammar

把“地”或“一边”填入适当的位置。Fill “地” or “一边” in the appropriate positions.

1. 慢慢_________向下扳动进给把手。
2. 清晰_________划线。
3. 一边钻，_________排屑。
4. 锉削时，双手一边下压，_________向前推锉刀。

课文理解 Text Comprehension

把下列句子按正确步骤排列。**Sort the following sentences according to the correct steps.**

1 再用平口钳夹紧工件。

2 慢慢地、不断地扳动进给把手，钻孔。

3 先在工件表面上划线，打样冲眼。

4 选择合适的钻头。

___③___ → ______ → ___④___ → ______

第13课 Lesson 13

Jiāgōng nèiluówén

加工内螺纹

Processing Internal Threads

复习 Revision

根据所给词语描述加工通孔的步骤。**Describe the steps of processing through holes based on the given vocabulary.**

划线　　样冲眼　　平口钳　　钻头　　进给把手　　钻孔　　切屑

热身 Warm-up

看图认读词语。**Recognize the words according to the pictures.**

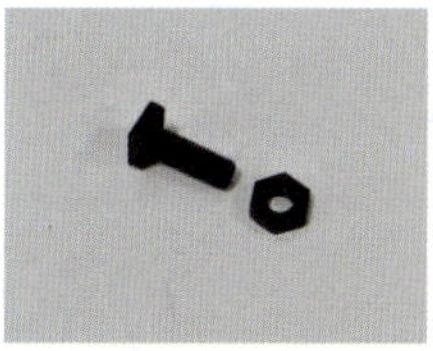

nèiluówén
内螺纹
internal thread

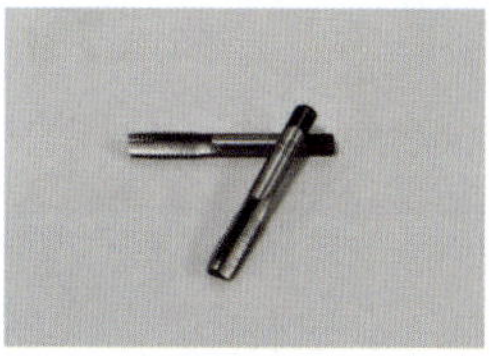

sīzhuī
丝锥
tap

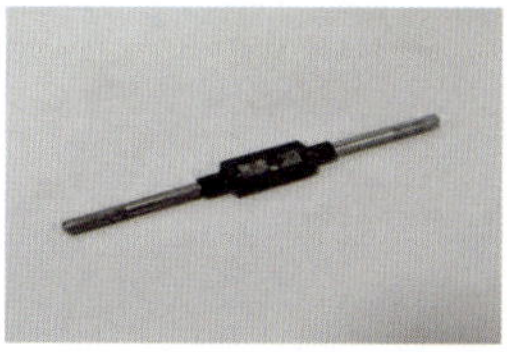

jiǎogàng
铰杠
tap wrench

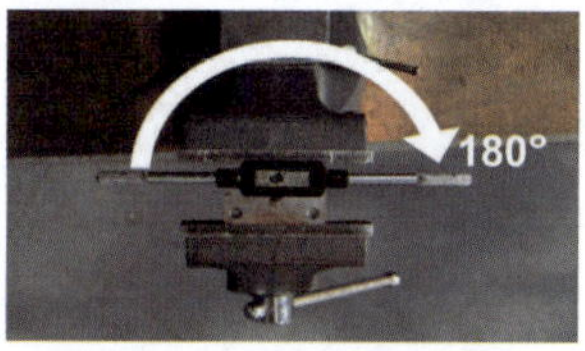

bàn quān
半圈
half turn

学习生词 Words and Expressions 13-01

1	内螺纹	nèiluówén	*n.*	internal thread
2	水平	shuǐpíng	*adj.*	horizontal
3	放置	fàngzhì	*v.*	to place
4	丝锥	sīzhuī	*n.*	tap
5	轻轻	qīngqīng		gently
6	转动	zhuàndòng	*v.*	to turn
7	铰杠	jiǎogàng	*n.*	tap wrench
8	旋进	xuánjìn	*phr.*	to screw in
9	半	bàn	*num.*	half
10	圈	quān	*m.*	turn
11	到	dào	*v.*	to
12	反向	fǎnxiàng	*v.*	(to be in the) opposite direction
13	旋出	xuánchū	*phr.*	to screw out
14	排出	páichū	*phr.*	to remove
15	旋转	xuánzhuǎn	*v.*	to revolve

词语练习 Word Exercises

1. 看图选词。Look at the pictures and choose the correct words.

❶ 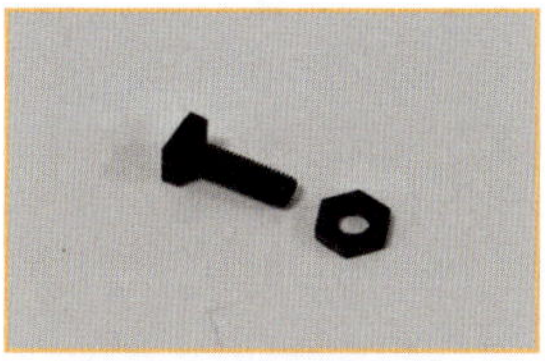

(   ) A. 平面   B. 内螺纹

❷ 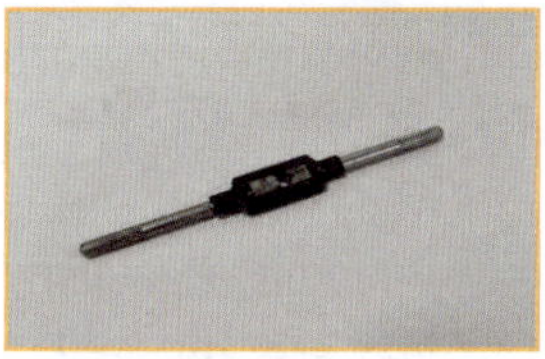

(   ) A. 铰杠   B. 丝锥

❸ 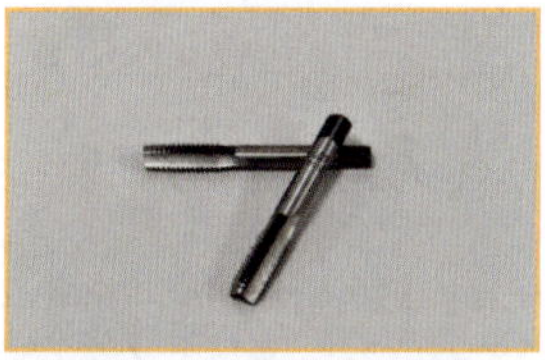

(   ) A. 铰杠   B. 丝锥

❹ 

(   ) A. 半圈   B. 一圈

2. 搭配练习。Matching.

❶ 夹紧	A. 丝锥
❷ 扶正	B. 工件
❸ 转动	C. 铰杠
❹ 排出	D. 切屑

学习课文 Text 13-02

Jiāgōng nèiluówén
加工内螺纹

Yòng táihǔqián jiājǐn gōngjiàn, jiāgōngmiàn yào shuǐpíng fàngzhì.
用台虎钳夹紧工件，加工面要水平放置。
Zuǒshǒu fúzhèng sīzhuī, xiàng xià yā, yòushǒu qīngqīng de zhuàndòng
左手扶正丝锥，向下压，右手轻轻地转动
jiǎogàng. Xiān xuánjìn bàn quān dào yì quān, ránhòu fǎnxiàng xuánchū
铰杠。先旋进半圈到一圈，然后反向旋出
bàn quān páichū qiēxiè. Yòng jiǎogàng fǎnxiàng xuánzhuǎn sīzhuī,
半圈，排出切屑。用铰杠反向旋转丝锥，
ránhòu yòng shǒu xuánchū sīzhuī.
然后用手旋出丝锥。

Processing Internal Threads

Clamp the workpiece with a bench vice and place the machining surface horizontally. Straighten the tap with the left hand and press it downward, while gently turning the tap wrench with the right hand. Screw the tap in by half to one turn firstly, and then reverse the direction to screw it out by half turn and remove the chips. Revolve the tap with the tap wrench in opposite direction, and then screw out the tap by hand.

课文练习 Text Exercises

1. 根据课文内容判断正误。**True or False.**

1. 用台虎钳夹紧工件，水平放置加工面。 (　　)
2. 左手扶正丝锥，向上压。 (　　)
3. 先旋进半圈到一圈，然后反向旋出半圈。 (　　)
4. 用铰杠反向旋转丝锥，再用手旋出丝锥。 (　　)

2. 选择合适的词语填空。**Choose the appropriate words to fill in the blanks.**

A. 铰杠	B. 内螺纹	C. 切屑	D. 丝锥

1. 左手扶正________，向下压。
2. 用________反向旋转丝锥。
3. 然后反向旋出半圈，排出________。
4. 加工________。

学习语法 Grammar

语法点 1 Grammar Point 1

先……，然后……

表示做事的先后顺序。

"先……，然后……" indicates the order of doing things.

Xiān xuánjìn bàn quān dào yì quān, ránhòu fǎnxiàng xuánchū bàn quān, páichū qiēxiè.
1 先 旋进 半 圈 到 一 圈，然后 反向 旋出 半 圈，排出 切屑。
Screw in by half to one turn first, and then reverse the direction to screw it out by half turn and remove the chips.

Xiān zài gōngjiàn biǎomiàn huàxiàn. ránhòu dǎ yàngchòngyǎn.
2 先 在 工件 表面 划线，然后 打 样冲眼。
First, scribe on the surface of the workpiece, and then punch.

Xiān fúzhèng yàngchòng, ránhòu yòng shǒuchuí qiāojī yàngchòng.
3 先 扶正 样冲，然后 用 手锤 敲击 样冲。
First, straighten the punch and then use a hammer to strike the punch.

语法点 1 练习 Exercise on Grammar Point 1

连词成句。**Rearrange the following words to make sentences.**

例如：

xuánjìn bàn quān dào yì quān　ránhòu　xiān　fǎnxiàng xuánchū bàn quān
①旋进 半 圈 到一圈　②然后　③先　④反向 旋出 半 圈

③①②④

xiān　ránhòu　zài gōngjiàn biǎomiàn huàxiàn　dǎ yàngchòngyǎn
1 ①先　②然后　③在 工件 表面 划线　④打 样冲眼

____

fúzhèng yàngchòng　xiān　ránhòu　yòng shǒuchuí qiāojī yàngchòng
2 ①扶正 样冲　②先　③然后　④用 手锤 敲击 样冲

____

xiān　ránhòu　dǎkāi zǒngdiànyuán　dǎkāi zuànchuáng diànyuán
3 ①先　②然后　③打开 总电源　④打开 钻床 电源

____

qǔxia jiù jùtiáo　ránhòu　xiān　zhuāngshang xīn jùtiáo
4 ①取下旧锯条　②然后　③先　④装上 新锯条

____

语法点 2 Grammar Point 2

动词 + 进 / 出　Verb + 进 / 出

“进”用在动词后，表示通过动作使人或物进入某个空间或范围；“出”用在动词后，表示通过动作使人或物离开某个空间或范围。

“进” is used after a verb to indicate that somebody or something is made to enter a certain space or range through an action, while “出” is used after a verb to indicate that somebody or something is made to leave a certain space or range through an action.

1. xiān xuánjìn bàn quān dào yì quān, ránhòu fǎnxiàng xuánchū bàn quān.
先旋进半圈到一圈，然后反向旋出半圈。
Screw in by half to one turn firstly, and then reverse the direction to screw it out by half turn.

2. Kāi zuànchuáng shí, bāndòng qǐdòng shǒubǐng, báchū jítíng ànniǔ.
开钻床时，扳动启动手柄，拔出急停按钮。
When switching on the drilling machine, pull the start handle and pull out the emergency stop button.

3. Yòng shǒu xuánchū sīzhuī.
用手旋出丝锥。
Screw out the tap by hand.

语法点 2 练习 Exercise on Grammar Point 2

把“进”或“出”填入适当的位置。Fill “进” or “出” in the appropriate positions.

1. Xiān xuán ________ bàn quān dào yì quān, ránhòu fǎnxiàng xuánchū bàn quān.
先旋________半圈到一圈，然后反向旋出半圈。

2. Kāi zuànchuáng shí, bāndòng qǐdòng shǒubǐng, bá ________ jítíng ànniǔ.
开钻床时，扳动启动手柄，拔________急停按钮。

3. Yòng shǒu xuán ________ sīzhuī.
用手旋________丝锥。

4. Pái ________ qiēxiè.
排________切屑。

汉字书写 Writing Chinese Characters

tài
太 太 太 太
太 太 太 太 太

quǎn
犬 犬 犬 犬
犬 犬 犬 犬 犬

fū
夫 夫 夫 夫
夫 夫 夫 夫 夫

tiān
天 天 天 天
天 天 天 天 天

文化拓展 Culture Insight

汉语

汉语是中国的官方语言，也是联合国六种工作语言之一。作为世界上最古老的语言之一，汉语拥有深厚的历史文化底蕴。汉语的起源可追溯至远古时期的黄河流域，随着华夏民族的兴起与发展，汉语逐渐形成并不断完善。汉语方言众多，大致分为北方方言、吴方言、湘方言、赣方言、客家方言、闽方言、粤方言等七大方言。这些方言在语音、词汇和语法上各有特色，反映了中国地域文化的多样性。

Chinese Language

Chinese is the official language of China and one of the six working languages of the United Nations. As one of the oldest languages in the world, Chinese embodies a profound historical and cultural legacy. The origin of Chinese can be traced back to ancient times in the Yellow River basin. With the rise and development of Chinese nation, the language gradually took shape and continued to evolve. There are many Chinese dialects, which can be roughly categorized into seven major groups: Northern dialects, Wu dialects, Xiang dialects, Gan dialects, Hakka dialects, Min dialects, and Yue dialects (Cantonese). These dialects have unique characteristics in pronunciation, vocabulary, and grammar, reflecting the diversity of Chinese regional cultures.

小结 Summary

词语 Words

朗读下列词语。Read the following words.

内螺纹	丝锥	铰杠
旋进	旋出	排出

语法 Grammar

把“先”“然后”或“进”“出”填入适当的位置。**Fill “先”, “然后” or “进”, “出” in the appropriate positions.**

1. ________旋进半圈到一圈，________反向旋出半圈，排出切屑。
2. ________在工件表面划线，________打样冲眼。
3. 先旋________半圈到一圈，然后反向旋出半圈。
4. 开钻床时，扳动启动手柄，拔________急停按钮。

课文理解 Text Comprehension

把下列句子按正确步骤排列。**Sort the following sentences according to the correct steps.**

1. 用铰杠反向旋转丝锥，然后用手旋出丝锥。
2. 先旋进半圈到一圈，然后反向旋出半圈，排出切屑。
3. 用台虎钳夹紧工件，加工面要水平放置。
4. 右手轻轻地转动铰杠。
5. 左手扶正丝锥，向下压。

___③___ → ________ → ___④___ → ________ → ________

第14课 Lesson 14

Jīchuáng jiāgōng ānquán

机床加工安全

The Safety of Machine Tool Processing

复习 Revision

根据词语选图片。**Choose the right pictures according to the words.**

A

B
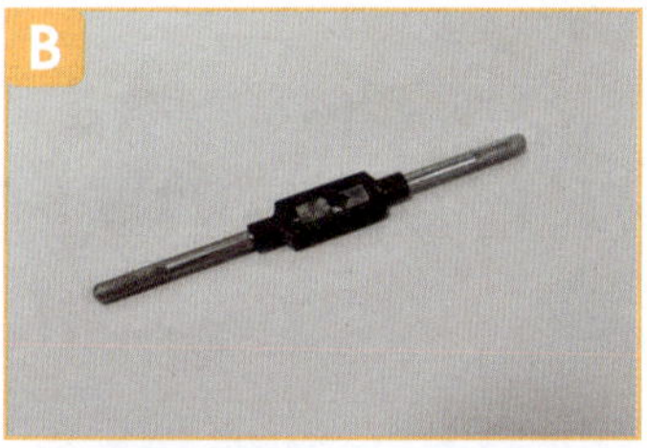

C
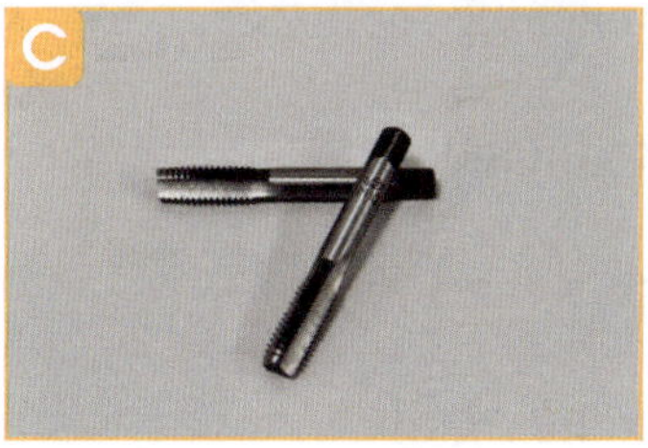

D
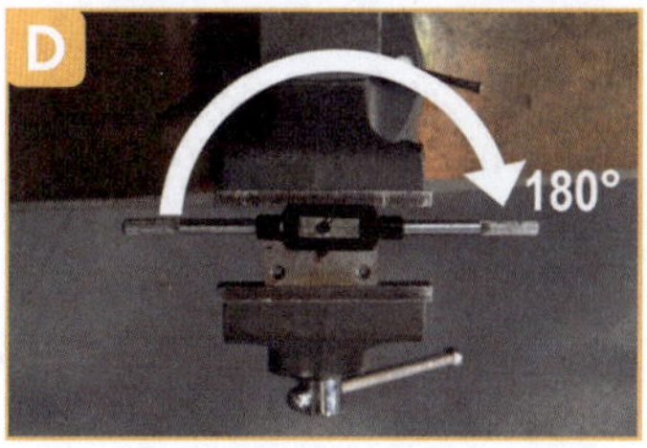

❶ 铰杠（　　）

❷ 丝锥（　　）

❸ 半圈（　　）

❹ 内螺纹（　　）

热身 Warm-up

选择正确的图片。Choose the right pictures.

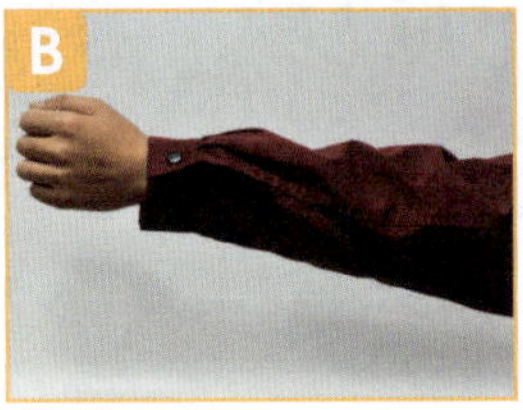

❶ 袖口 (xiùkǒu) cuff ( )

❷ 领口 (lǐngkǒu) neckband ( )

❸ 长发 (cháng fà) long hair ( )

❹ 机床 (jīchuáng) machine tool ( )

学习生词 Words and Expressions 14-01

1	机床	jīchuáng	*n.*	machine tool
2	包括	bāokuò	*v.*	to include
3	穿好	chuānhǎo	*phr.*	to wear; to put on
4	扎紧	zājǐn	*phr.*	to tie tightly
5	领口	lǐngkǒu	*n.*	neckband
6	袖口	xiùkǒu	*n.*	cuff
7	戴好	dàihǎo	*phr.*	to wear; to put on

8	长发	cháng fà	*phr.*	long hair
9	里	li	*n.*	inside
10	还	hái	*adv.*	else
11	别	bié	*adv.*	do not
12	手套	shǒutào	*n.*	gloves
13	周围	zhōuwéi	*n.*	around
14	站	zhàn	*v.*	to stand
15	人	rén	*n.*	person; people

词语练习 Word Exercises

1. 看图选词。Look at the pictures and choose the correct words.

❶  (　　) A. 机床　B. 钻床

❷  (　　) A. 安全帽　B. 长发

❸ 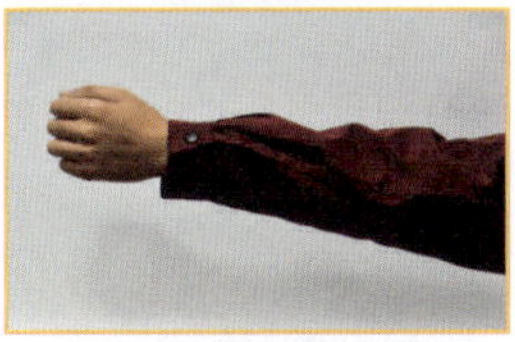 (　　) A. 袖口　B. 领口

❹ 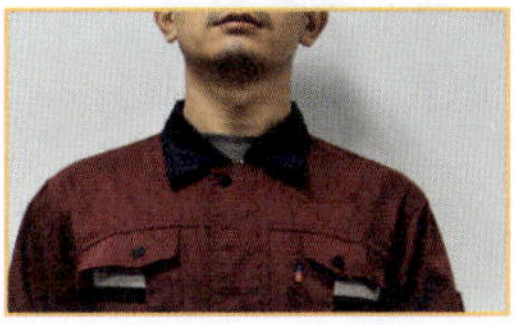 (　　) A. 领口　B. 袖口

2. 朗读词语搭配。**Read the collocations.**

❶ dàihǎo 戴好	ānquánmào 安全帽	❸ chuānhǎo 穿好	gōngzuòfú 工作服
	fánghù yǎnjìng 防护 眼镜		gōngzuòxié 工作鞋
❷ zājǐn 扎紧	lǐngkǒu 领口	❹ bié 别	dài shǒutào 戴 手套
	xiùkǒu 袖口		zhàn rén 站 人

学习课文 Text 14-02

Jīchuáng jiāgōng ānquán
机床加工安全

Jiékè: Jīchuáng jiāgōng ānquán bāokuò shénme?
杰克：机床 加工 安全 包括 什么？

Mǎ Míng: Chuānhǎo gōngzuòfú hé gōngzuòxié, zājǐn lǐngkǒu、xiùkǒu. Dàihǎo ānquánmào, bǎ cháng fà sāirù ānquánmào li.
马明：穿好 工作服 和 工作鞋，扎紧 领口、袖口。戴好 安全帽，把 长 发 塞入 安全帽 里。

Jiékè: Hái yào zhùyì shénme?
杰克：还 要 注意 什么？

Mǎ Míng: Dàihǎo fánghù yǎnjìng, bié dài shǒutào. Jīchuáng zhōuwéi bié zhàn rén.

马明：戴好防护眼镜，别戴手套。机床周围别站人。

The Safety of Machine Tool Processing

Jack: What should we be aware of regarding the processing safety of a machine tool?

Ma Ming: We should wear the safety clothes and safety shoes and tightly tie the neckband and cuffs. The safety cap should be worn and long hair should be tucked into it.

Jack: What else should we be aware of?

Ma Ming: We should wear protective glasses but avoid wearing gloves. There should be no others around the machine tool.

课文练习 Text Exercises

1. 根据课文内容选择正确答案。Choose the correct answers according to the text.

1 机床加工时，要穿什么？（　　）

A. 工作服和工作鞋　　B. 领口和袖口

2 机床加工时，要戴安全帽吗？（　　）

A. 要　　B. 不要

3 把长发塞入什么里？（　　）

A. 安全帽　　B. 工作服

4 机床加工时，要戴手套吗？ （ ）

A. 要 B. 不要

2. 一个学生发出指令，另一个学生做动作。**One student gives the instructions, and the other does the actions.**

1 穿好工作服和工作鞋。

2 扎紧领口、袖口。

3 戴好安全帽，把长发塞入安全帽里。

4 戴好防护眼镜。

学习语法 Grammar

语法点 1 Grammar Point 1

动词 + 好 Verb + 好

表示动作完成且完成情况较好。

"Verb + 好" indicates that the action has been completed and the result is satisfactory.

Cāozuò jīchuáng qián, chuānhǎo gōngzuòfú hé gōngzuòxié.
1 操作 机床 前， 穿好 工作服 和 工作鞋。
Wear work clothes and work shoes before operating the machine tool.

Zài chējiān gōngzuò shí, dàihǎo ānquánmào.
2 在 车间 工作 时，戴好 安全帽。
Wear a safety cap when working in the workshop.

Zuàn kǒng shí, dàihǎo fánghù yǎnjìng.
3 钻 孔 时，戴好 防护 眼镜。
Wear protective glasses when drilling.

语法点 1 练习 Exercise on Grammar Point 1

连词成句。**Rearrange the following words to make sentences.**

例如：

ānquánmào dài hǎo jīchuáng jiāgōng qián
①安全帽 ②戴 ③好 ④机床 加工 前

④②③①

1. hǎo gōngzuòfú hé gōngzuòxié chuān cāozuò jīchuáng qián
①好 ②工作服 和 工作鞋 ③穿 ④操作 机床 前

____

2. zài chējiān gōngzuò shí hǎo dài ānquánmào
①在 车间 工作 时 ②好 ③戴 ④安全帽

____

3. zuàn kǒng shí hǎo dài fánghù yǎnjìng
①钻 孔 时 ②好 ③戴 ④防护 眼镜

____

4. zā hǎo lǐngkǒu、xiùkǒu
①扎 ②好 ③领口、袖口

____

语法点 2 Grammar Point 2

副词：别 The Adverb: 别

表示阻止、禁止，意思是“不要”。

“别” indicates prohibition or prevention and means “do not”.

1. Dàihǎo fánghù yǎnjìng, bié dài shǒutào.
戴好 防护 眼镜，别 戴 手套。Wear protective glasses and do not wear gloves.

2. Jīchuáng zhōuwéi bié zhàn rén.
机床 周围 别 站 人。There should be no others around the machine tool.

3. Bié yòng shǒu qīnglǐ qiēxiè.
别 用 手 清理 切屑。Don’t use your hands to clean the chips.

语法点 2 练习 Exercise on Grammar Point 2

为“别”选择适当的位置。Fill “别” in the appropriate positions.

1 ________ （A）戴好（B）防护眼镜，（C）戴（D）手套。
(dài hǎo, fánghù yǎnjìng, dài, shǒutào)

2 ________ （A）机床（B）周围（C）站（D）人。
(jīchuáng, zhōuwéi, zhàn, rén)

3 ________ （A）用（B）手（C）清理（D）切屑。
(yòng, shǒu, qīnglǐ, qiēxiè)

4 ________ （A）把（B）台虎钳（C）放在（D）钳工台 上。
(bǎ, táihǔqián, fàng zài, qiángōngtái shang)

汉字书写 Writing Chinese Characters

lì 力 — 力 力

力 力 力 力

wàn 万 — 万 万 万

万 万 万 万

fāng 方 — 方 方 方 方

方 方 方 方

bàn 办 — 办 办 办 办

办 办 办 办

职业拓展 Career Insight

卧式车床

卧式车床是车床中应用最广泛的一种，约占车床总数的 65%，因其主轴以水平方式放置，故被称为卧式车床。卧式车床是能对轴、盘、环等多种类型工件进行多种工序加工的普通车床，常用于加工工件的内外回转表面、端面和各种内外螺纹。通过采用相应的刀具和附件，卧式车床还可进行钻孔、扩孔、攻丝和滚花等操作。

Horizontal Lathes

The horizontal lathe is the most widely used type of lathe, accounting for about 65% of the total number of lathes. It is called a horizontal lathe because its spindle is placed horizontally. A horizontal lathe is an ordinary lathe that can perform various machining operations on various types of workpieces such as shafts, discs, and rings. It is commonly used to process the inner and outer rotating surfaces, end faces, and various internal and external threads of workpieces. With the appropriate cutting tools and accessories, the horizontal lathe can also be used for drilling, expanding, tapping and knurling.

小结 Summary

词语 Words

朗读下列词语。Read the following words.

机床	穿好	扎紧
领口	袖口	手套

语法 Grammar

熟读句子。Read thc following sentences.

1. 操作机床前，穿好工作服和工作鞋。
2. 在车间工作时，戴好安全帽。
3. 机床周围别站人。
4. 别用手清理切屑。

课文理解 Text Comprchension

选择合适的词语填空。Choose the appropriate words to fill in the blanks.

A. 手套　　B. 领口、袖口　　C. 长发　　D. 机床

1. 机床加工时，穿好工作服和工作鞋，扎紧________。
2. 戴好安全帽，把________塞入安全帽里。
3. 戴好防护眼镜，别戴________。
4. ________周围别站人。

第15课
Lesson 15

Kāi guān chēchuáng
开关车床
Switching on/off Lathes

复习 Revision

根据词语选图片。**Choose the right pictures according to the words.**

A

B
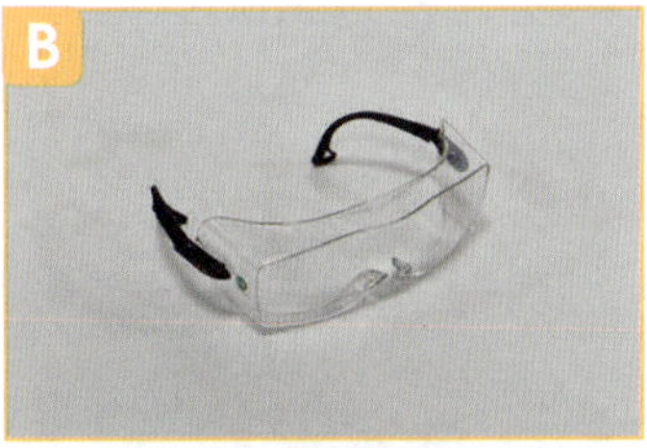

C
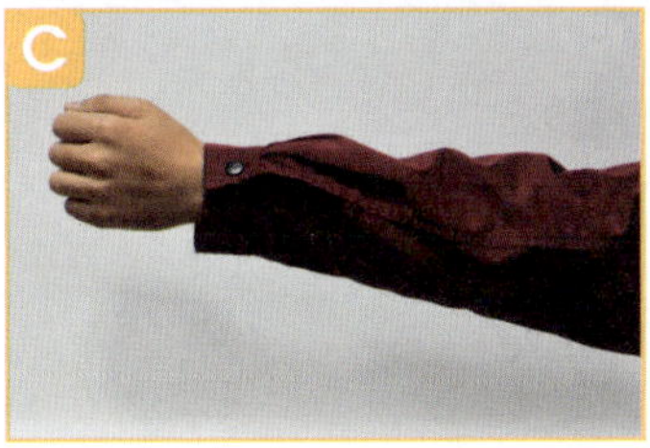

D
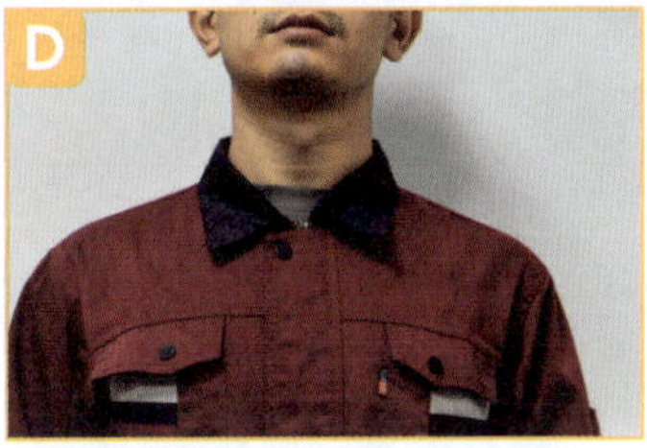

❶ 防护眼镜（　　）　　❷ 机床（　　）

❸ 领口（　　）　　❹ 袖口（　　）

热身 Warm-up

选择正确的图片。**Choose the right pictures.**

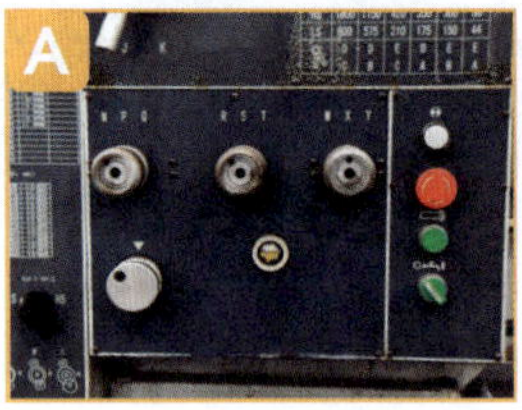

❶	chēchuáng diànyuán 车床 电源	power of the lathe	(　　)
❷	chēchuáng 车床	lathe	(　　)
❸	cāozònggǎn 操纵杆	control rod	(　　)
❹	biànsùxiāng 变速箱	gearbox	(　　)

学习生词 Words and Expressions 15-01

1	车床	chēchuáng	*n.*	lathe
2	前	qián	*n.*	before
3	确保	quèbǎo	*v.*	to make sure
4	变速箱	biànsùxiāng	*n.*	gearbox
5	正确	zhèngquè	*adj.*	correct

6	操纵杆	cāozònggǎn	*n.*	control rod
7	车床电源	chēchuáng diànyuán	*phr.*	power of the lathe
8	提起	tíqǐ	*phr.*	to lift
9	关闭	guānbì	*v.*	to switch off

词语练习 Word Exercises

1. 看图选词。**Look at the pictures and choose the correct words.**

❶ 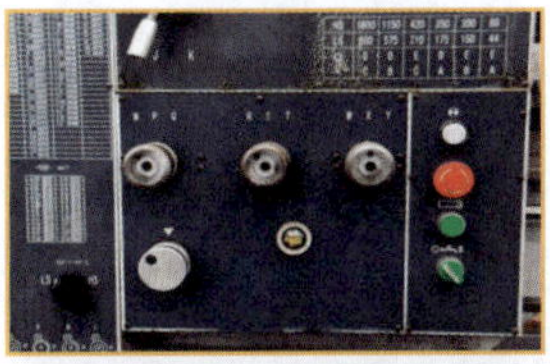 (　　) A. 变速箱　　B. 主轴箱

❷  (　　) A. 车床电源　　B. 急停按钮

❸  (　　) A. 车床　　B. 铣床

❹  (　　) A. 操纵杆　　B. 变速箱

2. 朗读词语搭配。**Read the collocations.**

❶	kāi chēchuáng 开 车床	qián 前	❷	kāi chēchuáng 开 车床	shí 时
	guān chēchuáng 关 车床			guān chēchuáng 关 车床	
❸	zhèngquè 正确	wèizhi 位置	❹	táiqǐ 抬起	cāozònggǎn 操纵杆
	kōngdǎng 空挡			bāndòng 扳动	

学习课文 Text 15-02

Kāi guān chēchuáng
开关车床

Kāi chēchuáng qián, yào quèbǎo biànsùxiāng shǒubǐng zài zhèngquè de wèizhì, cāozònggǎn zài kōngdǎng wèizhì.

开车床前，要确保变速箱手柄在正确的位置，操纵杆在空挡位置。

Kāi chēchuáng shí, dǎkāi chēchuáng diànyuán, báchū jítíng ànniǔ, ànxia qǐdòng ànniǔ, tíqǐ cāozònggǎn.

开车床时，打开车床电源，拔出急停按钮，按下启动按钮，提起操纵杆。

Guān chēchuáng shí, bāndòng cāozònggǎn zhì kōngdǎng wèizhì, ànxia jítíng ànniǔ, guānbì chēchuáng diànyuán.

关车床时，扳动操纵杆至空挡位置，按下急停按钮，关闭车床电源。

Switching on/off Lathes

Before switching on the lathe, make sure that the gearbox handle is in the correct position and that the control rod is in the neutral position.

When switching on the lathe, first switch on the power of the lathe, pull out the emergency stop button, press the start button and lift the control rod.

When switching off the lathe, pull the control rod to the neutral position, press the emergency stop button and switch off the power of the lathe.

课文练习 Text Exercises

1. 根据课文内容选择正确答案。Choose the correct answers according to the text.

1 开车床前，要确保变速箱手柄在（　　）位置。

A. 正确的　　　　B. 空挡

2 开车床前，操纵杆在（　　）位置。

A. 空挡　　　　B. 正确的

3 开车床时，打开车床电源，拔出急停按钮，按下启动按钮，提起（　　）。

A. 变速箱手柄　　　　B. 操纵杆

4 关车床时，要扳动操纵杆至空挡位置吗？（　　）

A. 要　　　　B. 不要

2. 一个学生发出指令，另一个学生做动作。**One student gives the instructions, and the other does the actions.**

1 打开车床电源，拔出急停按钮。

2 按下启动按钮，提起操纵杆。

3 扳动操纵杆至空挡位置。

4 按下急停按钮，关闭车床电源。

学习语法 Grammar

语法点 1 Grammar Point 1

动词：在　The Verb: 在

表示人或物的位置。

"在" indicates the position of a person or object.

Kāi chēchuáng qián, yào quèbǎo biànsùxiāng shǒubǐng zài zhèngquè de wèizhì.
1 开 车床 前，要 确保 变速箱 手柄 在 正确 的位置。
Before switching on the lathe, make sure the gearbox handle is in the correct position.

Kāi chēchuáng qián, yào quèbǎo cāozònggǎn zài kōngdǎng wèizhì.
2 开 车床 前，要 确保 操纵杆 在 空挡 位置。
Before switching on the lathe, make sure the control rod is in the neutral position.

Táihǔqián zài nǎr?
3 台虎钳在哪儿？ Where is the bench vice?

语法点 1 练习 Exercise on Grammar Point 1

为“在”选择适当的位置。Fill “在” in the appropriate positions.

1 ______ （A）开车床前，（B）要确保变速箱手柄（C）正确的位置。
kāi chēchuáng qián, yào quèbǎo biànsùxiāng shǒubǐng zhèngquè de wèizhì.

2 ______ （A）开车床前，（B）要确保操纵杆（C）空挡位置。
kāi chēchuáng qián, yào quèbǎo cāozònggǎn kōngdǎng wèizhì.

3 ______ （A）台虎钳（B）哪儿？
táihǔqián nǎr?

4 ______ （A）台虎钳（B）钳工台（C）上。
táihǔqián qiángōngtái shang.

语法点 2 Grammar Point 2

动词 + 下 Verb + 下

表示通过动作使人或物由高处向低处移动。

“Verb + 下” indicates that somebody or something is moved from a higher position to a lower position through an action.

1 Kāi chēchuáng shí, ànxia qǐdòng ànniǔ.
开车床时，按下启动按钮。
When switching on the lathe, press the start button.

2 Guān chēchuáng shí, ànxia jítíng ànniǔ.
关车床时，按下急停按钮。
When switching off the lathe, press the emergency stop button.

3 Sōngkāi V xíng luómǔ hé diànpiàn, qǔxia jiù jùtiáo.
松开V型螺母和垫片，取下旧锯条。
Loosen the V-nut and gasket, and remove the used saw blade.

语法点 2 练习 Exercise on Grammar Point 2

选择合适的词语填空。Choose the appropriate words to fill in the blanks.

àngxia A. 按下	qǔxia B. 取下

1. ________ jítíng ànniǔ 急停 按钮
2. ________ qǐdòng ànniǔ 启动 按钮
3. ________ jiù jùtiáo 旧 锯条
4. ________ jiù qiǎzhuǎ 旧 卡爪（jaw）

汉字书写 Writing Chinese Characters

rù 入 入

入 入 入 入 入

jiè 介 介 介 介

介 介 介 介 介

cóng 从 从 从 从

从 从 从 从 从

zhòng 众 众 众 众 众 众

众 众 众 众 众

文化拓展 Culture Insight

四大发明

中国古代有举世闻名的四大发明，它们是造纸术、印刷术、火药和指南针。造纸术发明于汉代，雕版印刷术发明于隋唐时期，火药是唐朝人发明的。活字印刷术是在宋代发明的。战国时，已有用天然磁铁矿磨制成的指南针，称“司南”。四大发明对中国古代政治、经济、文化的发展产生了巨大的推动作用，后经各种途径传至西方，对世界文明发展史产生了深远的影响。

The Four Great Inventions of Ancient China

In ancient China, there were world-famous Four Great Inventions: papermaking, printing, gunpowder, and the compass. Papermaking was invented in Han Dynasty, while woodblock printing was invented during Sui and Tang dynasties, and gunpowder were inventions of Tang Dynasty. Movable-type printing was invented in Song Dynasty. During Warring States Period, a compass made from natural magnetite, known as *sinan* had already been in use. The four inventions had a tremendous impact on the political, economic, and cultural development of ancient China, and were introduced to the West through various channels, profoundly influencing the development of world civilization.

小结 Summary

词语 Words

朗读下列词语。Read the following words.

车床	开车床	关车床
确保	变速箱	操纵杆

语法 Grammar

熟读句子。Read the following sentences.

1. 开车床前，要确保变速箱手柄在正确的位置。
2. 开车床前，要确保操纵杆在空挡位置。
3. 开车床时，按下启动按钮。
4. 关车床时，按下急停按钮。

课文理解 Text Comprehension

把下列句子按正确步骤排列。Sort the following sentences according to the correct steps.

1. 开车床时，打开车床电源，拔出急停按钮。
2. 开车床前，要确保变速箱手柄在正确的位置，操纵杆在空挡位置。
3. 开车床时，按下启动按钮，提起操纵杆。
4. 关车床时，扳动操纵杆至空挡位置，按下急停按钮，关闭车床电源。

________ → ________ → ________ → ________

第16课
Lesson 16

Zhuāngjiā zhóulèi máopījiàn
装夹轴类毛坯件
Clamping Shaft-Type Blanks

复习 Revision

根据词语选图片。**Choose the right pictures according to the words.**

A
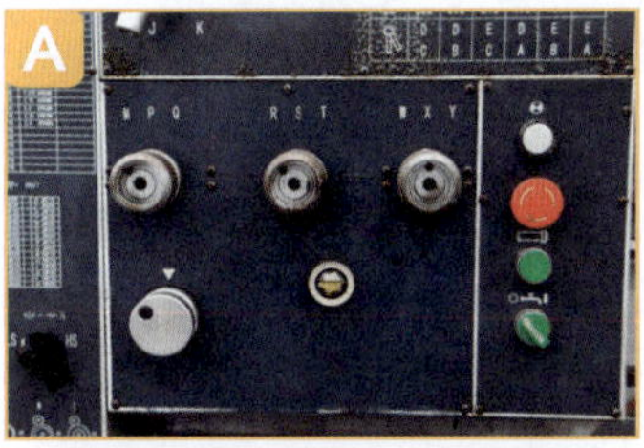

B

C

D
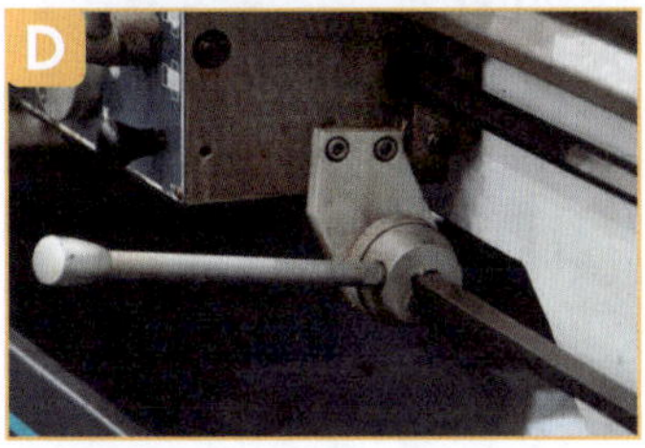

❶ 操纵杆（　　）
❷ 车床（　　）
❸ 车床电源（　　）
❹ 变速箱（　　）

热身 Warm-up

选择正确的图片。**Choose the right pictures.**

A

B

C

D

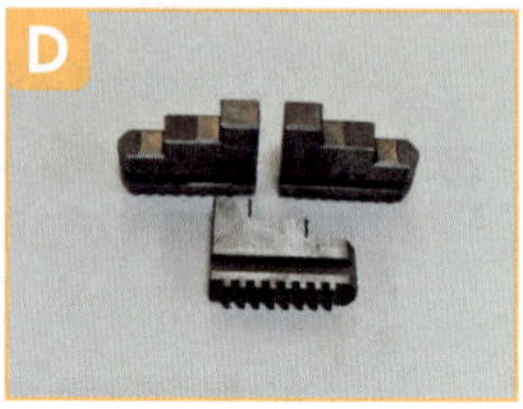

❶ 卡盘 扳手 (qiǎpán bānshou) chuck wrench (　　)

❷ 卡爪 (qiǎzhuǎ) jaw (　　)

❸ 轴类 毛坯件 (zhóulèi máopījiàn) shaft-type blank (　　)

❹ 开口 (kāikǒu) opening space (　　)

学习生词 Words and Expressions 16-01

1	轴类毛坯件	zhóulèi máopījiàn	*phr.*	shaft-type blank
2	卡盘扳手	qiǎpán bānshou	*phr.*	chuck wrench
3	卡爪	qiǎzhuǎ	*n.*	jaw
4	拿起	náqǐ	*phr.*	to pick up
5	放进	fàngjìn	*phr.*	to place in; to put in
6	开口	kāikǒu	*n.*	opening space
7	里边	lǐbian	*n.*	inside
8	部分	bùfen	*n.*	part

9	留	liú	*v.*	to leave
10	外边	wàibian	*n.*	outside
11	最后	zuìhòu	*n.*	finally
12	锁紧	suǒjǐn	*phr.*	to lock tightly
13	完成	wánchéng	*v.*	to complete

词语练习 Word Exercises

1. 看图选词。Look at the pictures and choose the correct words.

❶  (　　) A. 轴类毛坯件　B. 平面类毛坯件

❷  (　　) A. 卡盘扳手　B. 刀架扳手

❸  (　　) A. 卡盘　B. 卡爪

❹  (　　) A. 开口　B. 工件

2. 朗读词语搭配。**Read the collocations.**

❶	shùnshízhēn 顺时针	xuánzhuǎn 旋转
	nìshízhēn 逆时针	
❷	dǎkāi 打开	qiǎzhuǎ 卡爪
	bìhé 闭合	
❸	fúzhèng 扶正	gōngjiàn 工件
	náqǐ 拿起	
	jiājǐn 夹紧	

学习课文 Text 16-02

Zhuāngjiā zhóulèi máopījiàn
装夹 轴类毛坯件

Zuǒshǒu nìshízhēn xuánzhuǎn qiǎpán bānshou, dǎkāi sān gè qiǎzhuǎ; yòushǒu náqǐ gōngjiàn, fàngjìn kāikǒu lǐbian, bǎ yào jiāgōng de bùfen liú zài qiǎzhuǎ wàibian.

左手逆时针旋转卡盘扳手，打开三个卡爪；右手拿起工件，放进开口里边，把要加工的部分留在卡爪外边。

Fúzhèng gōngjiàn, shùnshízhēn xuánzhuǎn qiǎpán bānshou, bìhé qiǎzhuǎ, jiājǐn gōngjiàn.

扶正工件，顺时针旋转卡盘扳手，闭合卡爪，夹紧工件。

Zuìhòu yòng qiǎpán bānshou suǒjǐn sān gè qiǎzhuǎ, wánchéng zhuāngjiā.
最后用卡盘扳手锁紧三个卡爪，完成装夹。

Clamping Shaft-Type Blanks

Revolve the chuck wrench counterclockwise with the left hand to open the three jaws, pick up the workpiece with the right hand, place it inside the opening space, and leave the part to be processed outside the jaws.

Hold the workpiece straightly, rotate the chuck wrench clockwise to close the jaws, and clamp the workpiece tightly.

Finally, lock the three jaws tightly with a chuck wrench, and the workpiece is clamped completely.

课文练习 Text Exercises

1. 选择合适的词语填空。Choose the appropriate words to fill in the blanks.

A. 顺时针　B. 逆时针　C. 里边　D. 外边　E. 卡盘扳手

1. 左手________旋转卡盘扳手，打开三个卡爪。
2. 右手拿起工件，放进开口________，把要加工的部分留在卡爪________。

3 扶正工件，________旋转卡盘扳手，闭合卡爪，夹紧工件。

4 最后用________锁紧三个卡爪，完成装夹。

2. 一个学生发出指令，另一个学生做动作。**One student gives the instructions, and the other does the actions.**

1 左手逆时针旋转卡盘扳手，打开三个卡爪。

2 右手拿起工件，放进开口里边，把要加工的部分留在卡爪外边。

3 扶正工件，顺时针旋转卡盘扳手，闭合卡爪，夹紧工件。

4 用卡盘扳手锁紧三个卡爪。

学习语法 Grammar

语法点 1 Grammar Point 1

方位名词：里边 / 外边　The Directional Words: 里边 / 外边

表示某物在一定的空间以内或以外。

"里边/外边" indicates that something is inside or outside a specific space.

Yòushǒu náqǐ gōngjiàn, fàngjìn kāikǒu lǐbian.
1 右手 拿起 工件，放进 开口 里边。
Pick up the workpiece with the right hand, and place it inside the opening space.

Bǎ yào jiāgōng de bùfen liú zài qiǎzhuǎ wàibian.
2 把 要 加工 的 部分 留 在 卡爪 外边。
Leave the part to be processed outside the jaws.

Jiékè zài chējiān lǐbian.
3 杰克在 车间 里边。Jack is in the workshop.

语法点1练习 Exercise on Grammar Point 1

连词成句。**Rearrange the following words to make sentences.**

例如：

lǐbian	yǒu	chēchuáng	chējiān
①里边	②有	③车床	④车间

④①②③

1

lǐbian	yòushǒu náqǐ gōngjiàn	fàngjìn	kāikǒu
①里边	②右手 拿起 工件	③放进	④开口

____

2

wàibian	liú zài qiǎzhuǎ	yào jiāgōng de bùfen	bǎ
① 外边	②留 在 卡爪	③要 加工 的部分	④把

____

3

lǐbian	zài	chējiān	Jiékè
①里边	②在	③车间	④杰克

____

4

zài	Mǎ Míng	chējiān	wàibian
①在	②马 明	③车间	④外边

____

语法点2 Grammar Point 2

量词：个　The Measure Word: 个

汉语中最常用的量词，可以用于人，也可以用于东西。

"个" is the most commonly used measure word in Chinese. It can be used for both people and things.

sān gè qiǎzhuǎ
1 三个卡爪 three jaws

yí gè gōngjiàn
2 一个工件 one workpiece

Yí gè kǒng zhuāng zài yǒu luómǔ de lāgǎn shang.
3 一个孔装在有螺母的拉杆上。
A hole is installed on the pull rod with a nut.

语法点 2 练习 Exercise on Grammar Point 2

为“个”选择适当的位置。Fill “个” in the appropriate positions.

dǎkāi sān qiǎzhuǎ
1 ______ （A）打开（B）三（C）卡爪（D）。

yí kǒng zhuāng zài yǒu luómǔ de lāgǎn shang
2 ______ （A）一（B）孔（C）装在有螺母的（D）拉杆上。

bǎ yí gōngjiàn fàng zài qiángōngtái shang
3 ______ （A）把（B）一（C）工件（D）放在钳工台上。

yòng yí táihǔqián zhuāngjiā gōngjiàn
4 ______ （A）用一（B）台虎钳（C）装夹（D）工件。

汉字书写 Writing Chinese Characters

yòu 又 又

又 又 又 又 又

zhī 支 支 支 支

支 支 支 支 支

hàn 汉 汉 汉 汉 汉

汉 汉 汉 汉 汉

shuāng 双 双 双 双

双 双 双 双 双

职业拓展 Career Insight

落地车床

落地车床底座导轨采用矩形结构，跨距大，刚性好，适宜于低速重载切削。落地车床结构采用床头箱主轴垂直于托板运动的床身导轨，床头箱和横向床身连接在同一底座上，底座上为山形导轨结构，可手动调节托板的横向移动。落地车床操作方便，能够车削各种零件的内外圆柱面、端面、圆弧等成型表面，是加工各种轮胎模具及大平面盘类、环类零件的理想设备。

Floor-Type Lathes

The base guide rail of the floor-type lathe adopts a rectangular structure, with a large span and good rigidity. It is suitable for low-speed and heavy-duty cutting. The structure of the floor-type lathe features a bed guide rail with the spindle of the headstock perpendicular to the movement of the pallet. The headstock and the horizontal bed are connected to the same base, which has a mountain-shaped guide rail structure, allowing for manual adjustment of the pallet's lateral movement. The floor-type lathe is easy to operate and can turn the inner and outer cylindrical surfaces, end faces, arcs, and other formed surfaces of various parts. It is an ideal equipment for processing various tire molds as well as large flat disc and ring parts.

小结 Summary

词语 Words

朗读下列词语。**Read the following words.**

轴类毛坯件	卡盘扳手	卡爪
里边	外边	完成

语法 Grammar

熟读句子及短语。**Read the following sentences and phrases.**

1. 右手拿起工件，放进开口里边。
2. 把要加工的部分留在卡爪外边。
3. 三个卡爪
4. 一个工件

课文理解 Text Comprehension

把下列句子按正确步骤排列。Sort the following sentences according to the correct steps.

1 右手拿起工件，放进开口里边，把要加工的部分留在卡爪外边。

2 扶正工件，顺时针旋转卡盘扳手，闭合卡爪，夹紧工件。

3 左手逆时针旋转卡盘扳手，打开三个卡爪。

4 最后用卡盘扳手锁紧三个卡爪，完成装夹。

________ → ________ → ________ → ________

第17课 Lesson 17

Ānzhuāng chēdāo

安装车刀

Installing Turning Tools

复习 Revision

根据词语选图片。Choose the right pictures according to the words.

1. 卡盘扳手（　　）
2. 卡爪（　　）
3. 车床（　　）
4. 轴类毛坯件（　　）

热身 Warm-up

选择正确的图片。Choose the right pictures.

A 
B 
C 
D 

❶ chēxiāo 车削 turning ( )

❷ chēdāo 车刀 turning tool ( )

❸ yājǐn luóshuān 压紧 螺栓 compression bolt ( )

❹ dāojià 刀架 tool holder ( )

学习生词 Words and Expressions 17-01

1	安装	ānzhuāng	*v.*	to install
2	车刀	chēdāo	*n.*	turning tool
3	车削	chēxiāo	*v.*	to turn; to process on the turning machine
4	以前	yǐqián	*n.*	before
5	颗	kē	*m.*	*a measure word for small and round things*
6	压紧螺栓	yājǐn luóshuān	*phr.*	compression bolt
7	刀架	dāojià	*n.*	tool holder
8	以后	yǐhòu	*n.*	after

9	一定	yídìng	*adv.*	surely
10	检查	jiǎnchá	*v.*	to check
11	刀尖	dāojiān	*n.*	turning tool tip
12	高度	gāodù	*n.*	height
13	尾座顶尖	wěizuò dǐngjiān	*phr.*	tailstock
14	一致	yízhì	*adj.*	consistent

词语练习 Word Exercises

1. 看图选词。Look at the pictures and choose the correct words.

❶ 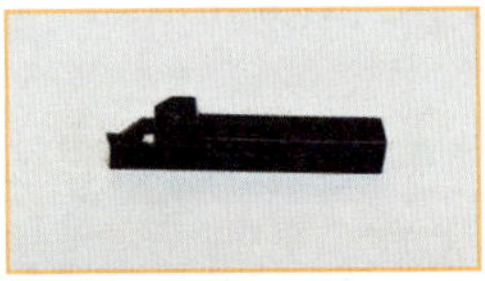 (　　) A. 车刀　B. 铣刀

❷  (　　) A. 刀架　B. 尾座

❸ 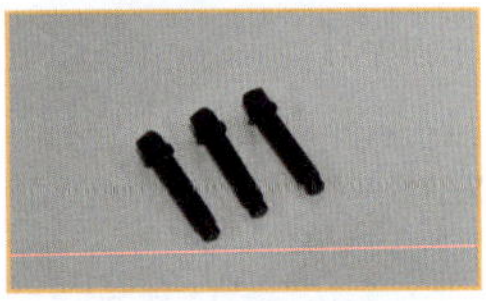 (　　) A. 压紧螺栓　B. 螺帽

❹  (　　) A. 钻孔　B. 车削

2. 根据拼音选择正确的词语。Choose the correct words based on Pinyin.

❶ dāojià (　　) A. 刀架　B. 刀柄

❷ chēdāo (　　) A. 车刀　B. 刀尖

❸ chēxiāo (　　) A. 安装　B. 车削

❹ yājǐn luóshuān (　　) A. 拧紧螺栓　B. 压紧螺栓

学习课文 Text 17-02

Ānzhuāng chēdāo
安装 车刀

Chēxiāo jiāgōng yǐqián, yào ānzhuāng chēdāo.
车削加工以前，要安装车刀。

Xiān nìshízhēn sōngkāi sān kē yājǐn luóshuān, bǎ chēdāo fàngjìn dāojià lǐbian, ránhòu shùnshízhēn nǐngjǐn yājǐn luóshuān. Ānzhuāng wánchéng.
先逆时针松开三颗压紧螺栓，把车刀放进刀架里边，然后顺时针拧紧压紧螺栓。安装完成。

Ānzhuāng chēdāo yǐhòu, yídìng yào jiǎnchá chēdāo dāojiān de wèizhì. Quèbǎo dāojiān gāodù yǔ wěizuò dǐngjiān de gāodù yízhì.
安装车刀以后，一定要检查车刀刀尖的位置。确保刀尖高度与尾座顶尖的高度一致。

Installing Turning Tools

Before turning, the turning tool needs to be installed .

First, loosen the three compression bolts counterclockwise to place the turning tool into the tool holder, and then tighten the compression bolts clockwise. The installation is completed.

After the installation of the turning tool is completed, the position of the turning tool tip must be checked to ensure that the height of the tool tip is consistent with the height of the tailstock.

课文练习 Text Exercises

1. 根据课文内容选择正确答案。Choose the correct answers according to the text.

1 车削加工以前，要安装________。

A. 车刀　　B. 卡盘扳手

2 先________松开三颗压紧螺栓，把车刀放进刀架里边。

A. 顺时针　　B. 逆时针

3 然后________拧紧压紧螺栓，安装完成。

A. 顺时针　　B. 逆时针

4 安装车刀以后，一定要检查________的位置。

A. 尾座顶尖　　B. 车刀刀尖

2. 选择合适的词语填空。Choose the appropriate words to fill in the blanks.

A. 顺时针　　B. 逆时针　　C. 车刀刀尖　　D. 车刀

1 车削加工以前，要安装________。

2 先________松开三颗压紧螺栓，把车刀放进刀架里边。

3 然后________拧紧压紧螺栓。

4 安装车刀以后，一定要检查________的位置。

学习语法 Grammar

语法点 1 Grammar Point 1

方位词：以前 / 以后 The Directional Words: 以前 / 以后

“以前”用于指某个时间点之前的一段时间，强调的是参照事件发生之前的情况或状态。“以后”用于指某个时间点之后的一段时间，强调的是参照事件发生之后的情况或状态。

“以前” is used to refer to a period of time prior to a certain point in time, emphasizing a situation or state prior to the occurrence of the referenced event. “以后” is used to refer to a period of time after a certain point in time, emphasizing the situation or state after the occurrence of the referenced event.

1. Chēxiāo jiāgōng yǐqián, yào ānzhuāng chēdāo.
   车削 加工 以前，要 安装 车刀。
   Before turning, the turning tool needs to be installed.
2. Chēdāo ānzhuāng wánchéng yǐhòu, yídìng yào jiǎnchá chēdāo dāojiān de wèizhì.
   车刀 安装 完成 以后，一定 要 检查 车刀 刀尖 的 位置。
   After the installation of the turning tool is completed, the position of the turning tool tip must be checked.
3. Huàxiàn yǐqián yào xiān fújǐn gōngjiàn.
   划线 以前 要 先 扶紧 工件。Before scribing, hold the workpiece tightly.

语法点 1 练习 Exercise on Grammar Point 1

连词成句。**Rearrange the following words to make sentences.**

例如：

yǐhòu ①以后 yào ②要 qīnglǐ qiángōngtái ③清理 钳工台 jiāgōng nèiluówén ④加工 内螺纹

④①②③

1. ①以前（yǐqián）　②车削加工（chēxiāo jiāgōng）　③安装车刀（ānzhuāng chēdāo）　④要（yào）

____

2. ①一定要（yídìng yào）　②车刀安装完成（chēdāo ānzhuāng wánchéng）　③以后（yǐhòu）　④检查车刀刀尖的位置（jiǎnchá chēdāo dāojiān de wèizhì）

____

3. ①以前（yǐqián）　②要（yào）　③划线（huàxiàn）　④先扶紧工件（xiān fújǐn gōngjiàn）

____

4. ①进入（jìnrù）　②要戴好安全帽（yào dàihǎo ānquánmào）　③车间（chējiān）　④以前（yǐqián）

____

语法点 2 Grammar Point 2

副词：一定　The Adverb: 一定

表示某事必然发生。

"一定" means that something must happen.

1. Chēdāo ānzhuāng wánchéng yǐhòu, yídìng yào jiǎnchá chēdāo dāojiān de wèizhì.
   车刀安装完成以后，一定要检查车刀刀尖的位置。
   After the installation of the turning tool is completed, the position of the turning tool tip should be double checked.

2. Yídìng yào xiān guān chēchuáng diànyuán.
   一定要先关车床电源。Be sure to switch off the power of the lathe first.

3. Zuànkǒng qián yídìng yào xuǎnzé héshì de zuàntóu.
   钻孔前一定要选择合适的钻头。
   Make sure to choose a suitable drill bit before drilling.

语法点 2 练习 Exercise on Grammar Point 2

判断下面四个含有“一定”的句子是否符合操作规定。Determine whether the following four sentences containing “一定” comply with the operational regulations.

Chēdāo ānzhuāng wánchéng yǐhòu, yídìng yào jiǎnchá chēdāo dāojiān de wèizhì.
1 车刀 安装 完成 以后，一定要检查车刀刀尖的位置。(   )

fúhé　　　　bù fúhé
A. 符合　　B. 不符合

Guān chēchuáng, yídìng yào xiān guān chēchuáng diànyuán.
2 关车床，一定要先关车床电源。(   )

fúhé　　　　bù fúhé
A. 符合　　B. 不符合

Zuànkǒng qián yídìng yào xuǎnzé héshì de zuàntóu.
3 钻孔前一定要选择合适的钻头。(   )

fúhé　　　　bù fúhé
A. 符合　　B. 不符合

Cuòxiāo qián yídìng yào xuǎnzé héshì de yàngchòng.
4 锉削前一定要选择合适的样冲。(   )

fúhé　　　　bù fúhé
A. 符合　　B. 不符合

汉字书写 Writing Chinese Characters

kuī 亏 亏 亏

亏 亏 亏 亏 亏

yún 云 云 云 云

云 云 云 云 云

jǐng

井 井 井 井 井

yuán

元 元 元 元 元

文化拓展 Culture Insight

火药

火药是中国古代的四大发明之一，它的起源可以追溯到中国春秋时期。唐朝时，火药被用于军事。在明代，火药的制造技术达到了一个新的高峰，其威力和使用范围得到了进一步的扩展。火药由中国传到欧洲后，促进了欧洲文艺复兴和宗教改革。它对人类社会的文明进步、经济和科学文化的发展起到了推动作用。

Gunpowder

Gunpowder is one of the Four Great Inventions in ancient China. Its origin can be traced back to Spring and Autumn Period of China. In Tang Dynasty, gunpowder was used for military purposes. During Ming Dynasty, the manufacturing technology of gunpowder reached a new peak, and its power and scope of use were further expanded. After gunpowder was introduced from China to Europe, it promoted the European Renaissance and religious reform, and played a driving role in the progress of human civilization as well as the development of economy, science and culture.

小结 Summary

词语 Words

朗读下列词语。Read the following words.

安装	车刀	车削
压紧螺栓	刀架	刀尖

语法 Grammar

熟读句子。Read the following sentences.

1. 车削加工以前，要安装车刀。
2. 划线以前要先扶紧工件。
3. 车刀安装完成以后，一定要检查车刀刀尖的位置。
4. 一定要先关车床电源。

课文理解 Text Comprehension

把下列句子按正确步骤排列。**Sort the following sentences according to the correct steps.**

1. 车削加工以前，要安装车刀。
2. 然后顺时针拧紧压紧螺栓，安装完成。
3. 先逆时针松开三颗压紧螺栓，把车刀放进刀架里边。
4. 安装车刀以后，一定要检查车刀刀尖的位置。确保刀尖高度与尾座顶尖的高度一致。

___①___ → ______ → ___②___ → ______

第18课 Lesson 18

Jiāgōng zhóulèi língjiàn
加工轴类零件
Processing Shaft-Type Parts

复习 Revision

根据词语选图片。**Choose the right pictures according to the words.**

A

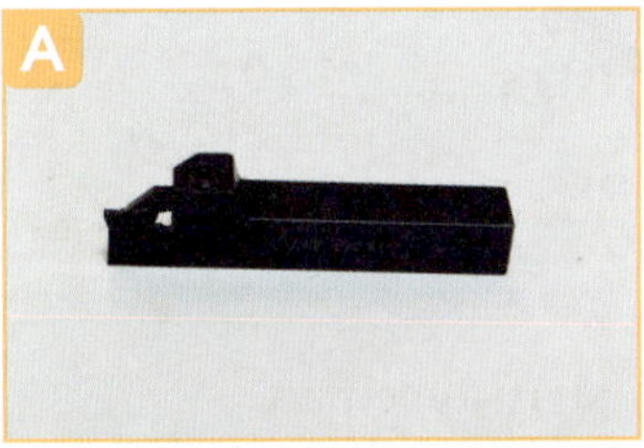

B

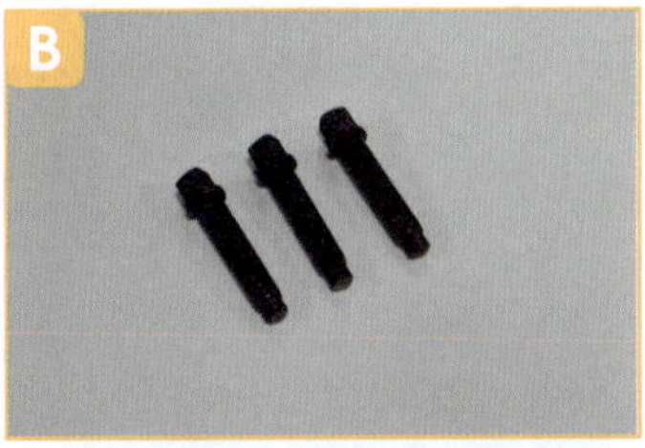

C

D

❶ 车削（　　）　❷ 车刀（　　）

❸ 压紧螺栓（　　）　❹ 刀架（　　）

热身 Warm-up

选择正确的图片。Choose the right pictures.

❶ 轴类零件 zhóulèi língjiàn shaft-type part (　　)

❷ 对刀 duìdāo set the tools (　　)

❸ 尺寸 chǐcùn size (　　)

❹ 刻度值 kèdùzhí scale value (　　)

学习生词 Words and Expressions 18-01

1	轴类零件	zhóulèi língjiàn	*phr.*	shaft-type part
2	对刀	duìdāo	*v.*	to set the tools
3	靠近	kàojìn	*v.*	to approach
4	接触	jiēchù	*v.*	to contact
5	产生	chǎnshēng	*v.*	to generate
6	少量	shǎoliàng	*adj.*	a small number of
7	刻度值	kèdùzhí	*n.*	scale value
8	以……为……	yǐ···wéi···		take…as…

9	起点	qǐdiǎn	*n.*	starting point
10	按照	ànzhào	*prep.*	according to
11	要求	yāoqiú	*n.*	requirement
12	尺寸	chǐcùn	*n.*	size
13	自动	zìdòng	*adv.*	automatic
14	到达	dàodá	*v.*	to reach
15	规定	guīdìng	*v.*	to be specified
16	停止	tíngzhǐ	*v.*	to stop

词语练习 Word Exercises

1. 看图选词。Look at the pictures and choose the correct words.

❶  (　　) A. 对刀　B. 测量

❷  (　　) A. 操纵杆　B. 刻度值

❸ 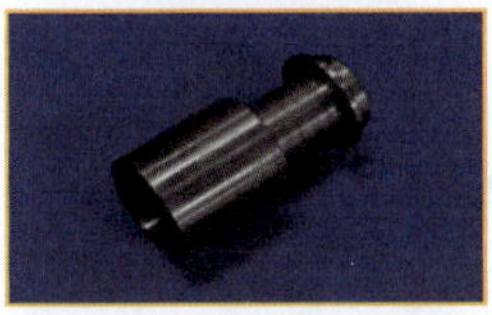 (　　) A. 轴类零件　B. 毛坯件

❹ 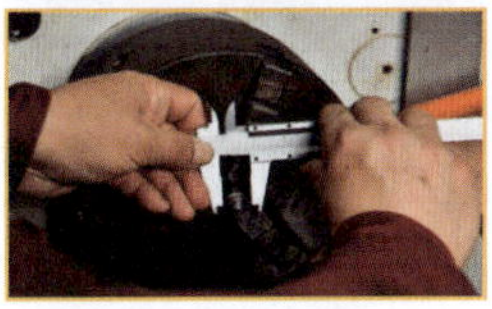 (　　) A. 刻度值　B. 尺寸

2. 根据拼音选择正确的词语。 **Choose the correct words based on Pinyin.**

1. duìdāo （ ） A. 车刀 B. 对刀
2. kèdùzhí （ ） A. 刻度值 B. 操纵杆
3. chǐcùn （ ） A. 尺寸 B. 大小
4. zhóulèi língjiàn （ ） A. 轴类零件 B. 图纸要求

学习课文 Text 18-02

Jiāgōng zhóulèi língjiàn
加工轴类零件

Jiāgōng shí xiān duìdāo. Dāojiān mànmàn de kàojìn gōngjiàn, zài dāojiān jiēchù dào gōngjiàn、chǎnshēng shǎoliàng qiēxiè shí, dúqǔ kèdùzhí.

加工时先对刀。刀尖慢慢地靠近工件，在刀尖接触到工件、产生少量切屑时，读取刻度值。

Yǐ kèdùzhí wéi qǐdiǎn, ànzhào túzhǐ yāoqiú, dāojiān jìnjǐ héshì de chǐcùn, tíqǐ zìdòng jìnjǐ cāozònggǎn, dāojiān dàodá guīdìng de chǐcùn yǐhòu, tíngzhǐ jìnjǐ.

以刻度值为起点，按照图纸要求，刀尖进给合适的尺寸，提起自动进给操纵杆，刀尖到达规定的尺寸以后，停止进给。

Processing Shaft-Type Parts

Tool setting should be operated before turning. Slowly approach the workpiece with the tool tip, and read the scale value when the tool tip slightly contacts the workpiece and a small number of chips are generated.

Take the scale value as the starting point and feed the tool tip to the appropriate size according to the requirements on the drawing. Lift the automatic feed control rod, and stop feeding after the tool tip reaches the specified size.

课文练习 Text Exercises

1. 根据课文内容选择正确答案。Choose the correct answers according to the text.

1 加工轴类零件时先________。

A. 对刀　　B. 车削加工

2 刀尖慢慢地靠近工件，在刀尖接触到工件、产生少量切屑时，读取________。

A. 刻度值　　B. 位置

3 以刻度值为起点，按照________要求，刀尖进给合适的尺寸。

A. 划线　　B. 图纸

4 提起________，刀尖到达规定的尺寸以后，停止进给。

A. 卡盘扳手　　B. 自动进给操纵杆

2. 选择合适的词语填空。**Choose the appropriate words to fill in the blanks.**

A. 图纸　　B. 慢慢地　　C. 刻度值　　D. 对刀　　E. 规定的尺寸

1. 加工时先________。
2. 刀尖________靠近工件，在刀尖接触到工件、产生少量切屑时，读取刻度值。
3. 以________为起点，按照________要求，刀尖进给合适的尺寸。
4. 提起自动进给操纵杆，刀尖到达________以后，停止进给。

学习语法 Grammar

语法点 1 Grammar Point 1

以……为……

表示“把……作为……”。

“以……为……” means “to take ... as...”.

Yǐ kèdùzhí wéi qǐdiǎn.
1. 以刻度值为起点。Take the scale value as the starting point.

Yǐ biǎncuò wéi gōngjù, cuòxiāo píngmiàn.
2. 以扁锉为工具，锉削平面。Take the flat file as a tool to file flat surfaces.

Yǐ sānjiǎocuò wéi gōngjù, cuòxiāo nèijiǎo.
3. 以三角锉为工具，锉削内角。
Take the triangular file as a tool to file the inner corners.

语法点 1 练习 Exercise on Grammar Point 1

连词成句。**Rearrange the following words to make sentences.**

例如：

túzhǐ yāoqiú	wéi	biāozhǔn	yǐ
①图纸要求	②为	③标准	④以

④①②③

1 ①以 (yǐ) ②为 (wéi) ③刻度值 (kèdùzhí) ④起点 (qǐdiǎn)

____

2 ①工具 (gōngjù) ②以 (yǐ) ③扁锉 (biǎncuò) ④为 (wéi)

____

3 ①工具 (gōngjù) ②为 (wéi) ③以 (yǐ) ④三角锉 (sānjiǎocuò)

____

4 ①工具 (gōngjù) ②为 (wéi) ③样冲 (yàngchòng) ④以 (yǐ)

____

语法点 2 Grammar Point 2

介词：按照 The Preposition: 按照

表示遵循某种标准。

"按照" means following a certain standard.

Ànzhào túzhǐ yāoqiú jìnxíng jiāgōng.
1 按照 图纸 要求 进行 加工。
Process according to the requirements on the drawing.

Ànzhào gōngjiàn xíngzhuàng xuǎnzé cuòdāo.
2 按照 工件 形状 选择 锉刀。
Choose a file according to the shape of the workpiece.

Ànzhào túzhǐ yāoqiú tiáo gāodùchǐ.
3 按照 图纸要求 调 高度尺。
Adjust the height gauge according to the requirements on the drawing.

语法点 2 练习 Exercise on Grammar Point 2

为“按照”选择适当的位置。Fill “按照” in the appropriate positions.

1 ________ 　（A）杰克（Jiékè）（B）图纸要求（túzhǐ yāoqiú）（C）进行（jìnxíng）（D）加工（jiāgōng）。

2 ________ 　（A）工件（gōngjiàn）（B）形状（xíngzhuàng）（C）选择（xuǎnzé）（D）锉刀（cuòdāo）。

3 ________ 　（A）新 员工（xīn yuángōng）（B）没有（méiyǒu）（C）要求（yāoqiú）（D）调高度尺（tiáo gāodùchǐ）。

4 ________ 　（A）安全（ānquán）（B）要求（yāoqiú）（C）穿（chuān）（D）工作服和工作鞋（gōngzuòfú hé gōngzuòxié）。

汉字书写 Writing Chinese Characters

gǔ
古 古 古 古 古
古 古 古 古 古

zhǐ
只 只 只 只 只
只 只 只 只 只

jiā

加 加 加 加 加

加 加 加 加 加

lǚ

吕 吕 吕 吕 吕 吕

吕 吕 吕 吕 吕

职业拓展 Career Insight

转塔式六角车床

转塔式六角车床除了有前刀架以外，还有一个转塔刀架。转塔式六角车床是以六角形旋转之转塔取代普通车床的尾座，刀座上可装置六支不同的刀具，可以节省一般车床更换刀具的时间，适合大量生产。转塔式六角车床主要用于车削外圆柱面及对内孔做钻、扩、铰或镗等加工。

Hexagonal Turret-Type Lathes

In addition to the front tool holder, the hexagonal turret-type lathe also has a turret tool holder. The hexagonal turret-type lathe replaces the tailstock of a regular lathe with a hexagonal rotating turret. Six different turning tools can be installed on the tool holder, which can save the time for replacing turning tools on general lathes and is suitable for large-scale production. The hexagonal turret-type lathe is mainly used for turning outer cylindrical surfaces and drilling, reaming, or boring inner holes.

小结 Summary

词语 Words

朗读下列词语。Read the following words.

轴类零件	对刀	靠近
接触	刻度值	要求

语法 Grammar

熟读句子。Read the following sentences.

1. 以刻度值为起点。
2. 以扁锉为工具，锉削平面。
3. 按照图纸要求进行加工。
4. 按照工件形状选择锉刀。

课文理解 Text Comprehension

把下列句子按正确步骤排列。Sort the following sentences according to the correct steps.

1. 以刻度值为起点，按照图纸要求，刀尖进给合适的尺寸。
2. 加工时先对刀。
3. 刀尖慢慢地靠近工件，在刀尖接触到工件、产生少量切屑时，读取刻度值。
4. 提起自动进给操纵杆，刀尖到达规定的尺寸以后，停止进给。

________ → ________ → ________ → ________

第19课 Lesson 19

Kāi guān xǐchuáng

开关铣床

Switching on/off Milling Machines

复习 Revision

根据词语选图片。**Choose the right pictures according to the words.**

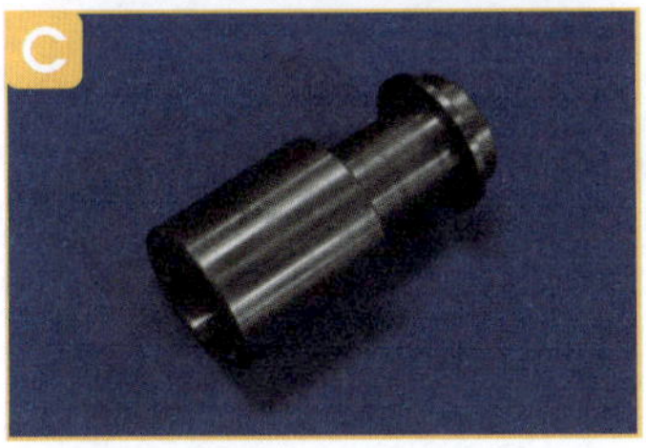

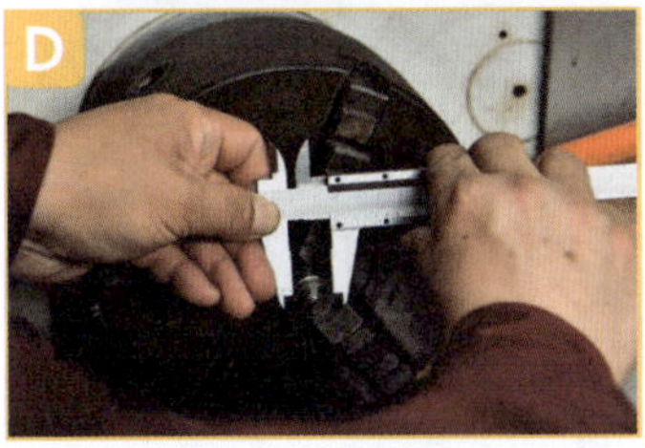

❶ 刻度值（　　）　　❷ 尺寸（　　）

❸ 轴类零件（　　）　　❹ 对刀（　　）

热身 Warm-up

选择正确的图片。Choose the right pictures.

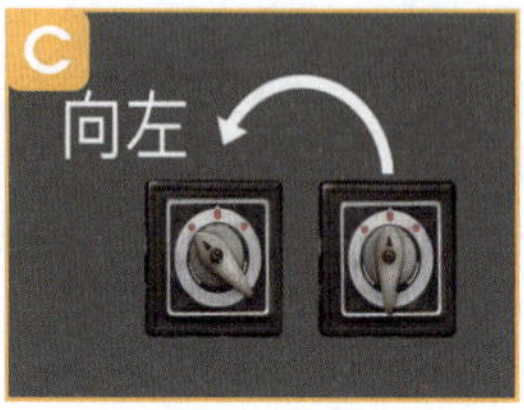

❶ 铣床 (xǐchuáng) milling machine (　　)　　❷ 电源 (diànyuán) power (　　)

❸ 主轴 (zhǔzhóu) spindle (　　)　　❹ 向左 (xiàng zuǒ) to the left (　　)

学习生词 Words and Expressions 19-01

1	铣床	xǐchuáng	*n.*	milling machine
2	首先	shǒuxiān	*adv.*	first
3	主轴	zhǔzhóu	*n.*	spindle
4	开关	kāiguān	*n.*	switch
5	应该	yīnggāi	*v.*	should
6	中间	zhōngjiān	*n.*	middle
7	停转	tíngzhuàn	*v.*	to stop rotating
8	接通	jiētōng	*v.*	to connect
9	左	zuǒ	*n.*	left

10	高速	gāosù	*adj.*	high speed
11	低速	dīsù	*adj.*	low speed
12	断开	duànkāi	*v.*	to switch off

词语练习 Word Exercises

1. 看图选词。Look at the pictures and choose the correct words.

❶ 
(　　) A. 车床　　B. 铣床

❷ 

(　　) A. 电源　　B. 按钮

❸ 
(　　) A. 主轴　　B. 扳手

❹ 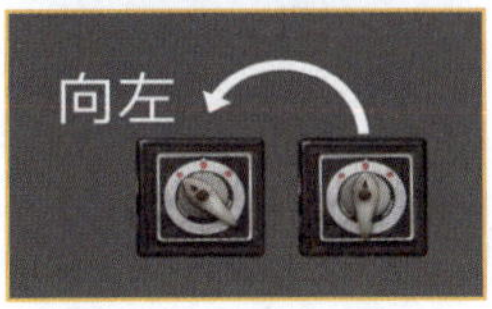

(　　) A. 尺寸　　B. 向左

2. 词语连线。Word Matching.

jiētōng 接通	jítíng ànniǔ 急停 按钮
báchū 拔出	zhǔzhóu kāiguān 主轴 开关
bāndòng 扳动	xǐchuáng diànyuán 铣床 电源
gāosù 高速	xuánzhuǎn 旋转

学习课文 Text 19-02

Kāi guān xǐchuáng
开关铣床

Kāi xǐchuáng:
（1）开铣床：

Shǒuxiān quèbǎo jìnjǐ cāozònggǎn zài kōngdǎng shang, zhǔzhóu kāiguān yīnggāi zài zhōngjiān tíngzhuàn wèizhì.
首先确保进给操纵杆在空挡上，主轴开关应该在中间停转位置。

Zài jiētōng xǐchuáng diànyuán, báchū jítíng ànniǔ, bāndòng zhǔzhóu kāiguān, xiàng zuǒ bān shì gāosù xuánzhuǎn, xiàng yòu bān shì dīsù xuánzhuǎn.
再接通铣床电源，拔出急停按钮，扳动主轴开关，向左扳是高速旋转，向右扳是低速旋转。

Guān xǐchuáng:
（2）关铣床：

Ànxia jítíng ànniǔ, bāndòng zhǔzhóu kāiguān zhì tíngzhuàn wèizhì, duànkāi xǐchuáng diànyuán.
按下急停按钮，扳动主轴开关至停转位置，断开铣床电源。

Switching on /off Milling Machines

I. Switching on the milling machine:

First, make sure that the feed control rod is in the neutral position and that the spindle switch is in the middle stop position.

Then, switch on the power of the milling machine, pull out the emergency stop button and pull the spindle switch. It rotates at a high speed when the switch is turned to the left, and at a low speed when turned to the right.

II. Switching off the milling machine

Press the emergency stop button, pull the spindle switch to the stop position and switch off the power of the milling machine.

课文练习 Text Exercises

1. 选择合适的词语填空。Choose the appropriate words to fill in the blanks.

A. 低速旋转　B. 高速旋转　C. 停转　D. 拔出　E. 空挡　F. 按下

1 开铣床时，首先确保进给操纵杆在 ________ 上，主轴开关应该在中间 ________ 位置。

2 接通铣床电源，________ 急停按钮，扳动主轴开关。

3 开铣床时，向左扳主轴开关是 ________，向右扳是 ________。

4 关铣床时，________ 急停按钮，扳动主轴开关至停转位置，断开铣床电源。

2. 一个学生发出指令，另一个学生做动作。**One student gives the instructions, and another student does the actions.**

1. 接通铣床电源，拔出急停按钮。
2. 扳动主轴开关，向左扳是高速旋转。
3. 扳动主轴开关，向右扳是低速旋转。
4. 按下急停按钮，扳动主轴开关至停转位置，断开铣床电源。

学习语法 Grammar

语法点 1 Grammar Point 1

能愿动词：应该 The Optative: 应该

表示某事的发生是理所当然的或者估计某事必然发生。

"应该" means that something is taken for granted to happen, or that it is expected to happen inevitably.

---

1. Zhǔzhóu kāiguān yīnggāi zài zhōngjiān tíngzhuàn wèizhi.
主轴 开关 应该 在 中间 停转 位置。
The spindle switch should be in the middle stop position.

2. Zài chējiān gōngzuò shí, yīnggāi chuān gōngzuòfú hé gōngzuòxié.
在 车间 工作 时，应该 穿 工作服 和 工作鞋。
When working in the workshop, we should wear work clothes and shoes.

3. Jìnjǐ cāozònggǎn yīnggāi zài zhèngquè wèizhi shang.
进给 操纵杆 应该 在 正确 位置 上。
The feed control rod should be in the correct position.

语法点 1 练习 Exercise on Grammar Point 1

连词成句。**Rearrange the following words to make sentences.**

例如：
①应该 (yīnggāi) ②戴好 (dàihǎo) ③防护 眼镜 (fánghù yǎnjìng) ④机床 加工 前 (jīchuáng jiāgōng qián)

④①②③

1 ①在 (zài) ②中间 停转 位置 (zhōngjiān tíngzhuàn wèizhì) ③应该 (yīnggāi) ④主轴 开关 (zhǔzhóu kāiguān)

______

2 ①在 车间 工作 时 (zài chējiān gōngzuò shí) ②应该 (yīnggāi) ③穿 (chuān) ④工作服和工作鞋 (gōngzuòfú hé gōngzuòxié)

______

3 ①正确 位置 上 (zhèngquè wèizhì shang) ②在 (zài) ③进给 操纵杆 (jìnjǐ cāozònggǎn) ④应该 (yīnggāi)

______

4 ①戴好 (dàihǎo) ②应该 (yīnggāi) ③安全帽 (ānquánmào) ④进 车间 工作 前 (jìn chējiān gōngzuò qián)

______

语法点 2 Grammar Point 2

"是"字句 "是" Sentence

由动词"是"充当谓语的句子，用来表达对事物的判断、说明或解释。

The verb "是" serves as the predicate in the sentence and is used to express judgments, explanations, or interpretations of matters.

Bāndòng zhǔzhóu kāiguān, xiàng zuǒ bān shì gāosù xuánzhuǎn.
1 扳动 主轴 开关，向 左 扳 是 高速 旋转。
Pull the spindle switch. It rotates at a high speed when the switch is turned to the left.

Bāndòng zhǔzhóu kāiguān, xiàng yòu bān shì dīsù xuánzhuǎn.
2 扳动 主轴 开关，向 右 扳 是低速 旋转。
Pull the spindle switch. It rotates at a low speed when the switch is turned to the right.

Xiàng yòu bāndòng shǒubǐng shì guān zuànchuáng.
3 向 右 扳动 手柄 是 关 钻床。
Pull the handle to the right to turn off the drilling machine.

语法点 2 练习 Exercise on Grammar Point 2

为“是”选择适当的位置。**Fill“是”in the appropriate positions.**

1 ______ bāndòng zhǔzhóu kāiguān xiàng zuǒ bān gāosù xuánzhuǎn
扳动（A）主轴 开关（B），（C）向 左 扳（D）高速 旋转。

2 ______ bandòng zhǔzhóu kāiguān, xiàng yòu bān dīsù xuánzhuǎn
扳动（A）主轴（B）开关，（C）向 右 扳（D）低速 旋转。

3 ______ xiàng yòu bāndòng shǒubǐng guān zuànchuáng
（A）向 右（B）扳动（C）手柄（D）关 钻床。

4 ______ xiàng zuǒ bāndòng shǒubǐng kāi zuànchuáng
（A）向 左（B）扳动（C）手柄（D）开 钻床。

汉字书写 Writing Chinese Characters

mǎ
马 马 马

马 马 马 马 马

wū 乌 乌 乌 乌

乌 乌 乌 乌 乌

mā 妈 妈 妈 妈 妈 妈

妈 妈 妈 妈 妈

ma 吗 吗 吗 吗 吗 吗

吗 吗 吗 吗 吗

文化拓展 Culture Insight

中国高铁

中国高铁的全称是“中国高速铁路”，是世界上发展最快、系统技术最全、集成能力最强、运营里程最长、运营速度最高、在建规模最大的高速铁路。

2003 年 10 月 11 日，秦沈客运专线全段建成通车，设计速度 250 千米 / 小时，为中国第一条高速国铁线路。2008 年 8 月 1 日，京津城际铁路开通运营，成为中国第一条设计速度 350 千米 / 小时级别的高速铁路。2023 年，中国铁路客运周转量、货物发送量、货运周转量以及运输密度均居世界首位。截至 2023 年底，中国铁路营业里程达到 15.9 万千米，其中高铁营业里程达到 4.5 万千米。

China's High-Speed Railway

The full name of China's High-Speed Railway is "China's High-Speed Passenger Railway". It is the fastest developing high-speed railway in the world, with the most comprehensive system technology, the strongest integration ability, the longest operating mileage, the highest operating speed, and the largest ongoing construction scale.

On October 11, 2003, the entire section of the Qinhuangdao-Shenyang Passenger Line was completed and put into service with a designed speed of 250 kilometers per hour, making it China's first national high-speed railway. On August 1, 2008, the Beijing-Tianjin Intercity Railway began operations, becoming the first high-speed railway in Chinese mainland with a designed speed of 350 kilometers per hour. In 2023, China's railway passenger turnover, freight volume, freight turnover, and transportation density all ranked first in the world. By the end of 2023, the operating mileage of China's railways has reached 159,000 kilometers, including 45,000 kilometers of high-speed railways.

小结 Summary

词语 Words

朗读下列词语。Read the following words.

铣床	首先	主轴
应该	中间	停转

语法 Grammar

熟读句子。**Read the following sentences.**

1. 主轴开关应该在中间停转位置。
2. 在车间工作时，应该穿工作服和工作鞋。
3. 扳动主轴开关，向左扳是高速旋转。
4. 扳动主轴开关，向右扳是低速旋转。

课文理解 Text Comprehension

把下列句子按正确步骤排列。**Sort the following sentences according to the correct steps.**

1. 开铣床时，接通铣床电源，拔出急停按钮。
2. 开铣床时，扳动主轴开关，向左扳是高速旋转，向右扳是低速旋转。
3. 开铣床时，首先确保进给操纵杆在空挡上，主轴开关应该在中间停转位置。
4. 关铣床时，按下急停按钮，扳动主轴开关至停转位置，断开铣床电源。

___③___ → ______ → ______ → ______

Zhuāngjiā píngmiànlèi máopījiàn

第20课 Lesson 20 装夹平面类毛坯件

Clamping Flat-Type Blanks

复习 Revision

根据词语选图片。Choose the right pictures according to the words.

A

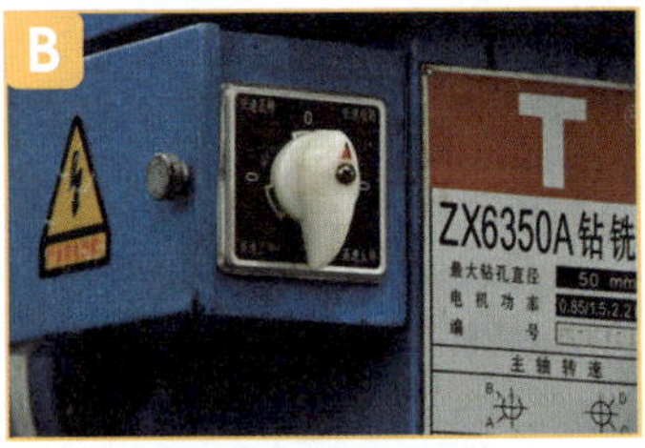

B

C

D

❶ 刻度值（　　）　❷ 铣床（　　）

❸ 电源（　　）　❹ 主轴（　　）

热身 Warm-up

选择正确的图片。**Choose the right pictures.**

A

B

C

D

❶ 平面类 毛坯件 (píngmiànlèi máopījiàn) flat-type blank ( )

❷ 铜皮 (tóngpí) copper foil ( )

❸ 导轨 (dǎoguǐ) guide rail ( )

❹ 垫铁 (diàntiě) shim ( )

学习生词 Words and Expressions 20-01

1	平面类毛坯件	píngmiànlèi máopījiàn	*phr.*	flat-type blank
2	大	dà	*adj.*	large
3	作为	zuòwéi	*v.*	to regard as
4	粗基准	cūjīzhǔn	*n.*	rough reference surface
5	它	tā	*pron.*	it
6	靠	kào	*v.*	to lean
7	固定	gùdìng	*v.*	to be fixed
8	铜皮	tóngpí	*n.*	copper foil

9	垫	diàn	*v.*	to place something between...
10	之间	zhījiān	*n.*	between...and...
11	导轨	dǎoguǐ	*n.*	guide rail
12	垫铁	diàntiě	*n.*	shim
13	敲	qiāo	*v.*	to knock
14	调整	tiáozhěng	*v.*	to adjust
15	不动	bú dòng	*phr.*	fixedly; immovably

词语练习 Word Exercises

1. 看图选词。Look at the pictures and choose the correct words.

❶  (　　) A. 平面类毛坯件　B. 轴类零件

❷  (　　) A. 垫铁　B. 铜皮

❸  (　　) A. 主轴　B. 导轨

❹  (　　) A. 垫铁　B. 导轨

2. 词语连线。**Word Matching.**

tiáozhěng 调整	gōngjiàn 工件
jiājǐn 夹紧	yí gè dà píngmiàn 一个大 平面
xuǎnzé 选择	wèizhì 位置
diànshang 垫上	diàntiě 垫铁

学习课文 Text 20-02

Zhuāngjiā píngmiànlèi máopījiàn
装夹平面类毛坯件

Xiān zài máopījiàn shang xuǎnzé yí gè dà píngmiàn zuòwéi
先在毛坯件上选择一个大平面作为

cūjīzhǔn, bǎ tā kào zài gùdìng qiánkǒumiàn shang.
粗基准，把它靠在固定钳口面上。

Zài bǎ tóngpí diàn zài qiánkǒu hé gōngjiàn máopīmiàn zhījiān.
再把铜皮垫在钳口和工件毛坯面之间。

Ránhòu zài gōngjiàn hé dǎoguǐ zhījiān diànshang diàntiě.
然后在工件和导轨之间垫上垫铁。

Zuìhòu qīngqīng de qiāo yì qiāo gōng jiàn, tiáozhěng hǎo wèizhì,
最后轻轻地敲一敲工件，调整好位置，

jiājǐn gōngjiàn, quèbǎo diàntiě bú dòng, wánchéng zhuāngjiā.
夹紧工件，确保垫铁不动，完成装夹。

Clamping Flat-Type Blanks

Select a large surface of the blank as the rough reference surface and lean it against the fixed jaw surface.

Place a copper foil between the jaw and the blank surface of the workpiece.

Then, place a shim between the workpiece and the guide rail.

Finally, gently knock the workpiece a few times to adjust the position. Clamp the workpiece tightly to ensure that the shim is fixed and then the whole process of clamping is completed.

课文练习 Text Exercises

1. 选择合适的词语填空。Choose the appropriate words to fill in the blanks.

A. 位置　　B. 垫铁　　C. 大平面　　D. 铜皮

1. 先在毛坯件上选择一个________作为粗基准，把它靠在固定钳口面上。
2. 再把________垫在钳口和工件毛坯面之间。
3. 然后在工件和导轨之间垫上________。
4. 最后轻轻地敲一敲工件，调整好________，夹紧工件，确保垫铁不动，完成装夹。

2. 一个学生发出指令，另一个学生做动作。One student gives the instructions, and the other does the actions.

1. 在毛坯件上选择一个大平面作为粗基准，把它靠在固定钳口面上。

2 把铜皮垫在钳口和工件毛坯面之间。

3 在工件和导轨之间垫上垫铁。

4 轻轻地敲一敲工件，调整好位置，夹紧工件，确保垫铁不动。

学习语法 Grammar

语法点 1 Grammar Point 1

动词重叠　Verb Reduplication

有些动词可以重叠，表示动作次数少、持续时间短或尝试的意思。

Some verbs can be reduplicated to indicate a small number of occurences, a short duration, or an attempt.

Zuìhòu qīngqīng de qiāo yì qiāo gōngjiàn, tiáozhěng hǎo wèizhì.
1 最后 轻轻 地 敲 一 敲 工件，调整 好 位置。
Finally, gently knock the workpiece to adjust the position.

Liáng yì liáng gōngjiàn chǐcùn.
2 量 一 量 工件 尺寸。Measure the workpiece.

Tiáo yì tiáo gāodùchǐ.
3 调 一 调 高度尺。Adjust the height gauge.

语法点 1 练习 Exercise on Grammar Point 1

连词成句。**Rearrange the following words to make sentences.**

例如：
yì ①一　jiā ②夹　hàntiáo ③焊条（welding rod）　jiā ④夹

②①④③ / ④①②③

1 ①调整（tiáozhěng） 好位置（hǎo wèizhì） ②敲一敲（qiāo yì qiāo） ③轻轻地（qīngqīng de） ④工件（gōngjiàn）

____

2 ①工件（gōngjiàn） 尺寸（chǐcùn） ②量（liáng） ③一（yì） ④量（liáng）

____

3 ①调（tiáo） ②高度尺（gāodùchǐ） ③一（yì） ④调（tiáo）

____

4 ①看（kàn） ②图纸（túzhǐ） ③看（kàn） ④一（yì）

____

语法点 2 Grammar Point 2

动词：作为 The Verb: 作为

意思是“当作、看成”。

It means “当作、看成”.

1 Xiān zài máopījiàn shang xuǎnzé yí gè dàpíngmiàn zuòwéi cūjīzhǔn.
先在毛坯件上选择一个大平面作为粗基准。
Select a large surface of the blank as the rough reference surface first.

2 Xuǎnzé biǎncuò zuòwéi cuòxiāo píngmiàn de gōngjù.
选择扁锉作为锉削平面的工具。
Choose a flat file as the tool for filing flat surfaces.

3 Bǎ gāodùchǐ hé fāngxiāng zuòwéi huàxiàn de gōngjù.
把高度尺和方箱作为划线的工具。
Choose a height gauge and a square box as the tools for scribing.

语法点 2 练习 Exercise on Grammar Point 2

判断下面四个句子是否符合操作规定。**Determine whether the following four sentences comply with the operational regulations.**

Xiān zài máopījiàn shang xuǎnzé yí gè dà píngmiàn zuòwéi cūjīzhǔn.
1 先在毛坯件上选择一个大平面作为粗基准。（ ）

fúhé / bù fúhé
A. 符合　　B. 不符合

Xuǎnzé biǎncuò zuòwéi cuòxiāo píngmiàn de gōngjù.
2 选择扁锉作为锉削平面的工具。（ ）

fúhé / bù fúhé
A. 符合　　B. 不符合

Bǎ gāodùchǐ hé fāngxiāng zuòwéi huàxiàn de gōngjù.
3 把高度尺和方箱作为划线的工具。（ ）

fúhé / bù fúhé
A. 符合　　B. 不符合

Xuǎnzé yàngchòng zuòwéi zhuāngjiā gōngjiàn de gōngjù.
4 选择样冲作为装夹工件的工具。（ ）

fúhé / bù fúhé
A. 符合　　B. 不符合

汉字书写 Writing Chinese Characters

shí
石 石 石 石 石

石 石 石 石 石

yòu
右 右 右 右 右

右 右 右 右 右

bǎi 百 百 百 百 百 百

百 百 百 百 百

zuǒ 左 左 左 左 左

左 左 左 左 左

职业拓展 Career Insight

立式车床

立式车床一般可分为单柱式和双柱式两种。立式车床的主要结构特点是它的主轴处于垂直位置。立式车床的主要优点是：工作台在水平面内，工件的安装、调整比较方便；工作台由导轨支撑，刚性好，切削平稳；有几个刀架，并能快速换刀。立式车床的加工精度可达到 IT9 ～ IT8，表面粗糙度 Ra 可达 3.2 ～ 1.6 um。立式车床的主参数为最大车削直径 D。

Vertical Lathes

Vertical lathes can generally be divided into single-column and double-column types. The main structural feature of a vertical lathe is that its spindle is positioned vertically. The main advantages of a vertical lathe are: the workbench is on the horizontal plane, making the installation and adjustment of workpieces relatively convenient; the workbench is supported by guide rails, providing good rigidity and stable cutting; and there are several tool holders, enabling quick tool changes. The machining accuracy of a vertical lathe can reach IT9 to IT8, and the surface roughness (Ra) can range from 3.2 to 1.6 um. The main parameter of a vertical lathe is the maximum turning diameter (D).

小结 Summary

词语 Words

朗读下列词语。**Read the following words.**

平面类毛坯件	粗基准	固定
铜皮	导轨	垫铁

语法 Grammar

熟读句子。**Read the following sentences.**

1. 最后轻轻地敲一敲工件，调整好位置。
2. 量一量工件尺寸。
3. 先在毛坯件上选择一个大平面作为粗基准。
4. 选择扁锉作为锉削平面的工具。

课文理解 Text Comprehension

把下列句子按正确步骤排列。**Sort the following sentences according to the correct steps.**

1. 再把铜皮垫在钳口和工件毛坯面之间。
2. 然后在工件和导轨之间垫上垫铁。
3. 先在毛坯件上选择一个大平面作为粗基准，把它靠在固定钳口面上。
4. 最后轻轻地敲一敲工件，调整好位置，夹紧工件，确保垫铁不动，完成装夹。

______ → ______ → ______ → ______

第21课 Lesson 21

Ānzhuāng xǐdāo
安装铣刀
Installing Milling Tools

复习 Revision

根据词语选图片。**Choose the right pictures according to the words.**

A
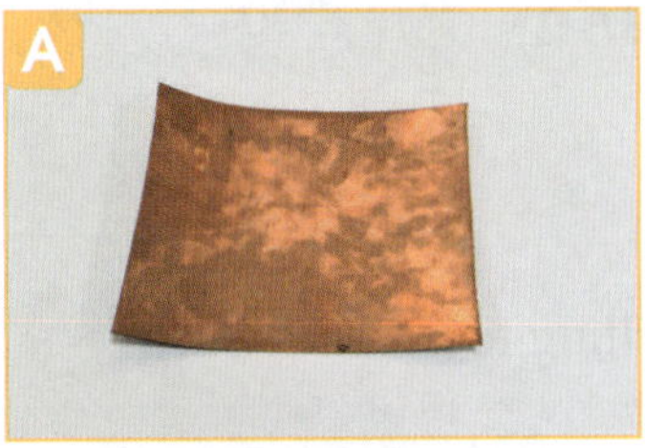

B

C

D

❶ 平面类毛坯件（　　）　❷ 铜皮（　　）

❸ 导轨（　　）　❹ 垫铁（　　）

热身 Warm-up

选择正确的图片。**Choose the right pictures.**

❶ 铣刀 (xǐdāo) milling tool (　　)

❷ 锥面 (zhuīmiàn) tapered surface (　　)

❸ 刀套 (dāotào) tool holder (　　)

❹ 螺帽 (luómào) nut (　　)

学习生词 Words and Expressions 21-01

1	铣刀	xǐdāo	*n.*	milling tool
2	清洁	qīngjié	*v.*	to clean
3	锥面	zhuīmiàn	*n.*	tapered surface
4	插进	chājìn	*phr.*	to insert
5	必须	bìxū	*adv.*	must
6	贴合	tiēhé	*v.*	to fit
7	螺杆	luógǎn	*n.*	screw
8	拉紧	lājǐn	*phr.*	to pull tightly

9	刀套	dāotào	*n.*	tool holder
10	螺帽	luómào	*n.*	nut
11	并且	bìngqiě	*conj.*	and
12	插入	chārù	*v.*	to insert
13	深度	shēndù	*n.*	depth

词语练习 Word Exercises

1. 看图选词。Look at the pictures and choose the correct words.

❶  (　　) A. 锥面　B. 螺杆

❷  (　　) A. 车刀　B. 铣刀

❸  (　　) A. 刀柄　B. 刀套

❹  (　　) A. 刀套　B. 螺帽

2. 朗读词语搭配。**Read the collocations.**

❶	ānzhuāng 安装	xǐdāo 铣刀	❸	xuǎnzé 选择	dāotào 刀套
	suǒjǐn 锁紧				
❷	qīngqié 清洁	dāobǐng 刀柄		chārù 插入	
	lājǐn 拉紧				

学习课文 Text 21-02

Ānzhuāng xǐdāo
安装铣刀

Shǒuxiān, qīngjié dāobǐng zhuīmiàn hé zhǔzhóukǒng, bǎ dāobǐng chājìn xǐchuáng zhǔzhóukǒng, dāobǐng zhuīmiàn gēn zhǔzhóukǒng bìxū tiēhé, yòng luógǎn lājǐn dāobǐng.
首先，清洁刀柄锥面和主轴孔，把刀柄插进铣床主轴孔，刀柄锥面跟主轴孔必须贴合，用螺杆拉紧刀柄。

Ránhòu, xuǎnzé héshì de dāotào, fàngjìn luómào li, bǎ xǐdāo chājìn dāotào li, bìngqiě quèbǎo héshì de chārù shēndù.
然后，选择合适的刀套，放进螺帽里，把铣刀插进刀套里，并且确保合适的插入深度。

Zuìhòu, suǒjǐn xǐdāo luómào, ānzhuāng wánchéng.
最后，锁紧铣刀螺帽，安装完成。

Installing Milling Tools

First, clean the tapered surface of the tool handle and the spindle hole. Insert the tool handle into the spindle hole of the milling machine. The tapered surface of the tool handle must fit precisely with the spindle hole, and the tool handle must be tightened with a screw.

Then, select the appropriate tool holder to place it in the nut, and then insert the milling tool into the tool holder, making sure that the inserting depth is appropriate.

Finally, tighten the milling tool nut and complete the installation.

课文练习 Text Exercises

1. 选择合适的词语填空。Choose the appropriate words to fill in the blanks.

A. 插入深度　B. 螺杆　C. 刀柄锥面　D. 主轴孔　E. 锁紧

1. 首先，清洁 ________ 和 ________，把刀柄插进铣床主轴孔。
2. 刀柄锥面跟主轴孔必须贴合，用 ________ 拉紧刀柄。
3. 然后，选择合适的刀套，放进螺帽里，把铣刀插进刀套里，并且确保合适的 ________。
4. 最后，________ 铣刀螺帽，安装完成。

2. 一个学生发出指令，另一个学生做动作。**One student gives the instructions, and another student does the actions.**

1 清洁刀柄锥面和主轴孔，把刀柄插进铣床主轴孔。

2 刀柄锥面跟主轴孔必须贴合，用螺杆拉紧刀柄。

3 选择合适的刀套，放进螺帽里。

4 把铣刀插进刀套里，并且确保合适的插入深度。

学习语法 Grammar

语法点 1 Grammar Point 1

连词：并且 The Conjunction: 并且

用于递进复句的后一分句，表示更进一层的意思。

"并且" is used to introduce the following clause in a progressive compound sentence, indicating a further step or progression.

1 Zài chējiān gōngzuò shí, yào dài ānquánmào, bìngqiě yào bǎ cháng fà sāirù ānquánmào li.
在车间工作时，要戴安全帽，并且要把长发塞入安全帽里。
When working in the workshop, it is necessary to wear a safety cap and tuck long hair into it.

2 Zài chējiān gōngzuò shí, chuānhǎo gōngzuòfú, bìngqiě zājǐn lǐngkǒu、xiùkǒu.
在车间工作时，穿好工作服，并且扎紧领口、袖口。
When working in the workshop, it is necessary to wear work clothes and tie the neckband and cuffs tightly.

3 Bǎ xǐdāo chājìn dāotào li, bìngqiě quèbǎo héshì de chārù shēndù.
把铣刀插进刀套里，并且确保合适的插入深度。
Insert the milling tool into the tool holder, making sure that the inserting depth is appropriate.

语法点1练习 Exercise on Grammar Point 1

连词成句。**Rearrange the following words to make sentences.**

例如：

dàihǎo ānquánmào / bìngqiě / dàihǎo fánghù yǎnjìng / jīchuáng jiāgōng shí

①戴好 安全帽　②并且　③戴好 防护 眼镜

④机床 加工 时

④①②③

1 zài chējiān gōngzuò shí / yào bǎ cháng fà sāirù ānquánmào li / yào dài ānquánmào / bìngqiě

①在 车间 工作 时　②要 把 长 发 塞入 安全帽 里

③要 戴 安全帽　④并且

______

2 zājǐn lǐngkǒu、xiùkǒu / zài chējiān gōngzuò shí / bìngqiě / chuānhǎo gōngzuòfú

①扎紧领口、袖口　②在 车间 工作 时　③并且

④穿好 工作服

______

3 bìngqiě / quèbǎo héshì de chārù shēndù / bǎ xǐdāo chājìn dāotào li

①并且　②确保合适的插入深度　③把铣刀 插进 刀套里

______

4 bìngqiě / xuéxí qiángōng / Jiékè xuéxí Zhōngwén

①并且　②学习 钳工　③杰克学习 中文

______

语法点 2 Grammar Point 2

副词：必须 The Adverb: 必须

表示在事理和情理上一定要，语气较重。

"必须" indicates that something is absolutely required in terms of reason and logic, with a strong tone.

Dāobǐng zhuīmiàn gēn zhǔzhóukǒng bìxū tiēhé.
1. 刀柄 锥面 跟 主轴孔 必须 贴合。
The tapered surface of the tool handle must fit precisely with the spindle hole.

Gōngjiàn bèicèmiàn bìxū yǔ huàxiàn píngtái tiējǐn.
2. 工件 被测面必须与 划线 平台 贴紧。
The measured surface of the workpiece must be tightly attached to the scribing platform.

Yàngchòng bìxū yǔ gōngjiàn biǎomiàn chuízhí.
3. 样冲 必须与 工件 表面 垂直。
The punch must be perpendicular to the surface of the workpiece.

语法点 2 练习 Exercise on Grammar Point 2

为"必须"选择适当的位置。**Fill "必须" in the appropriate positions.**

1. ________
dāobǐng zhuīmiàn gēn zhǔzhóukǒng tiēhé
刀柄 锥面（A）跟（B）主轴孔（C）贴合（D）。

2. ________
gōngjiàn bèicèmiàn yǔ huàxiàn píngtái tiējǐn
工件（A）被测面（B）与 划线 平台（C）贴紧（D）。

3. ________
yàngchòng yǔ gōngjiàn biǎomiàn chuízhí
（A）样冲（B）与（C）工件 表面（D）垂直。

4. ________
zài chējiān gōngzuò dài fánghù yǎnjìng
在 车间（A）工作（B）戴（C）防护 眼镜（D）。

汉字书写 Writing Chinese Characters

bā

巴 巴 巴 巴 巴

bɑ

吧 吧 吧 吧 吧

bǎ

把 把 把 把 把

bà

爸 爸 爸 爸 爸

文化拓展 Culture Insight

微信

微信（WeChat）是腾讯公司于2011年1月21日推出的一款为智能终端提供即时通信服务的免费应用程序。微信支持跨通信运营商、跨操作系统平台，通过网络快速发送免费（需消耗少量网络流量）语音短信、视频、图片和文字，同时，也可以使用通过共享流媒体内容的“朋友圈”“公众平台”等服务插件。微信提供公众平台、朋友圈、消息推送等功能，用户可以将内容分享给好友，也可以将自己看到的精彩内容分享到微信朋友圈。

WeChat

WeChat is a free application launched by Tencent on January 21st, 2011, providing instant messaging services for smart terminals. WeChat enables fast and free (with a small amount of mobile data consumption required) sending of voice messages, videos, images, and texts across communication operators and diverse operating system platforms. At the same time, service plugins such as the "Moments" and "Public Platform" for sharing streaming content can also be used. WeChat offers features such as the Public Platform, Moments, and message push notifications, allowing users to sharc content with friends and share interesting content they come across on their WeChat Moments.

小结 Summary

词语 Words

朗读下列词语。Read the following words.

铣刀	锥面	螺杆
刀套	螺帽	锁紧

语法 Grammar

熟读句子。Read the following sentences.

1. 在车间工作时，要戴安全帽，并且要把长发塞入安全帽里。
2. 在车间工作时，穿好工作服，并且扎紧领口、袖口。
3. 刀柄锥面跟主轴孔必须贴合。
4. 工件被测面必须与划线平台贴紧。

课文理解 Text Comprehension

把下列句子按正确步骤排列。Sort the following sentences according to the correct steps.

1. 首先，清洁刀柄锥面和主轴孔，把刀柄插进铣床主轴孔，刀柄锥面跟主轴孔必须贴合，用螺杆拉紧刀柄。
2. 最后，锁紧铣刀螺帽，安装完成。
3. 然后，选择合适的刀套，放进螺帽里，把铣刀插进刀套里，并且确保合适的插入深度。

________ → ________ → ________

第22课 Lesson 22

Jiāgōng píngmiànlèi língjiàn
加工平面类零件
Processing Flat-Type Parts

复习 Revision

根据词语选图片。Choose the right pictures according to the words.

A

B

C

D

❶ 刀套（　　）　　❷ 螺帽（　　）

❸ 锥面（　　）　　❹ 铣刀（　　）

热身 Warm-up

选择正确的图片。**Choose the right pictures.**

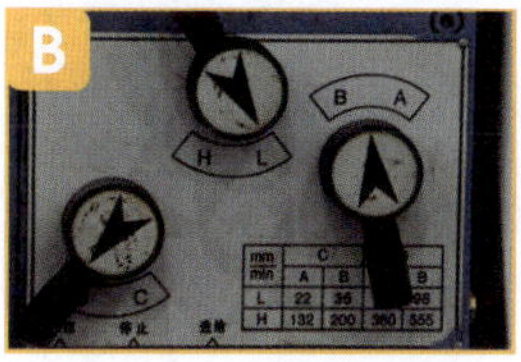

❶ píngmiànlèi língjiàn 平面类零件 flat-type part (　　)

❷ xǐxiāo 铣削 mill (　　)

❸ qiēxiāo cānshù 切削参数 cutting parameter (　　)

❹ chú máocì 除毛刺 debur (　　)

学习生词 Words and Expressions 22-01

1	平面类零件	píngmiànlèi língjiàn	*phr.*	flat-type part
2	精度	jīngdù	*n.*	accuracy
3	切削参数	qiēxiāo cānshù	*phr.*	cutting parameter
4	进行	jìnxíng	*v.*	to proceed
5	铣削	xǐxiāo	*v.*	to mill
6	去除	qùchú	*v.*	to remove
7	多余	duōyú	*adj.*	excess

8	后	hòu	*n.*	after
9	一方面……， 另一方面……	yì fāngmiàn…, lìng yì fāngmiàn…		on the one hand... on the other hand...
10	倒角	dǎojiǎo	*v.*	to chamfer
11	除毛刺	chú máocì	*phr.*	to deburr
12	处理	chǔlǐ	*v.*	to process
13	质量	zhìliàng	*n.*	quality
14	符合	fúhé	*v.*	to be in compliance with

词语练习 Word Exercises

1. 看图选词。**Look at the pictures and choose the words.**

❶  (　　) A. 铣削　　B. 车削

❷ 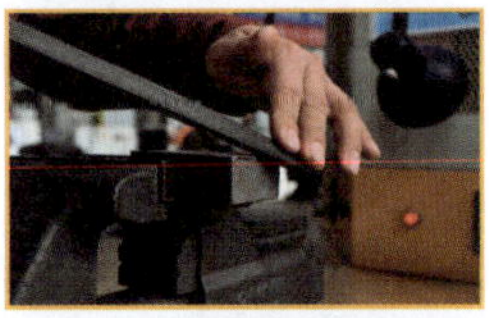 (　　) A. 除毛刺　　B. 铣削

❸  (　　) A. 切削参数　　B. 开关

❹  (　　) A. 平面类零件　　B. 毛坯件

2. 词语连线。**Word Matching.**

píngmiànlèi 平面类	túzhǐ yāoqiú 图纸要求
xuǎnzé héshì de 选择合适的	gōngjiàn 工件
gēnjù 根据	língjiàn 零件
xǐxiāo 铣削	qiēxiāo cānshù 切削参数
qùchú 去除	zhìliàng 质量
jiǎnchá 检查	duōyú bùfen 多余部分

学习课文 Text 22-02

Jiāgōng píngmiànlèi língjiàn 加工平面类零件

Shǒuxiān, gēnjù túzhǐ duì jiāgōng píngmiàn chǐcùn hé jīngdù de yāoqiú, xuǎnzé héshì de qiēxiāo cānshù.

首先，根据图纸对加工平面尺寸和精度的要求，选择合适的切削参数。

Ránhòu, duì gōngjiàn jìnxíng xǐxiāo, qùchú duōyú bùfen.

然后，对工件进行铣削，去除多余部分。

Xǐxiāo wánchéng hòu, yì fāngmiàn yào duì gōngjiàn jìnxíng dǎo-
铣削完成后，一方面要对工件进行倒
jiǎo、chú máocì chǔlǐ, lìng yì fāngmiàn hái yào jiǎnchá chǐcùn hé
角、除毛刺处理，另一方面还要检查尺寸和
biǎomiàn zhìliàng, quèbǎo fúhé túzhǐ yāoqiú.
表面质量，确保符合图纸要求。

Processing Flat-Type Parts

Firstly, select appropriate cutting parameters according to the requirements on the drawing for the size and accuracy of processing flat-type parts.

Then, mill the workpiece to remove excess parts.

After milling, on the one hand, the workpiece needs to be chamfered and deburred; on the other hand, the size and surface quality should be checked to ensure compliance with the requirements on the drawing.

课文练习 Text Exercises

1. 根据课文内容选择正确答案。Choose the correct answers according to the text.

1 首先，根据________对加工平面尺寸和精度的要求，选择合适的切削参数。

A. 起点　　　　B. 图纸

2 然后，对工件进行________，去除多余部分。

A. 铣削　　　　B. 清洁

3 铣削完成后，一方面要对工件进行 ________ 处理。

A. 倒角、除毛刺　　B. 铣削

4 铣削完成后，另一方面还要检查________，确保符合图纸要求。

A. 位置　　B. 尺寸和表面质量

2. 选择合适的词语填空。**Choose the appropriate words to fill in the blanks.**

A. 除毛刺　　B. 多余部分　　C. 精度　　D. 尺寸　　E. 图纸

1 首先，根据图纸对加工平面________和________的要求，选择合适的切削参数。

2 然后，对工件进行铣削，去除________。

3 铣削完成后，一方面要对工件进行倒角、________处理。

4 铣削完成后，另一方面还要检查尺寸和表面质量，确保符合________要求。

学习语法 Grammar

语法点 1 Grammar Point 1

介词：对　The Preposition: 对

引出动作的对象，表示对待。

"对" introduces the object of the action, indicating how it is treated.

Duì gōngjiàn jìnxíng xǐxiāo, qùchú duōyú bùfen.
1 对工件进行铣削，去除多余部分。
Mill the workpiece to remove excess parts.

Duì gōngjiàn jìnxíng dǎojiǎo、chú máocì chǔlǐ.
2 对工件进行倒角、除毛刺处理。
The workpiece needs to be chamfered and deburred.

Duì gōngjiàn jìnxíng huàxiàn.
3 对工件进行划线。Scribe on the workpiece.

语法点 1 练习 Exercise on Grammar Point 1

根据课文选择正确的词语。**Choose the correct words according to the text.**

1	Duì ________ jìnxíng xǐxiāo, qùchú duōyú bùfen. 对________进行铣削，去除多余部分。	gōngjiàn A. 工件	cuòdāo B. 锉刀
2	Duì ________ jìnxíng dǎojiǎo、chú máocì chǔlǐ. 对________进行倒角、除毛刺处理。	fāngcuò A. 方锉	gōngjiàn B. 工件
3	Duì ________ jìnxíng huàxiàn. 对________进行划线。	gāodùchǐ A. 高度尺	gōngjiàn B. 工件
4	Duì ________ jìnxíng cuòxiāo. 对________进行锉削。	píngmiàn A. 平面	dāobǐng B. 刀柄

语法点 2 Grammar Point 2

一方面……，另一方面……

一般用于解释、说明同时存在的两个方面的原因、情况。

"一方面……，另一方面……" is generally used to explain the simultaneous existence of two causes or situations.

Yì fāngmiàn yào duì gōngjiàn jìnxíng dǎojiǎo、chú máocì chǔlǐ, lìng yì fāngmiàn hái yào jiǎnchá chǐcùn hé biǎomiàn zhìliàng.
1 一方面要对工件进行倒角、除毛刺处理，另一方面还要检查尺寸和表面质量。
On the one hand, the workpiece needs to be chamfered and deburred; on the other hand, the size and surface quality should be checked.

Zài chējiān gōngzuò shí, yì fāngmiàn yào dàihǎo ānquánmào, lìng yì fāngmiàn yào zhùyì yòng diàn ānquán.
2 在车间工作时，一方面要戴好安全帽，另一方面要注意用电安全。
When working in the workshop, on the one hand, wear a safety cap; on the other hand, pay attention to the power safety.

Jiékè yì fāngmiàn xiǎng xuéhǎo Zhōngwén, lìng yì fāngmiàn yě xiǎng xuéhǎo jīchuáng cāozuò.
3 杰克一方面想学好中文，另一方面也想学好机床操作。
On the one hand, Jack wants to master Chinese; on the other hand, he also wants to master machine tool operations.

语法点 2 练习 Exercise on Grammar Point 2

选择正确的答案。Choose the right answers.

Yì fāngmiàn yào duì gōngjiàn jìnxíng dǎojiǎo、chú máocì chǔlǐ, lìng yì fāngmiàn
1 一方面要对工件进行倒角、除毛刺处理，另一方面________。

hái yào jiǎnchá chǐcùn hé biǎomiàn zhìliàng
A. 还要检查尺寸和表面质量

hái yào dàihǎo ānquánmào
B. 还要戴好安全帽

Zài chējiān gōngzuò shí, yì fāngmiàn yào dàihǎo ānquánmào, lìng yì fāngmiàn
2 在车间工作时，一方面要戴好安全帽，另一方面________。

yào zhùyì yòng diàn ānquán
A. 要注意用电安全

qǔxia jiù jùtiáo
B. 取下旧锯条

Jiékè yì fāngmiàn xiǎng xuéhǎo Zhōngwén, lìng yì fāngmiàn
3 杰克一方面想学好中文，另一方面________。

zhuāngjiā gōngjiàn
A. 装夹工件

yě xiǎng xuéhǎo jīchuáng cāozuò
B. 也想学好机床操作

Jiāgōng zhóulèi língjiàn shí, yì fāngmiàn yào ànzhào túzhǐ yāoqiú, lìng yì fāngmiàn
4 加工轴类零件时，一方面要按照图纸要求，另一方面________。

yào zhùyì ānquán
A. 要注意安全

guān diànyuán
B. 关电源

汉字书写 Writing Chinese Characters

zǐ

子 子 子 子 子

zì

字 字 字 字 字

lǐ

李 李 李 李 李

xué

学 学 学 学 学

职业拓展 Career Insight

6S 管理

6S 管理兴起于 20 世纪 50 年代的日本企业，它是一种管理模式，内容包括整理、整顿、清扫、安全、标准化、素养。

6S 管理是 5S 管理的升级，包括对员工行为品质、工作方法、作业流程的管理，以及对物品的规范管理。这种管理模式有利于提升企业形象、减少浪费、提高效率等。

6S Management

6S management was invented in Japanese companies in the 1950s. It is a management model that includes “sort”, “set in order”, “shine”, “safety”, “standardize” and “sustain”.

6S management is an upgrade of 5S, including the management of employee behavior, working methods, working processes, and standardized management of items. This management model is beneficial for enhancing company image, reducing waste, and improving efficiency.

小结 Summary

词语 Words

朗读下列词语。**Read the following words.**

平面类零件	精度	切削参数
铣削	倒角	除毛刺

语法 Grammar

熟读句子。**Read the following sentences.**

1 对工件进行铣削，去除多余部分。

2 对工件进行倒角、除毛刺处理。

3 一方面要对工件进行倒角、除毛刺处理，另一方面还要检查尺寸和表面质量。

4 在车间工作时，一方面要戴好安全帽，另一方面要注意用电安全。

课文理解 Text Comprehension

把下列句子按正确步骤排列。Sort the following sentences according to the correct steps.

1 铣削完成后，一方面要对工件进行倒角、除毛刺处理。

2 首先，根据图纸对加工平面尺寸和精度的要求，选择合适的切削参数。

3 另一方面还要检查尺寸和表面质量，确保符合图纸要求。

4 然后，对工件进行铣削，去除多余部分。

________ → ________ → ________ → ________

第23课 Lesson 23

Hànjiē ānquán

焊接安全 The Safety of Welding

复习 Revision

回答问题。**Answer the questions.**

1. 怎样铣削平面类零件？（用“首先……，然后……”回答）

   ____

2. 铣削完成后，还要做什么么？（用“一方面……，另一方面……”回答）

   ____

热身 Warm-up

选择正确的图片。**Choose the right pictures.**

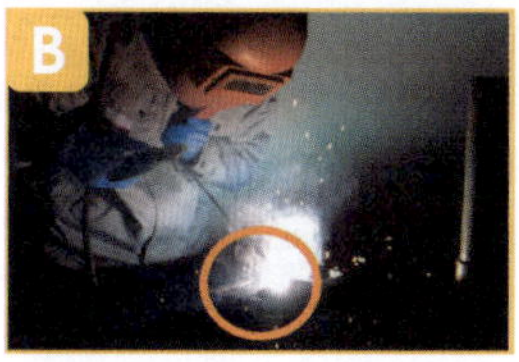

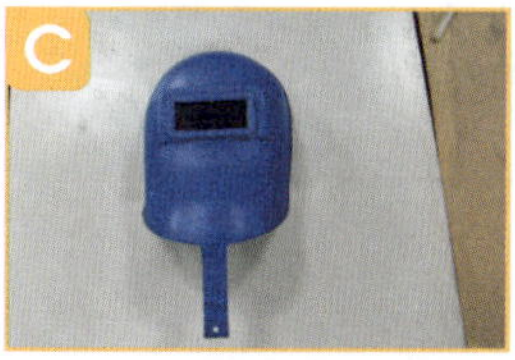

1. hànjiē miànzhào 焊接 面罩 welding mask （　　）
2. fángchén kǒuzhào 防尘 口罩 dust mask（　　）

❸ 焊接 手套 (hànjiē shǒutào) welding gloves (　　)　❹ 弧光 (húguāng) arc light (　　)

学习生词 Words and Expressions 23-01

1	焊接	hànjiē	*v.*	to weld
2	事项	shìxiàng	*n.*	event
3	防尘口罩	fángchén kǒuzhào	*phr.*	dust mask
4	面罩	miànzhào	*n.*	mask
5	为什么	wèi shénme	*pron.*	why
6	因为	yīnwèi	*conj.*	because
7	弧光	húguāng	*n.*	arc light
8	伤	shāng	*v.*	to harm
9	眼睛	yǎnjing	*n.*	eye
10	米	mǐ	*m.*	meter
11	以内	yǐnèi	*n.*	within
12	不能	bù néng	*phr.*	cannot
13	危险物品	wēixiǎn wùpǐn	*phr.*	hazardous materials

词语练习 Word Exercises

1. 看图选词。Look at the pictures and choose the correct words.

❶ 

(　　) A. 焊接手套 (hànjiē shǒutào)　B. 工作鞋 (gōngzuòxié)

❷ 

(　　) A. 防尘 口罩 (fángchén kǒuzhào)　B. 防护眼镜 (fánghù yǎnjìng)

❸ 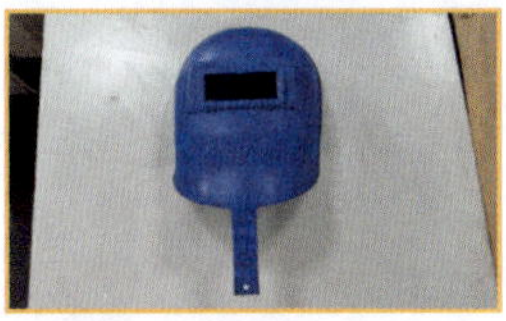

(　　) A. 安全帽 (ānquánmào)　B. 焊接面罩 (hànjiē miànzhào)

❹ 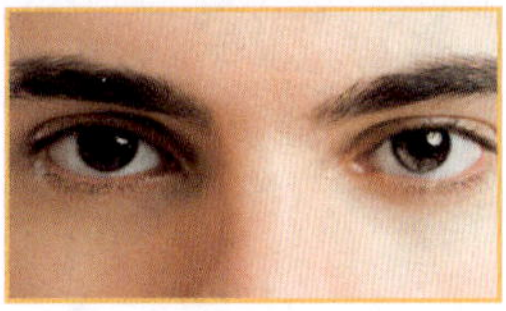

(　　) A. 眼睛 (yǎnjing)　B. 眼镜 (yǎnjìng)

2. 朗读词语搭配。Read the collocations.

<table>
<tr><td rowspan="4">❶ hànjiē
焊接</td><td>ānquán
安全</td><td rowspan="2">❷ zhùyì
注意</td><td>shìxiàng
事项</td></tr>
<tr><td>miànzhào
面罩</td><td>ānquán
安全</td></tr>
<tr><td rowspan="2">shǒutào
手套</td><td rowspan="2">❸ dàihǎo
戴好</td><td>fángchén kǒuzhào
防尘 口罩</td></tr>
<tr><td>ānquánmào
安全帽</td></tr>
</table>

学习课文 Text 23-02

Hànjiē ānquán
焊接安全

Jiékè: Hànjiē qián yǒu nǎxiē zhùyì shìxiàng?
杰克：焊接前有哪些注意事项？

Mǎ Míng: Yào chuānhǎo gōngzuòfú hé gōngzuòxié, dàihǎo hànjiē shǒutào hé fángchén kǒuzhào.
马明：要穿好工作服和工作鞋，戴好焊接手套和防尘口罩。

Jiékè: Hànjiē shí yào zhùyì shénme?
杰克：焊接时要注意什么？

Mǎ Míng: Yào dàihǎo hànjiē miànzhào.
马明：要戴好焊接面罩。

Jiékè: Wèi shénme?
杰克：为什么？

Mǎ Míng: Yīnwèi húguāng shāng yǎnjing.
马明：因为弧光伤眼睛。

Jiékè: Hái yào zhùyì shénme?
杰克：还要注意什么？

Mǎ Míng: 10 mǐ yǐnèi bù néng fàng wēixiǎn wùpǐn.
马明：10米以内不能放危险物品。

The Safety of Welding

Jack: What are the precautions before welding?

Ma Ming: You need to wear work clothes and shoes, welding gloves, and dust masks.

Jack: What should I be aware of when welding?

Ma Ming: You need to wear a welding mask.

Jack: Why?

Ma Ming: Because arc light can harm eyes.

Jack: What else should I be aware of?

Ma Ming: There should not be any hazardous materials within ten meters.

课文练习 Text Exercises

1. 根据课文内容选择正确答案。Choose the correct answers according to the text.

1 焊接前，要穿好________，戴好________。

A. 工作服和工作鞋　　　　B. 焊接手套和防尘口罩

2 焊接时，要戴好________。

A. 护目眼镜　　　　B. 焊接面罩

3 焊接时要注意弧光，不要________眼睛。

A. 抬　　　　B. 伤

4 焊接时，10________以内不要放危险物品。

A. 米　　　　B. 个

2. 根据课文内容判断正误。**True or False.**

1 焊接前，别穿工作服和工作鞋。 ( )

2 焊接时，危险物品要放在 10 米以内。 ( )

3 焊接时，应该戴好焊接面罩。 ( )

4 焊接完成，必须戴好护目眼镜。 ( )

学习语法 Grammar

语法点 1 Grammar Point 1

疑问代词：为什么 The Interrogative Pronoun: 为什么

用来询问原因。

"为什么" is used to ask about the reason.

Hànjiē shí wèi shénme yào dàihǎo hànjiē miànzhào?
1 焊接时为什么要戴好焊接面罩？
Why is it necessary to wear a welding mask when welding?

Gōngzuò shí wèi shénme yào chuān gōngzuòfú?
2 工作时为什么要穿工作服？
Why is it necessary to wear work clothes when working?

Jiékè wèi shénme yào xué Zhōngwén?
3 杰克为什么要学中文？ Why does Jack need to learn Chinese?

语法点 1 练习 Exercise on Grammar Point 1

用"为什么"改写下列句子，并朗读出来。**Rewrite the following sentences with "为什么" and read them aloud.**

例如：

Hànjiē shí yào dàihǎo hànjiē miànzhào.
焊接时要戴好焊接面罩。

Hànjiē shí wèi shénme yào dàihǎo hànjiē miànzhào?
焊接时为什么要戴好焊接面罩？

Gōngzuò shí yào chuān gōngzuòfú.
1 工作 时 要 穿 工作服。

____

Jiékè yào xué Zhōngwén.
2 杰克 要 学 中文。

____

Jiāgōng tōngkǒng shí yào mànmàn de、 bú duàn de xiàng xià bāndòng jìnjǐ bǎshou.
3 加工 通孔 时 要 慢慢 地、不 断 地 向 下 扳动 进给把手。

____

Yòng shuāzi qīnglǐ qiēxiè.
4 用 刷子 清理 切屑。

____

语法点 2 Grammar Point 2

连词：因为 The Conjunction: 因为

表示原因。

"因为" indicates the reason.

Yīnwèi húguāng shāng yǎnjing.
1 因为 弧光 伤 眼睛。 Because arc light can harm the eyes.

Yīnwèi yào quèbǎo ānquán.
2 因为 要 确保 安全。 Because we need to ensure the safety.

Yīnwèi yào cuòxiāo nèijiǎo.
3 因为 要 锉削 内角。 Because we need to file the inner corners.

语法点 2 练习 Exercise on Grammar Point 2

搭配练习。Matching.

Hànjiē shí wèi shénme yào dài hànjiē miànzhào?
焊接时为什么要戴焊接面罩？

Hànjiē qián wèi shénme yào chuānhǎo gōngzuòfú hé gōngzuòxié?
焊接前为什么要穿好工作服和工作鞋？

Wèi shénme xǐxiāo qián yào kàn túzhǐ?
为什么铣削前要看图纸？

Jīchuáng jiāgōng shí wèi shénme bìxū yào dàihǎo hùmù yǎnjìng?
机床加工时为什么必须要戴好护目眼镜？

Wèi shénme yào xuǎnzé sānjiǎocuò?
为什么要选择三角锉？

Yīnwèi yào quèbǎo jiāgōng jiéguǒ fúhé yāoqiú.
因为要确保加工结果符合要求。

Yīnwèi húguāng shāng yǎnjing.
因为弧光伤眼睛。

Yīnwèi yào quèbǎo ānquán.
因为要确保安全。

Yīnwèi yào fángzhǐ tiěxiè shāngdào yǎnjing.
因为要防止（to prevent）铁屑伤到眼睛。

Yīnwèi yào cuòxiāo nèijiǎo.
因为要锉削内角。

汉字书写 Writing Chinese Characters

chǎng
厂

guǎng
广

zhuāng 庄

庄	庄	庄	庄	庄						

chuáng 床

床	床	床	床	床						

文化拓展 Culture Insight

中秋节

中秋节是中国传统节日，为农历八月十五日，因这一天是一年秋季的中期而得名。在中国，八月是农作物收获的季节，庆祝丰收、祝贺团圆便成了中秋节的主题。

每年的八月十五日，当夜幕降临，明月东升，一家人相聚在一起，观赏着又大又圆的月亮，吃着又香又甜的月饼，其乐融融。因此，中秋节家人团聚这种风俗一直延续到今天。而他乡的游子在这一天也会望着天上的明月，寄托着自己对故乡和亲人的思念。

Mid-Autumn Festival

Mid-Autumn Festival, which falls on the 15th of the eighth month in the lunar calendar, is a traditional Chinese festival and named for being at the midpoint of autumn. Since August is the harvest season in China, celebrating the harvest and rejoicing in the reunion have become the themes of Mid-Autumn Festival.

Every year on the 15th of the eighth month in the lunar calendar, when night falls and the bright moon rises in the east, families gather together watching the big and round moon, eating delicious and sweet mooncakes, and enjoying happiness. Therefore, the custom of family reunions on Mid-Autumn Festival has continued down to the present day. And wanderers will also gaze at the bright moon in the sky on this day, expressing their longing for their hometown and loved ones.

小结 Summary

词语 Words

朗读下列词语。**Read the following words.**

防护服	焊接面罩	防尘口罩	因为
危险物品	为什么	弧光	眼睛

语法 Grammar

选择合适的词语填空。**Choose the appropriate words to fill in the blanks.**

A. 为什么　　　　B. 因为

1 焊接时________要戴好焊接面罩？

2 焊接前________要穿好工作服？

3 ________弧光伤眼睛。

4 ________要确保安全。

课文理解 Text Comprehension

回答问题。 Answer the questions.

杰克：焊接前有哪些注意事项？

马明：______________________________。

杰克：焊接时要注意什么？

马明：要戴好焊接面罩。

杰克：为什么？

马明：因为______________________________。

杰克：还要注意什么？

马明：10 米______________________________。

第24课
Lesson 24

Zhǔnbèi diànhúhànjī
准备电弧焊机
Preparing Arc Welding Machines

复习 Revision

认读词语。**Recognize the words.**

焊接手套

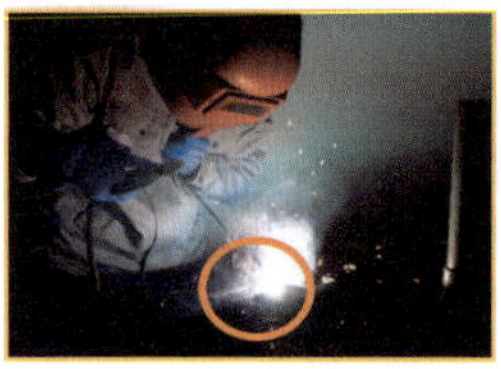
弧光

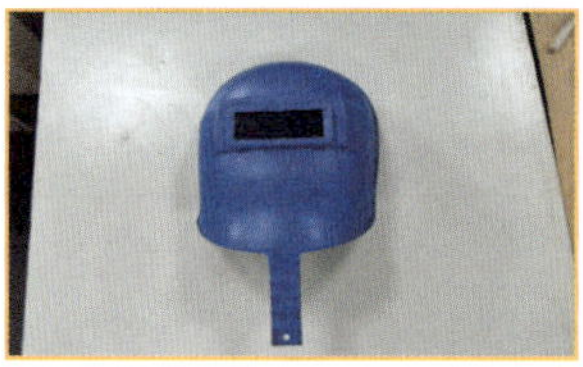
焊接面罩

防尘口罩

热身 Warm-up

选择正确的图片。**Choose the right pictures.**

D

E
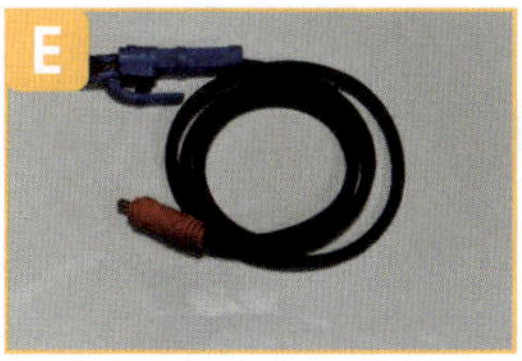

❶	dìxiàn 地线	ground wire	(　　)
❷	hànqián 焊钳	electrode holder	(　　)
❸	dìxiànjiā 地线夹	ground wire clamp	(　　)
❹	kòngzhì miànbǎn 控制 面板	control panel	(　　)
❺	diànhúhànjī 电弧焊机	arc welding machine	(　　)

学习生词 Words and Expressions 24-01

1	电弧焊机	diànhúhànjī	*n.*	arc welding machine
2	地线	dìxiàn	*n.*	ground wire
3	接地	jiēdì	*v.*	to ground
4	地线夹	dìxiànjiā	*n.*	ground wire clamp
5	连接	liánjiē	*v.*	to connect
6	正极接口	zhèngjí jiēkǒu	*phr.*	positive electrode interface
7	焊钳	hànqián	*n.*	electrode holder

8	负极接口	fùjí jiēkǒu	*phr.*	negative electrode interface
9	只要……，就……	zhǐyào…，jiù…		so long as
10	控制面板	kòngzhì miànbǎn	*phr.*	control panel
11	亮	liàng	*v.*	to light

词语练习 Word Exercises

1. 判断图片与词语是否相符。Judge whether the pictures match the words.

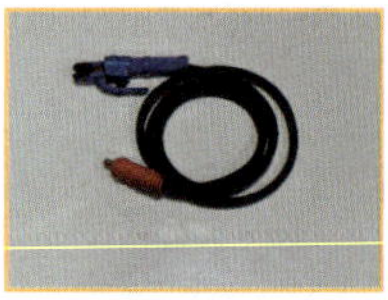

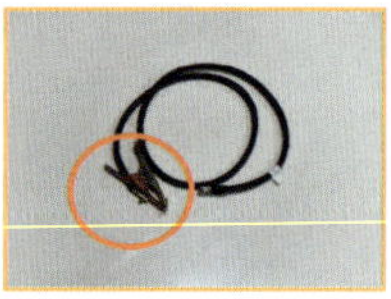
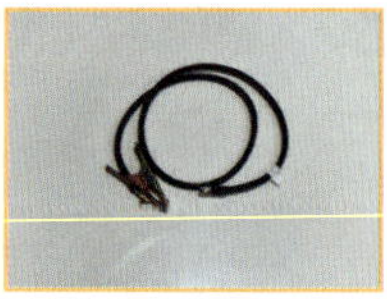

电弧焊机	焊钳	地线夹	控制面板	地线
(　　)	(　　)	(　　)	(　　)	(　　)

2. 词语连线。 Word Matching.

jiētōng 接通	diànhúhànjī kāiguān 电弧焊机 开关
xiàng shàng tuī 向 上 推	diànhúhànjī 电弧焊机
zhǔnbèi 准备	diànhúhànjī diànyuán 电弧焊机 电源
dìxiàn 地线	jiēdì 接地

学习课文 Text 24-02

Zhǔnbèi diànhúhànjī
准备电弧焊机

Zhǔnbèi diànhúhànjī yīnggāi zhùyì:
准备 电弧焊机 应该 注意:

Zài jiētōng diànhúhànjī diànyuán qián, dìxiàn yīnggāi jiēdì.
在 接通 电弧焊机电源 前，地线应该接地。

Jiāng dìxiànjiā liánjiē dào diànhúhànjī de zhèngjí jiēkǒu shang,
将 地线夹连接到 电弧焊机的正极接口 上，
jiāng hànqián liánjiē dào diànhúhànjī de fùjí jiēkǒu shang.
将 焊钳 连接到电弧焊机的负极接口 上。

Jiāng diànhúhànjī de kāiguān xiàng shàng tuī.
将 电弧焊机的开关 向 上 推。

Zhǐyào kòngzhì miànbǎn liàng le, diànhúhànjī jiù zhǔnbèi hǎo le.
只要 控制 面板 亮 了，电弧焊机 就 准备 好了。

Preparing Arc Welding Machines

When preparing an arc welding machine, follow the instructions below:

Before connecting the power to the arc welding machine, the ground wire should be grounded.

Connect the ground wire clamp to the positive electrode interface of the arc welding machine, and connect the electrode holder to the negative electrode interface of the arc welding machine.

Push the switch on the arc welding machine upwards.

As long as the control panel light is on, the arc welding machine is ready for use.

课文练习 Text Exercises

1. 根据课文内容判断正误。True or False.

1. 接通电弧焊机电源后，地线接地。 (　　)
2. 地线夹要连接到电弧焊机上。 (　　)
3. 开电弧焊机时，要把电弧焊机的开关向下推。 (　　)
4. 焊钳要连接到电弧焊机的负极接口上。 (　　)

2. 选择正确的答案。Choose the right answers.

1. 安装电弧焊设备时，要先________，再________。

   A. 接通电弧焊机的电源　　B. 将地线接地

2. 将地线夹连接到电弧焊机的________上，将焊钳连接到电弧焊机的________上。

   A. 正极接口　　B. 负极接口

3 将电弧焊机的________向上推。

A. 开关　　　　B. 按钮

4 ________亮了，________就准备好了。

A. 电弧焊机　　　　B. 控制面板

学习语法 Grammar

语法点 1 Grammar Point 1

介词：将 The Preposition: 将

用法与“把”基本相同，用于书面语中。

“将” is used in a similar way to “把”, and is commonly used in written language.

Jiāng dìxiànjiā liánjiē dào diànhúhànjī de zhèngjí jiēkǒu shang.
1 将 地线夹 连接 到 电弧焊机 的 正极 接口 上。
Connect the ground wire clamp to the positive electrode interface of the arc welding machine.

Yào jiāng hànqián liánjiē dào diànhúhànjī de fùjí jiēkǒu shang.
2 要 将 焊钳 连接 到电弧焊机的负极接口 上。
Connect the electrode holder to the negative electrode interface of the arc welding machine.

Bìxū jiāng cháng fà sāirù ānquánmào li.
3 必须 将 长 发塞入安全帽 里。
Make sure to tuck your long hair into the safety cap.

语法点 1 练习 Exercise on Grammar Point 1

连词成句。**Rearrange the following words to make sentences.**

例如：

dìxiànjiā ①地线夹　liánjiē ②连接　dào ③到　diànhúhànjī de ④电弧焊机的

jiāng ⑤将　zhèngjí jiēkǒu shang ⑥正极 接口 上

⑤①②③④⑥

1. dào ①到　hànqián ②焊钳　diànhúhànjī de ③电弧焊机的　liánjiē ④连接　jiāng ⑤将

   fùjí jiēkǒu shang ⑥负极接口 上

   ____

2. ānquánmào ①安全帽　li ②里　sāirù ③塞入　cháng fà ④长 发　bìxū ⑤必须　jiāng ⑥将

   ____

3. shuǐpíng fàngzhì ①水平 放置　jiāgōngmiàn ②加工面　jiāng ③将　yào ④要

   ____

4. kōngdǎng wèizhì ①空挡 位置　bāndòng ②扳动　zhì ③至　cāozònggǎn ④操纵杆　yào ⑤要　jiāng ⑥将

   ____

语法点 2 Grammar Point 2

条件复句：只要……，就……

Conditional Compound Sentence: 只要……，就……

表示在前一分句的条件下，就能产生后一分句的结果。

"只要……，就……" means that under the condition in the first clause, the result in the second clause will be produced.

1. Zhǐyào kòngzhì miànbǎn liàng le, diànhúhànjī jiù zhǔnbèi hǎo le.
   只要控制面板亮了，电弧焊机就准备好了。
   As long as the control panel light is on, the arc welding machine is ready for use.

2. Zhǐyào ànxia jítíng ànniǔ, jīchuáng jiù tíngzhǐ gōngzuò.
   只要按下急停按钮，机床就停止工作。
   As long as the emergency stop button is pressed, the machine tool will stop working.

3. Zhǐyào dàihǎo hànjiē miànzhào, jiù néng fángzhǐ húguāng shāng yǎnjing.
   只要戴好焊接面罩，就能防止弧光伤眼睛。
   As long as you wear a welding mask, you can protect your eyes from the harm of the arc light.

语法点 2 练习 Exercise on Grammar Point 2

用"只要……，就……"改写下列句子，并朗读出来。**Rewrite the following sentences with "只要……，就……" and read them aloud.**

例如：

Kòngzhì miànbǎn liàng le, diànhúhànjī jiù zhǔnbèi hǎo le.
控制面板亮了，电弧焊机就准备好了。

Zhǐyào kòngzhì miànbǎn liàng le, diànhúhànjī jiù zhǔnbèi hǎo le.
只要控制面板亮了，电弧焊机就准备好了。

1. Ànxia jítíng ànniǔ, jīchuáng tíngzhǐ gōngzuò.
   按下急停按钮，机床停止工作。

   ____

2. Dàihǎo hànjiē miànzhào, néng fángzhǐ húguāng shāng yǎnjing.
   戴好焊接面罩，能防止弧光伤眼睛。

   ____

Zài chējiān gōngzuò, yào dàihǎo ānquánmào, chuānhǎo gōngzuòfú.
3 在车间工作，要戴好安全帽，穿好工作服。

____

Wánchéng jiāgōng, yào guānbì chēchuáng diànyuán.
4 完成加工，要关闭车床电源。

____

汉字书写 Writing Chinese Characters

tián
田 田 田 田 田

yóu
由 由 由 由 由

jiǎ
甲 甲 甲 甲 甲

shēn
申 申 申 申 申

职业拓展 Career Insight

盾构机

盾构机，全名叫盾构隧道掘进机，是一种使用盾构法的隧道掘进机，是隧道掘进的专用工程机械。

盾构机自问世至今已有近 200 年的历史，其起源于英国，发展于日本、德国。盾构机在中国得到了广泛应用，截至目前，中国最大的盾构机是由中铁十四局建造的，直径达到 16.07 米。

现代盾构机集光、机、电、液、传感、信息技术于一体，具有自动化程度高、节省人力、施工速度快、一次成洞、不受气候影响、开挖时可控制地面沉降、减少对地面建筑物的影响和在水下开挖时不影响地面交通等特点，现广泛应用于地铁、铁路、公路、市政、水电等隧道工程。

Shield Machines

The shield machine, with its full name as shield tunneling machine, is a type of tunnel boring machine that uses shield tunneling method and is a specialized piece of engineering machinery for tunnel excavation.

Shield tunneling machines have a history of nearly 200 years since their inception, starting in the UK and developing in Japan and Germany. Shield tunneling machines have been widely used in China and to date the largest shield tunneling machine in China was built by China Railway 14th Bureau, with a diameter of 16.07 meters.

Modern shield tunneling machines integrate light, machinery, electricity, fluid, sensing, and information technology. With the characteristics of high automation, labor efficiency, fast construction, one-time tunneling, immunity to climate conditions, controllable ground settlement during excavation, reduced impact on ground buildings, and no disruption to ground traffic during underwater excavation, they have been widely used in tunnel engineering such as subways, railways, highways, municipal engineering, and hydropower.

小结 Summary

词语 Words

朗读下列词语。**Read the following words.**

电弧焊机	焊钳	地线夹	正极接口	负极接口
控制面板	亮	连接	只要……，就……	

语法 Grammar

熟读句子。**Read the following sentences.**

1. 将焊钳连接到电弧焊机的负极接口上。
2. 将长发塞入安全帽里。
3. 只要控制面板亮了，电弧焊机就准备好了。

4 只要按下急停按钮，机床就停止工作。

课文理解 Text Comprehension

选择合适的词语填空。**Choose the appropriate words to fill in the blanks.**

A. 前　B. 地线夹　C. 地线　D. 焊钳　E. 控制面板

1. 在接通电弧焊机电源________，________应该接地。
2. 将________连接到电弧焊机的正极接口上，将________连接到电弧焊机的负极接口上。
3. 将电弧焊机的开关向上推。只要________亮了，电弧焊机就准备好了。

第25课 Lesson 25

Diànhúhàn de cāozuò
电弧焊的操作
Operating Arc Welding

复习 Revision

认读词语。Recognize the words.

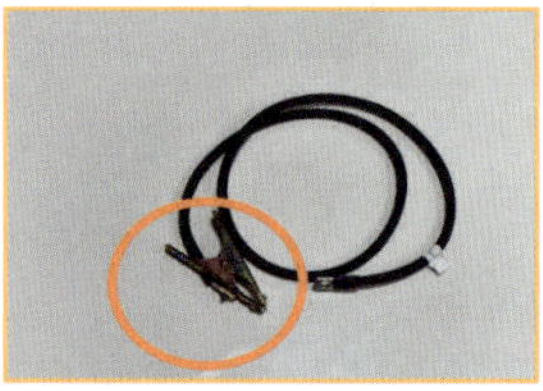

地线夹

电弧焊机

地线

控制面板

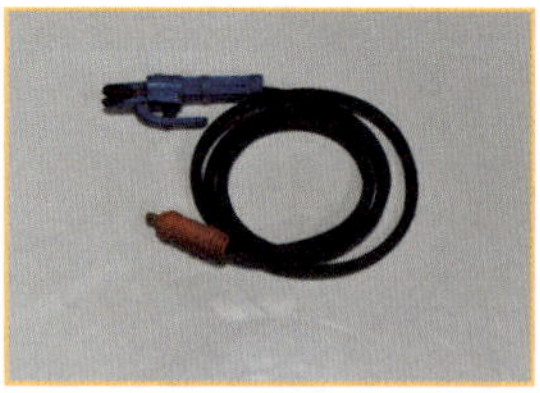

焊钳

热身 Warm-up

选择正确的图片。**Choose the right pictures.**

A

B
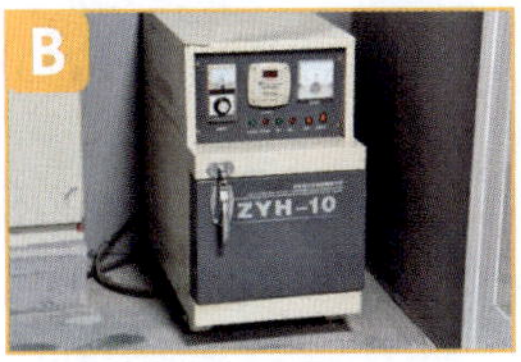

C
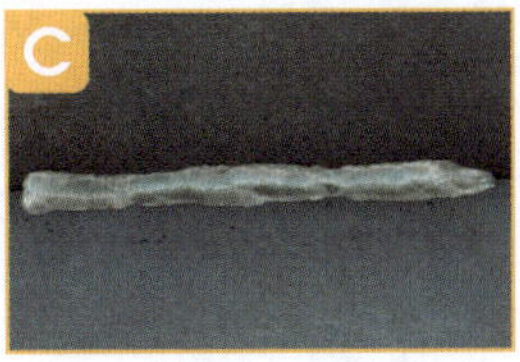

D
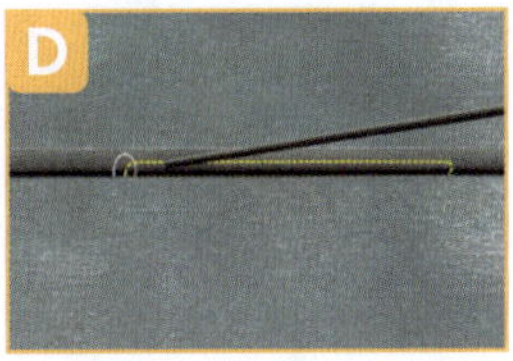

1	hōnggānxiāng 烘干箱	drying oven	(　　)
2	hàntiáo 焊条	welding rod	(　　)
3	hànfèng 焊缝	welding seam	(　　)
4	zhíxiàn yùntiáofǎ 直线 运条法	the method of straight-line welding	(　　)

学习生词 Words and Expressions 25-01

1	电弧焊	diànhúhàn	*n.*	arc welding
2	操作	cāozuò	*v.*	to operate
3	从	cóng	*prep.*	from
4	烘干箱	hōnggānxiāng	*n.*	drying oven
5	焊条	hàntiáo	*n.*	welding rod

6	烫伤	tàngshāng	*phr.*	to burn
7	夹住	jiāzhù	*phr.*	to clamp
8	让	ràng	*v.*	to let
9	顶端	dǐngduān	*n.*	top
10	金属面	jīnshǔmiàn	*n.*	metal surface
11	焊缝	hànfèng	*n.*	welding seam
12	处	chù	*n.*	place
13	起弧	qǐhú	*v.*	to start the arc
14	移回	yíhuí	*phr.*	to move back
15	直线运条法	zhíxiàn yùntiáofǎ	*phr.*	the method of straight-line welding

词语练习 Word Exercises

1. 判断图片与词语是否相符。**Judge whether the pictures match the words.**

焊条

(　　)

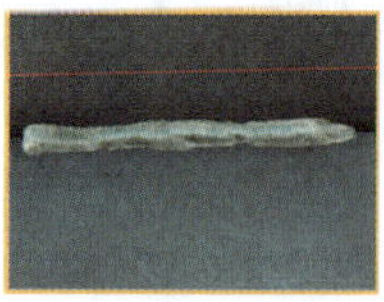

烘干箱

(　　)

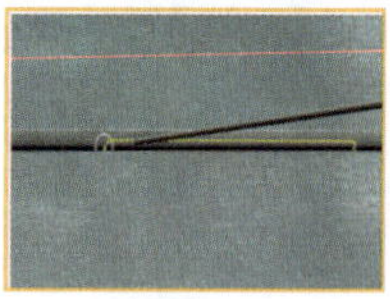

焊缝

(　　)

直线运条法

(　　)

2. 词语连线。 **Word Matching.**

jiāzhù 夹住	qǐdiǎn 起点
fángzhǐ 防止	hàntiáo 焊条
hànfèng 焊缝	tàngshāng 烫伤
cāozuò 操作	diànhúhàn 电弧焊

学习课文 Text 25-02

Diànhúhàn de cāozuò

电弧焊的操作

Diànhú hànjiē zhīqián, xiān cóng hōnggānxiāng li náchū hàntiáo.
电弧焊接之前，先从烘干箱里拿出焊条。

Ná hàntiáo shí, wèile fángzhǐ tàngshāng shǒu, yào dàihǎo shǒutào.
拿焊条时，为了防止烫伤手，要戴好手套。

Diànhú hànjiē shí, yòng hànqián jiāzhù hàntiáo, ràng hàntiáo dǐngduān de
电弧焊接时，用焊钳夹住焊条，让焊条顶端的

jīnshǔmiàn jiēchù gōngjiàn biǎomiàn.
金属面接触工件表面。

Zài hànfèng qǐdiǎn qián 10 mm chù qǐhú, ránhòu bǎ hàntiáo
在焊缝起点前 10 mm 处起弧，然后把焊条

yíhuí hànfèng qǐdiǎn, yòng zhíxiàn yùntiáofǎ hànjiē.
移回焊缝起点，用直线运条法焊接。

Operating Arc Welding

Before arc welding, take out the welding rod from the drying oven. Wear gloves when holding welding rods to avoid burning your hands. During arc welding, clamp the welding rod with an electrode holder, and the metal surface at the top of the welding rod contacts the surface of the workpiece.

Start the arc 10mm before the starting point of the welding seam, and then move the welding rod back to the starting point of the welding seam. Weld with the method of straight-line welding.

课文练习 Text Exercises

1. 选择正确的答案。Choose the right answers.

1 从烘干机里拿出________。 A. 焊条 B. 焊机

2 戴手套是为了________烫伤手。 A. 防止 B. 确保

3 电弧焊接时，用焊钳________焊条。 A. 抬起 B. 夹住

4 让焊条顶端的金属面接触________。 A. 被测面 B. 工件表面

2. 选择合适的词语填空。**Choose the appropriate words to fill in the blanks.**

A. 戴好　　B. 起弧　　C. 接触　　D. 直线运条法

1. 电弧焊接之前，先从烘干箱里拿出焊条。拿焊条时要________手套，这是为了防止烫伤手。
2. 电弧焊接时，用焊钳夹住焊条，让焊条顶端的金属面________工件表面。
3. 在焊缝起点前 10 mm 处________，然后把焊条移回焊缝起点，用_____焊接。

学习语法 Grammar

语法点 1 Grammar Point 1

介词：从　The Preposition: 从

引出动作经过的路线、场所。

"从" introduces the route or location through which the action passes.

1. Cóng hōnggānxiāng li qǔchū hàntiáo.
从 烘干箱 里取出 焊条。
Take out the welding rod from the drying oven.
2. Cóng dāotào lǐbian qǔchū xǐdāo.
从 刀套 里边 取出 铣刀。
Take out the milling tool from the tool holder.
3. Cóng shǒujù shang qǔxia jiù jùtiáo.
从 手锯 上 取下 旧 锯条。
Remove the used saw blade from the hand saw.

语法点 1 练习 Exercise on Grammar Point 1

为“从”选择适当的位置。**Fill “从” in the appropriate positions.**

例如：　A　　（A）烘干箱 里（B）取出（C）焊条（D）。
hōnggānxiāng li　qǔchū　hàntiáo

1. ______　（A）刀套（B）里边（C）取出（D）铣刀。
dāotào　lǐbian　qǔchū　xǐdāo

2. ______　（A）手锯 上（B）取下（C）旧锯条（D）。
shǒujù shang　qǔxia　jiù jùtiáo

3. ______　（A）划线 平台（B）上（C）拿起（D）工件。
huàxiàn píngtái　shang　náqǐ　gōngjiàn

4. ______　（A）钳工台（B）上（C）拿起（D）手锤。
qiángōngtái　shang　náqǐ　shǒuchuí

语法点 2 Grammar Point 2

介词：为了　The Preposition: 为了

引出动作、行为的目的。

“为了” introduces the purpose of actions or behaviors.

1. Wèile fángzhǐ tàngshāng shǒu, ná hàntiáo shí yào dàihǎo shǒutào.
为了防止烫伤手，拿焊条时要戴好手套。
Wear gloves when holding welding rods to avoid burning your hands.

2. Wèile ānquán, yīnggāi chuān gōngzuòfú、dài ānquánmào.
为了安全，应该穿工作服、戴安全帽。
For the sake of safety, make sure to wear the work clothes and safety cap/helmet.

3. Wèile zhǔnquè jiǎncè píngmiàndù, jiǎncè qián yào xiān qīnglǐ sāichǐ hé gōngjiàn biǎomiàn.
为了准确检测平面度，检测前要先清理塞尺和工件表面。
For the accuracy of flatness testing, the surface of the feeler gauge and workpiece should be cleaned before testing.

语法点 2 练习 Exercise on Grammar Point 2

为"为了"选择适当的位置。**Fill "为了" in the appropriate positions.**

例如：<u>A</u>

fángzhǐ tàngshāng shǒu ná hàntiáo shí yào dàihǎo shǒutào
（A）防止烫伤手（B），（C）拿焊条时要戴好手套（D）。

1 ________

ānquán gōngzuò shí yīnggāi chuān gōngzuòfú、dài ānquánmào
（A）安全（B），（C）工作时应该穿工作服、戴安全帽（D）。

2 ________

hànjiē shí yào dàihǎo hànjiē miànzhào zhè shì fángzhǐ húguāng shāng dào yǎnjing
（A）焊接时要戴好焊接面罩（B），这是（C）防止弧光伤到眼睛（D）。

3 ________

fángzhǐ tiěxiè shāng dào yǎnjing jiāgōng shí jīchuáng duìmiàn bú yào zhàn rén
（A）防止铁屑伤到眼睛（B），（C）加工时（D）机床对面不要站人。

4 ________

ná hàntiáo shí yào dàihǎo shǒutào zhè shì fángzhǐ tàngshāng shǒu
（A）拿焊条时要戴好手套（B），这是（C）防止烫伤手（D）

汉字书写 Writing Chinese Characters

huǒ
火 火 火 火

火

miè 灭 灭 灭 灭 灭

灭	灭	灭	灭	灭						

huǒ 伙 伙 伙 伙 伙 伙

伙	伙	伙	伙	伙						

yán 炎 炎 炎 炎 炎 炎 炎 炎

炎	炎	炎	炎	炎						

文化拓展 Culture Insight

印刷术

印刷术是中国古代劳动人民的发明之一。雕版印刷术发明于隋唐时期，并在唐朝中后期普遍使用。到了北宋时期，毕昇发明了活字印刷术。

印刷术具有方便灵活、省时省力等特点，它使文字和图书能够大量进入社会，为世界范围内知识的广泛传播、交流创造了条件。随着时间的推移，印刷术先后传到朝鲜、日本等国家及中亚、西亚和欧洲等地区，加速了这些国家和地区社会发展的进程，为现代社会的建立提供了必要前提。

Printing

Printing is one of the inventions of ancient Chinese working people. Woodblock printing was invented in the Sui and Tang dynasties and widely used in mid to late Tang Dynasty. During Northern Song Dynasty, Bi Sheng invented the movable-type printing technology.

Printing technology is characterized by its convenience, flexibility, and ability to save time and labor. It enables a large number of texts and books to enter society, creating conditions for the widespread dissemination and exchange of knowledge worldwide. With passage of time, printing technology was successively introduced to North Korea, Japan, Central Asia, Western Asia, and Europe, accelerating the process of social development in these countries and regions and providing necessary prerequisites for the establishment of modern society.

小结 Summary

词语 Words

朗读下列词语。**Read the following words.**

焊缝	顶端	移回
起弧	焊条	直线运条法

语法 Grammar

选择合适的词语填空。Choose the appropriate words to fill in the blanks.

A. 从　　B. 为了

1 （　　）防止烫伤手，拿焊条时要戴好手套。

2 （　　）防止弧光伤到眼睛，焊接时要戴好焊接面罩。

3 （　　）烘干箱里取出焊条。

4 （　　）手锯上取下旧锯条。

课文理解 Text Comprehension

选择合适的词语填空。Choose the appropriate words to fill in the blanks.

A. 顶端　　B. 直线运条法　　C. 拿　　D. 10 mm

1 拿焊条：从烘干箱里________出焊条。拿焊条时，为了防止烫伤手，要戴好手套。

2 焊接时：用焊钳夹住焊条，让焊条________的金属面接触工件表面。

3 在焊缝起点前________处起弧，然后把焊条移回焊缝起点，用________焊接。

第26课 Lesson 26

Qīnglǐ hànfèng
清理焊缝
Cleaning Welding Seams

复习 Revision

认读词语。Recognize the words.

烘干箱

焊条

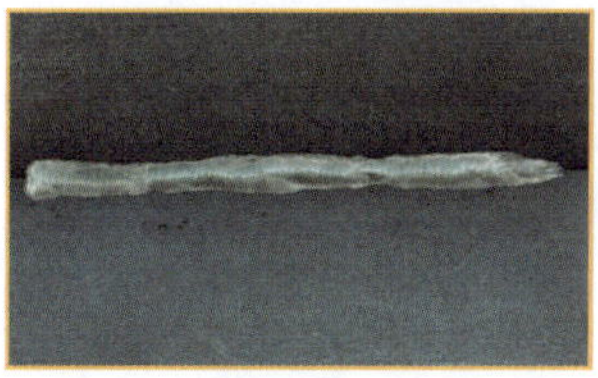

焊缝

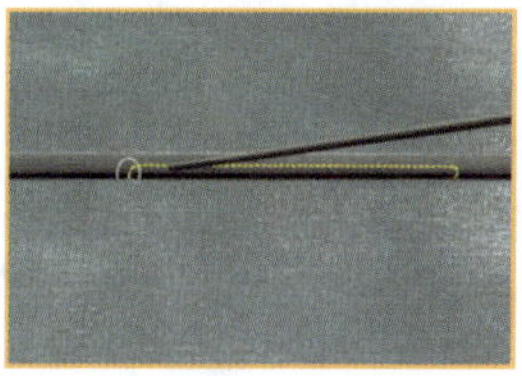

直线运条法

热身 Warm-up

选择正确的图片。Choose the right pictures.

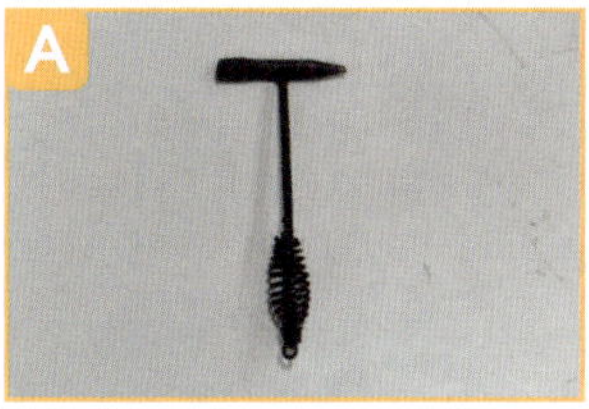

A

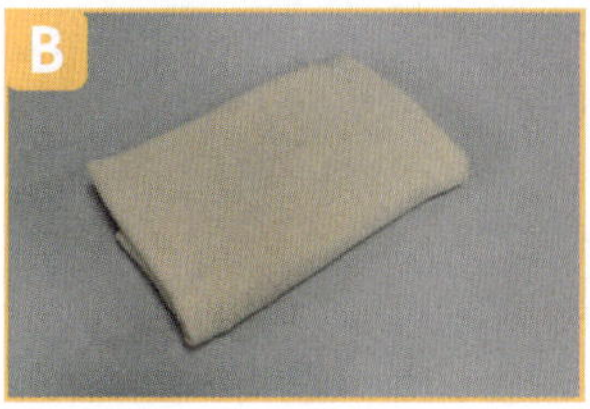

B

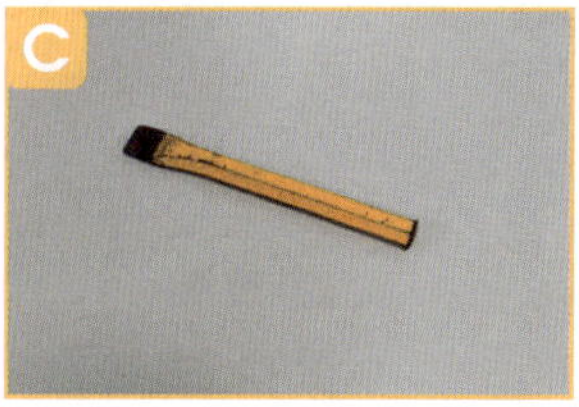

C

D

E

F

❶ píngtóu zànzi 平头 錾子 flat chisel （　　）	❷ hànliú 焊瘤 overlap （　　）
❸ qīngjiébù 清洁布 cleaning cloth （　　）	❹ xiùjì 锈迹 rust （　　）
❺ gāngsīshuā 钢丝刷 wire brush （　　）	❻ qiāozhāchuí 敲渣锤 slag hammer （　　）

学习生词 Words and Expressions 26-01

1	优化	yōuhuà	*v.*	to optimize
2	外观	wàiguān	*n.*	appearance
3	如果……，就……	rúguǒ…, jiù…		if ... (then) ...
4	凹凸处	āotūchù	*n.*	unsmooth spot
5	打磨	dǎmó	*v.*	to polish
6	一下儿	yíxiàr	*q.*	for a while
7	药皮	yàopí	*n.*	flux coating
8	锈迹	xiùjì	*n.*	rust

9	钢丝刷	gāngsīshuā	*n.*	wire brush
10	焊瘤	hànliú	*n.*	overlap
11	平头錾子	píngtóu zànzi	*phr.*	flat chisel
12	铲平	chǎnpíng	*phr.*	to smooth out
13	敲渣锤	qiāozhāchuí	*n.*	slag hammer
14	敲平	qiāopíng	*phr.*	to flatten
15	清洁布	qīngjiébù	*n.*	cleaning cloth
16	擦拭	cāshì	*v.*	to wipe
17	灰尘	huīchén	*n.*	dust

词语练习 Word Exercises

1. 图文连线。Match the pictures with the words.

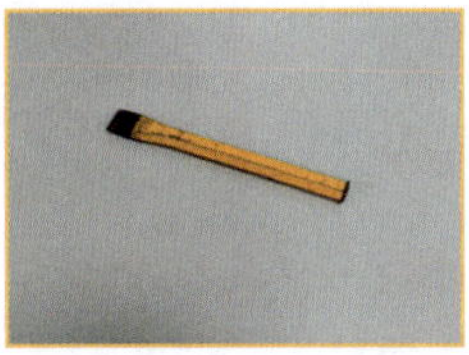

焊瘤　　清洁布　　钢丝刷　　敲渣锤　　平头錾子　　锈迹

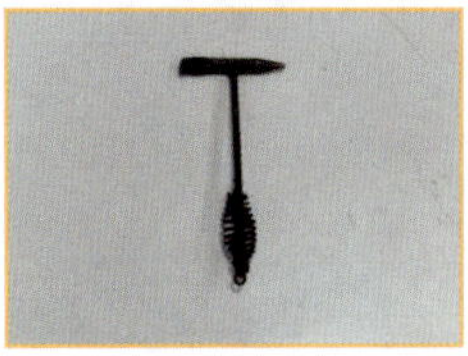

2. 朗读词语搭配。**Read the collocations.**

❶ qīnglǐ 清理	hànfèng 焊缝	❷ yōuhuà 优化	hànfèng zhìliàng 焊缝 质量
	yàopí 药皮		hànfèng wàiguān 焊缝 外观
	xiùjì 锈迹		
❸ yòng 用	dǎmójī dǎmó yíxiàr 打磨机打磨一下儿		
	gāngsīshuā qīnglǐ yíxiàr 钢丝刷 清理一下儿		

学习课文 Text 26-02

Qīnglǐ hànfèng
清理 焊缝

Wèile yōuhuà hànfèng de zhìliàng hé wàiguān, hànjiē hòu,
为了优化 焊缝 的 质量 和 外观，焊接 后，

yào xuǎnzé héshì de gōngjù qīnglǐ hànfèng:
要选择合适的 工具 清理 焊缝：

Rúguǒ hànfèng yǒu āotūchù, jiù yòng dǎmójī dǎmó
如果焊缝 有凹凸处， 就 用 打磨机打磨

yíxiàr.
一下儿。

Rúguǒ hànfèng yǒu yàopí hé xiùjì, jiù yòng gāngsīshuā qīnglǐ yíxiàr.
如果焊缝有药皮和锈迹，就用钢丝刷清理一下儿。

Rúguǒ hànfèng biǎomiàn yǒu hànliú, jiù yòng píngtóu zànzi chǎnpíng huòzhě yòng qiāozhāchuí qiāopíng.
如果焊缝表面有焊瘤，就用平头錾子铲平或者用敲渣锤敲平。

Zuìhòu, yòng qīngjiébù cāshì hànfèng huīchén.
最后，用清洁布擦拭焊缝灰尘。

Cleaning Welding Seams

After welding, choose the appropriate tools to clean the welding seam, in order to optimize its quality and appearance.

If there are unsmooth spots on the welding seam, use a grinder to polish them.

If there are flux coating and rust on the welding seam, use a wire brush to clean them.

If there are overlaps on the surface of the welding seam, use a flat chisel to smooth them out or a slag hammer to flatten them.

Finally, use a cleaning cloth to wipe the dust off the welding seam.

课文练习 Text Exercises

1. 根据课文内容判断正误。True or False.

1. 清理焊缝需要在焊接后操作。（　　）
2. 打磨机是用来清理药皮的工具。（　　）
3. 如果焊缝表面有焊瘤，就用平头錾子敲平。（　　）
4. 如果焊缝表面有灰尘，就用清洁布擦拭。（　　）

2. 选择合适的词语填空。Choose the appropriate words to fill in the blanks.

A. 为了　B. 钢丝刷　C. 凹凸处　D. 工具　E. 擦拭　F. 焊瘤

1. ________优化焊缝的质量和外观，焊接后，要选择合适的________清理焊缝。
2. 如果焊缝有________，就用打磨机打磨一下儿。
3. 如果焊缝有药皮和锈迹，就用________清理一下儿。
4. 如果焊缝表面有________，就用平头錾子铲平或者用敲渣锤敲平。
5. 最后，用清洁布________焊缝灰尘。

学习语法 Grammar

语法点 1 Grammar Point 1

假设复句：如果……，就……

Hypothetical Compound Sentence: 如果……，就……

第一个分句表示假设的前提，第二个分句表示在第一个分句的前提下能够得到的结果。

The first clause represents the premise of the hypothesis, and the second clause represents the result that can be obtained under the premise of the first clause.

1. Rúguǒ hànfèng biǎomiàn yǒu hànliú, jiù yòng píngtóu zànzi chǎnpíng.
如果焊缝表面有焊瘤，就用平头錾子铲平。
If there are overlaps on the surface of the welding seam, use a flat chisel to spade them.

2. Rúguǒ hànfèng biǎomiàn yǒu huīchén, jiù yòng qīngjiébù cāshì.
如果焊缝表面有灰尘，就用清洁布擦拭。
If there is dust on the welding seam, wipe it with a cleaning cloth.

3. Rúguǒ yào cuòxiāo nèijiǎo, jiù xuǎnzé sānjiǎocuò.
如果要锉削内角，就选择三角锉。
If you want to file the inner corners, choose a triangular file.

语法点 1 练习 Exercise on Grammar Point 1

搭配练习。**Matching.**

Rúguǒ hànfèng biǎomiàn yǒu hànliú, 如果焊缝表面有焊瘤，	jiù xuǎnzé sānjiǎocuò. 就选择三角锉。
Rúguǒ yào cuòxiāo nèijiǎo, 如果要锉削内角，	jiù yòng qīngjiébù cāshì. 就用清洁布擦拭。
Rúguǒ hànfèng shang yǒu āotūchù, 如果焊缝上有凹凸处，	jiù yòng gāngsīshuā qīnglǐ. 就用钢丝刷清理。
Rúguǒ hànfèng biǎomiàn yǒu huīchén, 如果焊缝表面有灰尘，	jiù yòng píngtóu zànzi chǎnpíng. 就用平头錾子铲平。
Rúguǒ hànfèng shang yǒu xiùjì, 如果焊缝上有锈迹，	jiù yòng dǎmójī dǎmó. 就用打磨机打磨。

语法点 2 Grammar Point 2

动词 + 一下儿 Verb + 一下儿

“一下儿”用在动词后，有动作的时间短或语气缓和的意思。

“一下儿” is used after a verb to indicate a short duration of the action or soften the tone of the expression.

Yòng qīngjiébù cāshì yíxiàr.
1 用 清洁布 擦拭一下儿。 Wipe it with a cleaning cloth.

Yòng dǎmójī dǎmó yíxiàr.
2 用 打磨机打磨一下儿。 Polish it with a polishing machine.

Yòng gāngsīshuā qīnglǐ yíxiàr.
3 用 钢丝刷 清理一下儿。 Clean it with a wire brush.

语法点 2 练习 Exercise on Grammar Point 2

为“一下儿”选择适当的位置。**Fill “一下儿” in the appropriate positions.**

例如： D （A）用（B）清洁布（C）擦拭（D）。
yòng qīngjiébù cāshì

1 ______ （A）用（B）打磨机（C）打磨（D）。
yòng dǎmojī dǎmó

2 ______ （A）用（B）钢丝刷（C）清理（D）。
yòng gāngsīshuā qīnglǐ

3 ______ （A）调整（B）高度尺 的（C）位置（D）。
tiáozhěng gāodùchǐ de wèizhì

4 ______ （A）确认（B）图纸 的（C）要求（D）。
quèrèn túzhǐ de yāoqiú

汉字书写 Writing Chinese Characters

xīn
心 心 心 心 心

bì
必 必 必 必 必

zhōng
忠 忠 忠 忠 忠

sī
思 思 思 思 思

职业拓展 Career Insight

激光清理焊缝

激光清理焊缝是一种有效的清理焊缝的方式。它通过将激光光束辐照在待处理工件表面，从而产生巨大的能量，击碎污染层，使污物瞬间剥离基材，恢复材料的本来面目。激光清理的过程不会产生新的物质和污染，适用于清洗工业生产中的金属基材和产品，特别适合清洗不规则、不平整的表面。

Laser Cleaning of Welding Seams

Laser cleaning of welding seams is an effective way to clean welding seams. The laser beam is irradiated on the surface of the workpiece, generating enormous energy to break down the contaminated layer, causing the dirt to instantly peel off the substrate and restoring the original appearance of the material. The process of laser cleaning does not generate new substances or pollution, making it suitable for cleaning metal substrates and products in industrial production, especially for cleaning irregular and uneven surface.

小结 Summary

词语 Words

朗读下列词语。**Read the following words.**

敲渣锤	平头錾子	打磨机	钢丝刷	焊瘤
药皮	锈迹	铲平	敲平	清洁布

语法 Grammar

熟读句子。**Read the following sentences.**

1 如果焊缝表面有焊瘤，就用平头錾子铲平或者用敲渣锤敲平。

2 如果焊缝表面有灰尘，就用清洁布擦拭。

3 如果焊缝有凹凸处，就用打磨机打磨一下儿。

4 如果焊缝有药皮和锈迹，就用钢丝刷清理一下儿。

课文理解 Text Comprehension

选择合适的词语填空。**Choose the appropriate words to fill in the blanks.**

A. 敲渣锤　　B. 平头錾子　　C. 钢丝刷　　D. 打磨机　　E. 清洁布

1 打磨焊缝凹凸处的工具是：________。

2 清理焊缝药皮和锈迹的工具是：________。

3 铲平焊瘤的工具是：________。敲平焊瘤的工具是：________。

4 擦拭灰尘的工具是：________。

Mùcè hànjiē jiéguǒ

第27课 目测焊接结果

Lesson 27 Visually Inspecting Welding Results

复习 Revision

认读词语。**Recognize the words.**

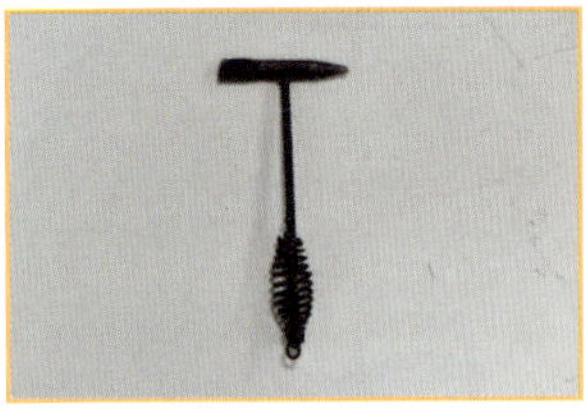

敲渣锤

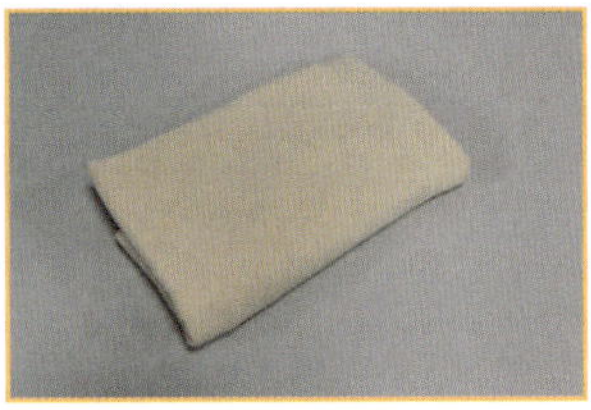

清洁布

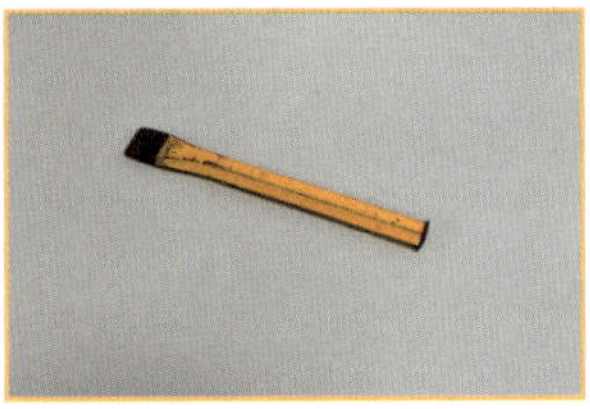

平头錾子

钢丝刷

焊瘤

锈迹

热身 Warm-up

选择正确的图片。**Choose the right pictures.**

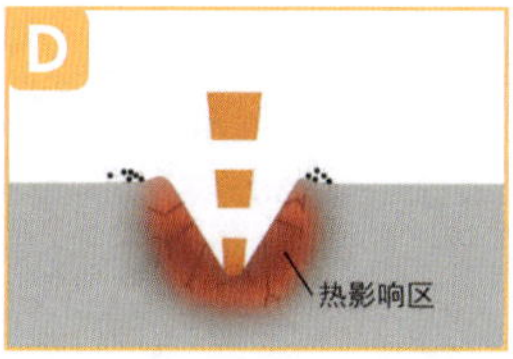

1. qìkǒng 气孔 pore (　　)
2. lièwén 裂纹 crack (　　)
3. jiāzhā 夹渣 slag inclusion (　　)
4. rèyǐngxiǎng qūyù 热影响 区域 heat-affected area (　　)

学习生词 Words and Expressions 27-01

1	目测	mùcè	*v.*	to inspect visually
2	结果	jiéguǒ	*n.*	result
3	裂纹	lièwén	*n.*	crack
4	气孔	qìkǒng	*n.*	pore

5	特别	tèbié	*adv.*	specially
6	两端	liǎngduān	*n.*	both ends
7	连接处	liánjiēchù	*n.*	connection
8	出现	chūxiàn	*v.*	to appear
9	夹渣	jiāzhā	*n.*	slag inclusion
10	余高	yúgāo	*n.*	weld reinforcement
11	过高	guò gāo	*phr.*	excessively high
12	情况	qíngkuàng	*n.*	situation
13	热影响区域	rèyǐngxiǎng qūyù	*phr.*	heat-affected area
14	每	měi	*pron.*	every
15	都	dōu	*adv.*	all
16	变色	biànsè	*v.*	to discolour

词语练习 Word Exercises

1. 判断图片与词语是否相符。**Judge whether the pictures match the words.**

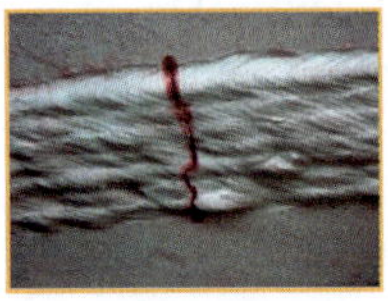
裂纹
（　　）

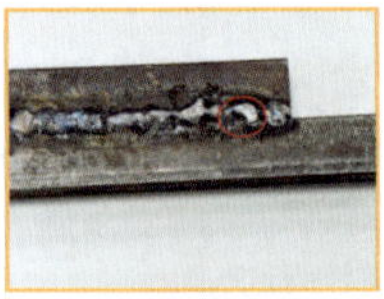
夹渣
（　　）

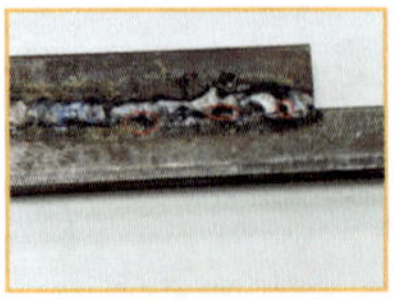
热影响区域
（　　）

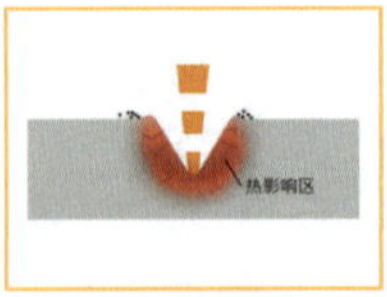
气孔
（　　）

2. 朗读词语搭配。**Read the collocations.**

❶ jiǎnchá 检查	hànfèng 焊缝	❷ hànfèng 焊缝	chǐcùn 尺寸
	rèyǐngxiǎng qūyù 热影响 区域		liǎngduān 两端
			liánjiēchù 连接处

学习课文 Text 27-02

Mùcè hànjiē jiéguǒ
目测 焊接 结果

Hànjiē wánchéng hòu, xiān yào jiǎnchá hànfèng, quèbǎo hànfèng
焊接 完成 后，先 要检查焊缝，确保焊缝
méiyǒu lièwén hé qìkǒng, hái yào tèbié zhùyì hànfèng liǎngduān hé
没有裂纹和 气孔，还要特别注意焊缝 两端和
liánjiēchù, bú yào chūxiàn jiāzhā huò yúgāo guò gāo de qíngkuàng.
连接处，不要出现夹渣 或 余高 过 高 的 情况。

Ránhòu, gēnjù túzhǐ yāoqiú jiǎncè hànfèng chǐcùn, quèbǎo
然后，根据图纸要求检测焊缝尺寸，确保
jiéguǒ fúhé yāoqiú.
结果符合 要求。

Zuìhòu, hái yào jiǎnchá rèyǐngxiǎng qūyù. Měi gè wèizhì dōu
最后，还要检查热影响区域。每个位置都
bù néng biànsè huò biànxíng.
不 能 变色 或 变形 。

Visually Inspecting Welding Results

After welding is completed, the welding seam should be inspected to ensure that there are no cracks or pores. Special attention should also be paid to both ends and connections of the welding seam to avoid slag inclusion or excess weld reinforcement.

Then, check the size of the welding seam in accordance with the requirements on the drawing to ensure that the result meets the specifications.

Finally, check the heat-affected area to ensure that there is no discoloration or deformation anywhere.

课文练习 Text Exercises

1. 根据课文内容判断正误。True or False.

1 焊缝应该出现裂纹和气孔。（ ）

2 焊接完，要检查焊缝两端和连接处，一定要出现夹渣或余高过高的情况。（ ）

3 焊缝尺寸应该符合图纸要求。（ ）

4 热影响区域的每个位置都要变色和变形。（ ）

2. 选择合适的词语填空。Choose the appropriate words to fill in the blanks.

A. 特别　　B. 焊缝尺寸　　C. 检查　　D. 热影响区域

1 焊接完成后，先要________焊缝，确保焊缝没有裂纹和气孔，还要________注意焊缝两端和连接处，不要出现夹渣或余高过高的情况。

2 然后，根据图纸要求检测________，确保结果符合要求。

3 最后，还要检查________。每个位置都不能变色或变形。

学习语法 Grammar

语法点 1 Grammar Point 1

程度副词：特别　The Adverb of Degree: 特别

意思是“非常、格外”，表示程度超过一般。

“特别” means “very” or “extraordinarily”. It indicates a degree exceeding the average.

1 Hái yào tèbié zhùyì hànfèng liǎngduān hé liánjiēchù, bú yào chūxiàn jiāzhā huò yúgāo guò gāo de qíngkuàng.
还要特别注意焊缝两端和连接处，不要出现夹渣或余高过高的情况。
Special attention should also be paid to both ends and connections of the welding seam to avoid slag inclusion or excess weld reinforcement.

2 Yào tèbié zhùyì píngkǒuqián de wèizhì hé fāngxiàng.
要特别注意平口钳的位置和方向。
Pay special attention to the position and direction of the flat nose holders.

3 Qǔ hàntiáo shí, yào tèbié zhùyì hàntiáo de wēndù.
取焊条时，要特别注意焊条的温度。
When taking welding rods, special attention should be paid to the temperature of the welding rods.

语法点 1 练习 Exercise on Grammar Point 1

为“特别”选择适当的位置。**Fill “特别” in the appropriate positions.**

例如： ___B___ hái yào（A）zhùyì（B）hànfèng liǎngduān hé liánjiēchù（C）。
还要（A）注意（B）焊缝两端和连接处（C）。

1 ________ （A）yào（B）zhùyì（C）píngkǒuqián de fāngxiàng hé wèizhì。
（A）要（B）注意（C）平口钳的方向和位置。

2 ________ qǔ hàntiáo shí,（A）yào（B）zhùyì hàntiáo de wēndù（C）。
取焊条时，（A）要（B）注意焊条的温度（C）。

3 ________ zài chējiān gōngzuò shí,（A）yào（B）zhùyì ānquán（C）。
在车间工作时，（A）要（B）注意安全（C）。

4 ________ ānzhuāng chēdāo shí,（A）yào（B）zhùyì chēdāo dāojiān de wèizhì（C）。
安装车刀时，（A）要（B）注意车刀刀尖的位置（C）。

语法点 2 Grammar Point 2

指示代词：每 The Demonstrative Pronoun: 每

表示特定范围内的任何一个或一组，侧重“全部”，强调个体之间的共性，常与“都”配合使用，构成“每……都……”格式。

“每” represents any individual or group within a specific range, emphasizing the concept of “all” and highlighting the commonalities among individuals. It is often used in conjunction with “都” to form the structure of “每……都……”.

1 Měi gè wèizhì dōu bù néng biànsè huò biànxíng.
每个位置都不能变色或变形。
There should be no discoloration or deformation anywhere.

2 Zhuāngjiā zhóulèi língjiàn shí, měi gè qiǎzhuǎ dōu yào nǐngjǐn.
装夹轴类零件时，每个卡爪都要拧紧。
When clamping shaft parts, each claw must be tightened.

3 Zài chējiān gōngzuò shí, měi gè yuángōng dōu yào chuān gōngzuòxié.
在车间工作时，每个员工都要穿工作鞋。
When working in the workshop, every employee is required to wear work shoes.

语法点 2 练习 Exercise on Grammar Point 2

用“每”回答问题，并朗读出来。**Answer the questions with “每” and read them aloud.**

例如：

Nǎxiē wèizhì bù néng yǒu biànsè huò biànxíng?
哪些位置不能有变色或变形？

Měi gè wèizhì dōu bù néng yǒu biànsè huò biànxíng.
每个位置都不能有变色或变形。

Zhuāngjiā zhóulèi língjiàn shí, nǎxiē qiǎzhuǎ yào nǐngjǐn?
1 装夹轴类零件时，哪些卡爪要拧紧？

____

Zài chējiān gōngzuò shí, nǎxiē yuángōng yào chuān gōngzuòxié?
2 在车间工作时，哪些员工要穿工作鞋？

____

Ānzhuāng chēdāo shí, nǎxiē yājǐn luóshuān yào sōngkāi?
3 安装车刀时，哪些压紧螺栓要松开？

____

Chēdāo fàngjìn dāojià lǐbian hòu, nǎxiē yājǐn luóshuān yào nǐngjǐn?
4 车刀放进刀架里边后，哪些压紧螺栓要拧紧？

____

汉字书写 Writing Chinese Characters

huā
花 花 花 花 花 花 花

花	花	花	花	花						

kǔ

苦 苦 苦 苦 苦 苦 苦 苦

苦 苦 苦 苦 苦

cǎo

草 草 草 草 草 草 草 草 草

草 草 草 草 草

chá

茶 茶 茶 茶 茶 茶 茶 茶 茶

茶 茶 茶 茶 茶

文化拓展 Culture Insight

饺子

饺子是中国人的传统美食。它的制作方法很简单：将多种原材料切碎调成馅儿，把和好的面擀成圆圆的面皮，再将馅儿包在面皮中，最后把包好的饺子放入水中煮熟，即可食用。

中国人非常喜欢吃饺子，各地习俗不同，饺子的品种也五花八门。有纯肉馅儿的、蔬菜馅儿的，也有菜肉馅儿的。沿海地区还喜欢用墨鱼、鲅鱼和黄鱼等做成馅料包饺子。每逢节假日，中国人的餐桌上总免不了一大碗热气腾腾的饺子。所以，每年的冬至、春节，吃饺子也就成了中国人的重要习俗。此外，饺子也有团圆的寓意，每当外地的游子回家时，一家人也会吃上一碗美味可口的饺子。

Dumplings

Dumplings are a traditional Chinese delicacy, made using a simple method: finely chop various ingredients and mix them into a filling; flatten the dough into round wrappers; wrap the filling in the wrapper; and finally, place the wrapped dumplings in boiling water until they are fully cooked and ready to be enjoyed.

Chinese people love to eat dumplings very much. The customs vary in different regions, and there are also a variety of dumplings. There are meat dumplings, vegetable dumplings, as well as mixed vegetable and meat dumplings. Coastal areas also like to make dumplings with squid, mackerel, and yellow croaker. On festival days, Chinese people always have a large bowl of steaming dumplings on their dining table, and eating dumplings has become an important custom for Chinese people every year during the Winter Solstice and Spring Festival. In addition, dumplings also have the meaning of reunion. Whenever the wanderers return home from afar, the whole family will also eat delicious dumplings.

小结 Summary

词语 Words

朗读下列词语。**Read the following words.**

裂纹	气孔	夹渣	余高
过高	每	变色	变形

语法 Grammar

选择合适的词语填空。Choose the appropriate words to fill in the blanks.

A. 特别　　B. 每

1. 还要（　　）注意焊缝两端和连接处，不要出现夹渣或余高过高的情况。
2. 要（　　）注意平口钳的位置和方向。
3. （　　）个位置都不能变色或变形。
4. 装夹轴类零件时，（　　）个卡爪都要拧紧。

课文理解 Text Comprehension

根据课文内容填空。Fill in the blanks according to the text.

1. 焊接完成后，先要检查焊缝，确保焊缝没有________和________，还要特别注意________和________，不要出现夹渣或余高过高的情况。
2. 然后，根据图纸要求检测________，确保结果________。
3. 最后，还要检查________。每个位置都不能________。

第28课 Lesson 28

Chāoshēngbō jiǎncè

超声波检测

Ultrasonic Testing

复习 Revision

认读词语。**Recognize the words.**

裂纹

夹渣

气孔

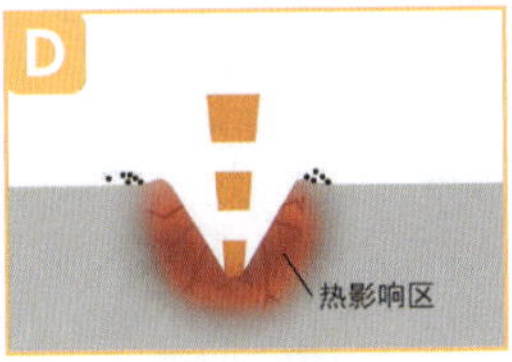

热影响区域

热身 Warm-up

选择正确的图片。**Choose the right pictures.**

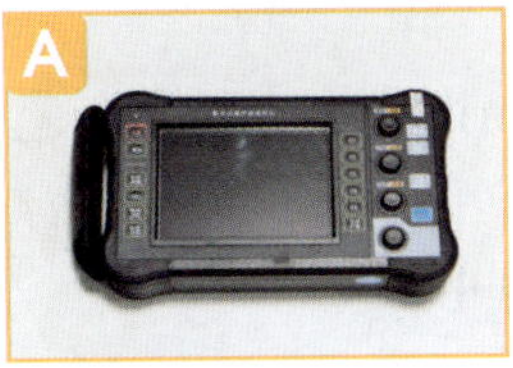

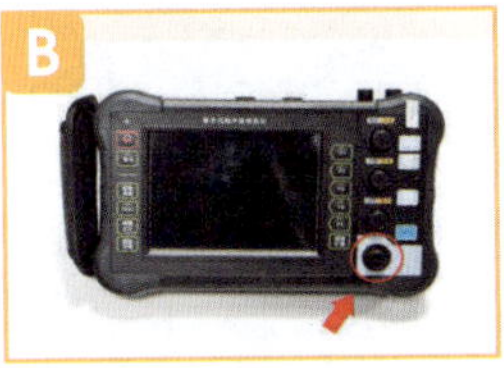

❶ 探头 (tàntóu) probe　　(　　)

❷ 水平 旋钮 (shuǐpíng xuánniǔ) horizontal knob （　　）

❸ 超声波 检测仪 (chāoshēngbō jiǎncèyí) ultrasonic detector （　　）

❹ 耦合剂 (ǒuhéjì) coupling agent （　　）

学习生词 Words and Expressions 28-01

1	超声波检测	chāoshēngbō jiǎncè	*phr.*	ultrasonic testing
2	比	bǐ	*prep.*	to compare
3	高效	gāoxiào	*adj.*	efficient
4	准确	zhǔnquè	*adj.*	accurate
5	超声波检测仪	chāoshēngbō jiǎncèyí	*phr.*	ultrasonic detector
6	水平旋钮	shuǐpíng xuánniǔ	*phr.*	horizontal knob
7	探头	tàntóu	*n.*	probe
8	中心线	zhōngxīnxiàn	*n.*	center line
9	水平面	shuǐpíngmiàn	*n.*	horizontal plane
10	耦合剂	ǒuhéjì	*n.*	coupling agent
11	填充	tiánchōng	*v.*	to fill

12	拿着	názhe	*phr.*	to hold
13	扫描	sǎomiáo	*v.*	to scan
14	区域	qūyù	*n.*	area
15	查看	chákàn	*v.*	to check

词语练习 Word Exercises

1. 判断图片与词语是否相符。**Judge whether the pictures match the words.**

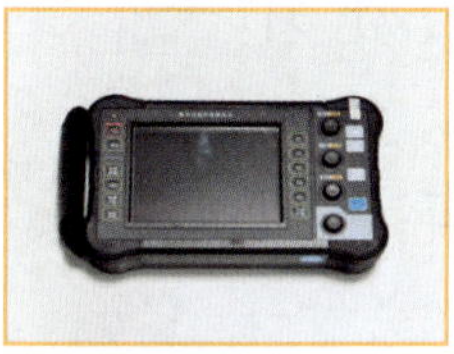

超声波检测仪 (　　)

耦合剂 (　　)

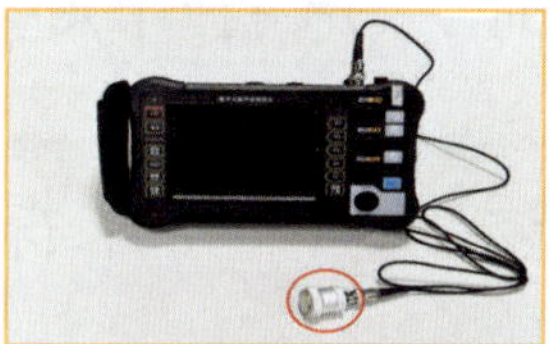

探头 (　　)

水平旋钮 (　　)

2. 词语连线。**Word Matching.**

xuánzhuǎn 旋转	tàntóu 探头
názhe 拿着	shuǐpíng xuánniǔ 水平 旋钮
chákàn 查看	hànfèng qūyù 焊缝 区域
sǎomiáo 扫描	hànjiē jiéguǒ 焊接 结果

学习课文 Text 28-02

Chāoshēngbō jiǎncè
超声波检测

Chāoshēngbō jiǎncè hànfèng bǐ mùcè hànfèng gāoxiào、zhǔnquè.
超声波检测焊缝比目测焊缝高效、准确。

Jiǎncè qián, xiān dǎkāi chāoshēngbō jiǎncèyí de diànyuán kāiguān,
检测前，先打开超声波检测仪的电源开关，

xuánzhuǎn shuǐpíng xuánniǔ, quèbǎo tàntóu zhōngxīnxiàn gēn shuǐpíngmiàn chuízhí.
旋转水平旋钮，确保探头中心线跟水平面垂直。

Ránhòu, bǎ ǒuhéjì tiánchōng dào tàntóu hé hànfèng zhījiān.
然后，把耦合剂填充到探头和焊缝之间。

Yòng shǒu názhe tàntóu, sǎomiáo hànfèng qūyù, chákàn hànjiē jiéguǒ.
用手拿着探头，扫描焊缝区域，查看焊接结果。

Ultrasonic Testing

Ultrasonic testing of welding seams is more efficient and accurate than visual inspection.

Before testing, turn on the power switch of the ultrasonic detector, rotate the horizontal knob, and ensure that the center line of the probe is perpendicular to the horizontal plane. Then, fill the coupling agent between the probe and the welding seam.

Hold the probe by hand and scan the welding area to check the welding results.

课文练习 Text Exercises

1. 根据课文内容判断正误。True or False.

1 超声波检测前，首先要打开超声波检测仪的电源开关，然后再按下启动按钮。 (　　)

2 探头的中心线要与水平面垂直。 (　　)

3 耦合剂要填充到水平旋钮和焊缝之间。 (　　)

4 超声波检测时，要用手拿着探头，用探头扫描焊缝区域。 (　　)

2. 选择合适的词语填空。Choose the appropriate words to fill in the blanks.

A. 高效　　B. 耦合剂　　C. 垂直　　D. 电源开关　　E. 扫描

1 超声波检测焊缝比目测焊缝________、准确。

2 检测前，先打开超声波检测仪的________，旋转水平旋钮，确保探头中心线跟水平面________。然后，把________填充到探头和焊缝之间。

3 用手拿着探头，________焊缝区域，查看焊接结果。

学习语法 Grammar

语法点 1 Grammar Point 1

比较句：A 比 B + 形容词 Comparative Sentence: A 比 B + Adjective

表示 A 在某方面的程度超过 B。

It indicates that A exceeds B in a certain aspect.

Chāoshēngbō jiǎncè hànfèng bǐ mùcè hànfèng gāoxiào.
1 超声波 检测 焊缝 比目测 焊缝 高效。
Ultrasonic testing of welding seams is more efficient than visual inspection.

Chāoshēngbō jiǎncè jiéguǒ bǐ mùcè jiéguǒ zhǔnquè.
2 超声波 检测 结果比目测结果 准确。
Ultrasonic testing results are more accurate than visual inspection results.

Rúguǒ yào qīnglǐ hànfèng shang de xiùjì, gāngsīshuā bǐ píngtóu zànzi héshì.
3 如果 要 清理 焊缝 上 的锈迹，钢丝刷 比 平头錾子合适。
If you want to clean the rust on the welding seam, a wire brush is more suitable than a flat chisel.

语法点 1 练习 Exercise on Grammar Point 1

用“比”回答问题，并朗读出来。**Answer the questions with “比”, and read them aloud.**

例如：

Chāoshēngbō jiǎncè hànfèng hé mùcè hànfèng, nǎge gāoxiào?
超声波 检测 焊缝 和 目测 焊缝，哪个 高效？

Chāoshēngbō jiǎncè hànfèng bǐ mùcè hànfèng gāoxiào.
超声波 检测 焊缝 比目测 焊缝 高效。

Chāoshēngbō jiǎncè hànfèng hé mùcè hànfèng, nǎge zhǔnquè?
1 超声波 检测 焊缝 和目测 焊缝，哪个 准确？

____

Rúguǒ yào qīnglǐ hànfèng shang de xiùjì, gāngsīshuā hé píngtóu zànzi nǎge héshì?
2 如果 要 清理 焊缝 上 的锈迹，钢丝刷 和 平头 錾子 哪个合适？

____

Rúguǒ yào cuòxiāo píngmiàn, biǎncuò hé sānjiǎocuò nǎge héshì?
3 如果 要 锉削 平面，扁锉 和 三角锉 哪个合适？

____

Rúguǒ yào cuòxiāo nèiyuánhúmiàn, bànyuáncuò hé sānjiǎocuò nǎge héshì?
4 如果 要 锉削 内圆弧面，半圆锉 和 三角锉 哪个合适？

____

语法点 2 Grammar Point 2

持续态：V + 着 Continuous Tense: V + 着

表示某种动作或状态的持续。

"V +着" indicates the continuation of a certain action or state.

Yòng shǒu názhe tàntóu sǎomiáo hànfèng qūyù, chákàn hànjiē jiéguǒ.
1 用 手 拿着探头 扫描 焊缝 区域，查看 焊接 结果。
Hold the probe by hand and scan the welding area to check the welding results.

Jiékè chuānzhe gōngzuòfú.
2 杰克 穿着 工作服。 Jack is wearing the work clothes.

jīchuáng kāizhe.
3 机床 开着。 The machine tool is on.

语法点 2 练习 Exercise on Grammar Point 2

为“着”选择适当的位置。**Fill “着” in the appropriate positions.**

例如： B
yòng shǒu ná tàntóu sǎomiáo hànfèng qūyù
用（A）手拿（B）探头（C）扫描 焊缝区域。

1. ________ （A）杰克（B）穿（C）工作服。
   Jiékè chuān gōngzuòfú
2. ________ （A）机床（B）开（C）。
   jīchuáng kāi
3. ________ （A）右手（B）拿（C）工件。
   yòushǒu ná gōngjiàn
4. ________ （A）左手 手掌（B）压（C）锉刀的另一端。
   zuǒshǒu shǒuzhǎng yā cuòdāo de lìng yì duān

汉字书写 Writing Chinese Characters

mén 门 门 门
门 门 门 门 门

men 们 们 们 们 们
们 们 们 们 们

wèn 问 问 问 问 问 问
问 问 问 问 问

jiān 间 间 间 间 间 间 间
间 间 间 间 间

职业拓展 Career Insight

电磁脉冲焊接

电磁脉冲焊接是一种先进的焊接技术。它可通过洛伦兹力产生的强大能量，把熔点相差很大的异种金属在 20 μs 内焊接在一起，形成原子间的结合。和电弧焊、二保焊、氩弧焊相比，电磁脉冲焊接在焊接过程中没有热输入，不会造成材料物理特性的损失，焊缝强度还可大于较弱一方母材的强度。

在中国，电磁脉冲焊接已广泛运用于新能源汽车领域，如电池的焊接和回收、汽车车身结构轻量化设计，以及高端医药行业。

Electromagnetic Pulse Welding

Electromagnetic pulse welding is an advanced welding technology. It can use the powerful energy generated by the Lorentz force to weld dissimilar metals with significantly different melting points together in just 20 microseconds, forming a bond between atoms. Compared with arc welding, CO_2 welding, and argon arc welding, electromagnetic pulse welding has no heat input during the welding process and does not cause the loss of physical properties of the material. Moreover, the strength of the weld can also be greater than that of the weaker parent material.

In China, electromagnetic pulse welding has been widely used in the field of new energy vehicles, such as welding and recycling of batteries, lightweight design of automotive body structures, and high-end pharmaceutical industries.

小结 Summary

词语 Words

朗读下列词语。Read the following words.

超声波检测仪	水平旋钮	探头	中心线
水平面	耦合剂	填充	扫描

语法 Grammar

熟读句子。Read the following sentences.

1. 超声波检测焊缝比目测焊缝高效。
2. 如果要清理焊缝上的锈迹，钢丝刷比平头錾子合适。
3. 用手拿着探头扫描焊缝区域，查看焊接结果。
4. 杰克穿着工作服。

课文理解 Text Comprehension

选择合适的词语。Choose the appropriate words.

1. 超声波检测焊缝（A. 比　B. 和）目测焊缝高效、准确。
2. 检测前，先打开超声波检测仪的（A. 电源开关　B. 急停按钮），（A. 旋转　B. 按下）水平旋钮，确保探头中心线跟水平面（A. 垂直　B. 贴合）。然后，把耦合剂填充到探头和焊缝之间。
3. 用手（A. 拿着　B. 压着）探头，扫描焊缝区域，查看焊接结果。

Zhǔnbèi èrbǎohàn

第29课 准备二保焊

Lesson 29 Preparing for CO_2 Welding

复习 Revision

认读词语。Recognize the words.

水平旋钮

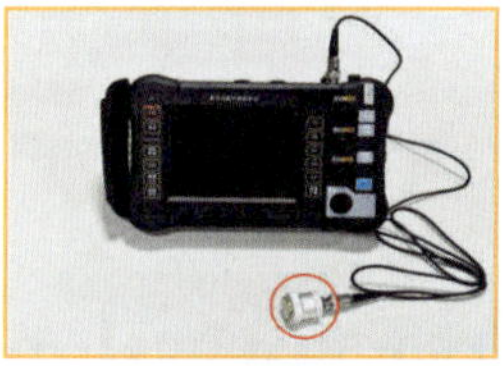

探头

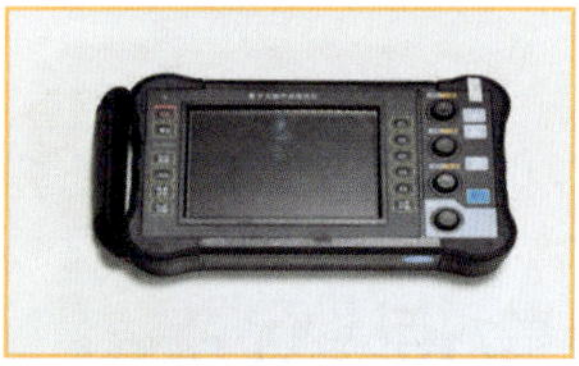

超声波检测仪

耦合剂

热身 Warm-up

选择正确的图片。Choose the right pictures.

A

B

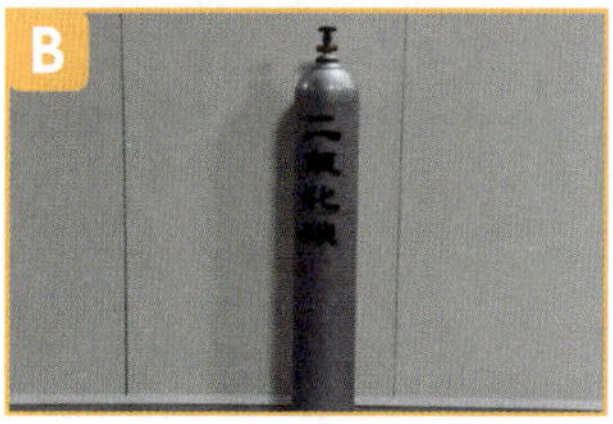

C

D

E
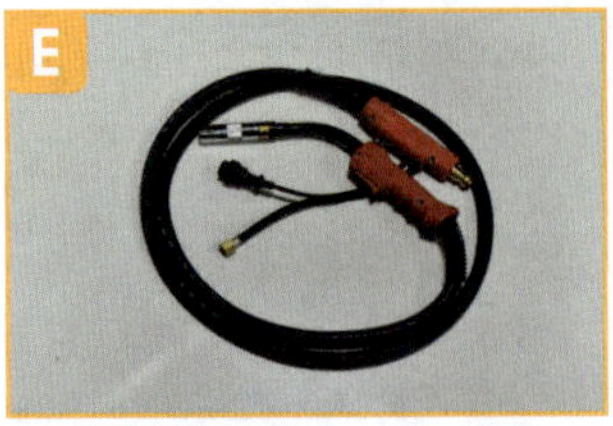

F
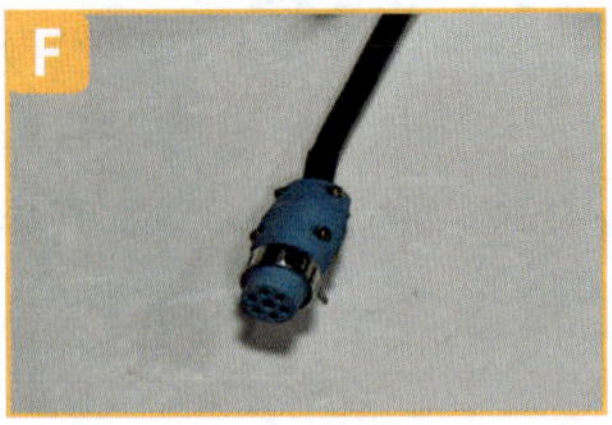

❶	èrbǎohànqiāng 二保焊枪	CO_2 welding torch	(　　)
❷	tōngxìn diànlǎn 通信 电缆	communication cable	(　　)
❸	hànsī 焊丝	welding wire	(　　)
❹	sòngsījī 送丝机	wire feeder	(　　)
❺	qìliúbiǎo 气流表	airflow meter	(　　)
❻	qìpíng 气瓶	gas cylinder	(　　)

学习生词 Words and Expressions 29-01

1	二保焊	èrbǎohàn	*n.*	CO_2 welding
2	二保焊机	èrbǎohànjī	*n.*	CO_2 welding machine
3	焊丝	hànsī	*n.*	welding wire
4	送丝机	sòngsījī	*n.*	wire feeder
5	气流表	qìliúbiǎo	*n.*	airflow meter
6	气瓶	qìpíng	*n.*	gas cylinder
7	通信电缆	tōngxìn diànlǎn	*phr.*	communication cable

8	二保焊枪	èrbǎohànqiāng	*n.*	CO_2 welding torch
9	枪缆	qiānglǎn	*n.*	welding torch cable
10	务必	wùbì	*adv.*	surely
11	一旦……， 就……	yídàn…， jiù…		once ... (then) ...
12	小于	xiǎoyú	*v.*	less than
13	更换	gēnghuàn	*v.*	to replace

词语练习 Word Exercises

1. 看图选词。Look at the pictures and choose the correct words.

❶ 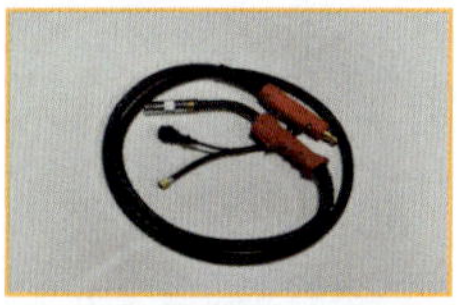 (　　) A. 二保焊枪　B. 焊钳

❷ 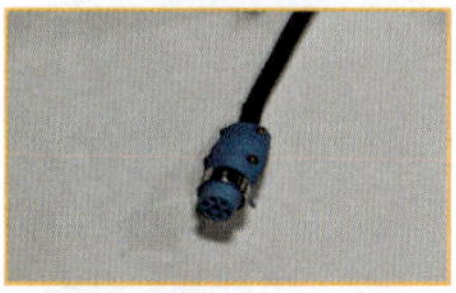 (　　) A. 地线　B. 通信电缆

❸  (　　) A. 焊丝　B. 地线夹

❹  (　　) A. 送丝机　B. 焊机

2. 词语连线。 **Word Matching.**

zhǔnbèi 准备	qìpíng 气瓶
ānzhuāng 安装	qìliúbiǎo 气流表
zhùyì 注意	qìliúbiǎo de shùzhí 气流表的 数值
gēnghuàn 更换	èrbǎohàn 二保焊

学习课文 Text 29-02

Zhǔnbèi èrbǎohàn
准备二保焊

Xiān bǎ dìxiànjiā liánjiē dào èrbǎohànjī de fùjí jiēkǒu
先把地线夹连接到二保焊机的负极接口
shang, bǎ hànsī zhuāngjìn sòngsījī li, bǎ qìliúbiǎo ānzhuāng dào
上，把焊丝装进送丝机里，把气流表安装到
qìpíng shang.
气瓶上。

Ránhòu, liánjiē sòngsījī de tōngxìn diànlǎn hé èrbǎohànjī,
然后，连接送丝机的通信电缆和二保焊机，
zài bǎ èrbǎohànqiāng de qiānglǎn liánjiē dào sòngsījī shang.
再把二保焊枪的枪缆连接到送丝机上。

Hànjiē qián, wùbì zhùyì qìliúbiǎo de shùzhí. yídàn
焊接前，务必注意气流表的数值。一旦

shùzhí xiǎoyú 3 MPa, jiù yào gēnghuàn qìpíng.
数值小于 3 MPa，就要更换气瓶。

Preparing for CO_2 Welding

First, connect the ground wire clamp to the negative electrode interface of the CO_2 welding machine. Insert the welding wire into the wire feeder. Install the airflow meter onto the gas cylinder.

Then, connect the communication cable of the wire feeder to the CO_2 welding machine, and then connect the cable of the CO_2 welding torch to the wire feeder.

Before welding, sure to pay attention to the value of the airflow meter. Once the value is less than 3MPa, the gas cylinder needs to be replaced.

课文练习 Text Exercises

1. 根据课文内容选择正确答案。Choose the correct answers according to the text.

1 准备二保焊时，要把地线夹连接到二保焊机的________上。

A. 正极接口　　　B. 负极接口

2 气流表要安装到________上。

A. 气瓶　　　B. 气孔

3 连接________的通信电缆和二保焊机。

A. 送丝机　　B. 焊机

4 一旦气流表的数值小于 3 MPa，就要________气瓶。

A. 更换　　B. 安装

2. 根据课文内容判断正误。True or False.

1 焊接前，要把焊丝装进送丝机里。（　　）

2 焊接前，要确保气流表的数值不小于 3 MPa。（　　）

3 二保焊枪的枪缆要连接到二保焊机上。（　　）

4 气流表要连接到二保焊机的正极接口上。（　　）

学习语法 Grammar

语法点 1 Grammar Point 1

程度副词：务必 The Adverb of Degree: 务必

意思是“一定、必须”。

“务必” means “must” or “should”.

1 Hànjiē qián wùbì zhùyì qìliúbiǎo de shùzhí.
焊接前，务必注意气流表的数值。
Before welding, closely monitor the airflow meter readings.

2 Zài chējiān gōngzuò shí, wùbì zhùyì ānquán.
在车间工作时，务必注意安全。
Safety must be strictly when working in the workshop.

3 Jiǎncè píngmiàndù shí, gāodùchǐ wùbì tiējǐn píngtái.
检测平面度时，高度尺务必贴紧平台。
When testing the planeness, the height gauge must be tightly attached to the platform.

语法点 1 练习 Exercise on Grammar Point 1

用“务必”改写下列句子，并朗读出来。**Rewrite the following sentences with “务必” and read them aloud.**

例如：
Hànjiē qián bìxū zhùyì qìliúbiǎo de shùzhí.
焊接前，必须注意气流表的数值。
Hànjiē qián wùbì zhùyì qìliúbiǎo de shùzhí.
焊接前，务必注意气流表的数值。

1. Zài chējiān gōngzuò shí, yídìng yào zhùyì ānquán.
在车间工作时，一定要注意安全。
____

2. Qǔ hàntiáo shí, bìxū yào zhùyì hàntiáo de wēndù.
取焊条时，必须要注意焊条的温度。
____

3. Jiǎncè píngmiàndù shí, gāodùchǐ bìxū tiējǐn píngtái.
检测平面度时，高度尺必须贴紧平台。
____

4. Chēdāo ānzhuāng wánchéng yǐhòu, yídìng yào jiǎnchá chēdāo dāojiān de wèizhì.
车刀安装完成以后，一定要检查车刀刀尖的位置。
____

语法点 2 Grammar Point 2

假设复句：一旦……，就……

Hypothetical Compound Sentence: 一旦……，就……

表示如果有新情况出现，事情就会随着新情况的产生而发生变化。

“一旦……，就……” means that if any changes occur, things will change accordingly.

Yídàn qìliúbiǎo de shùzhí xiǎoyú 3 MPa, jiù yào gēnghuàn qìpíng.
1 一旦气流表的数值小于 3 MPa，就要更换气瓶。
Once the airflow meter reading is less than 3MPa, the gas cylinder needs to be replaced.

Yídàn hànfèng shang yǒu yàopí, jiù yào yòng gāngsīshuā qīnglǐ.
2 一旦焊缝上有药皮，就要用钢丝刷清理。
Once there is flux coating on the welding seam, it needs to be cleaned with a wire brush.

Yídàn hànfèng shang yǒu huīchén, jiù yào yòng qīngjiébù cāshì.
3 一旦焊缝上有灰尘，就要用清洁布擦拭。
Once there is dust on the welding seam, it should be wiped with a cleaning cloth.

语法点 2 练习 Exercise on Grammar Point 2

用"一旦……，就……"改写下列句子，并朗读出来。**Rewrite the following sentences with "一旦……，就……" and read them aloud.**

例如：

Rúguǒ qìliúbiǎo de shùzhí xiǎoyú 3 MPa, jiù yào gēnghuàn qìpíng.
如果气流表的数值小于 3 MPa，就要更换气瓶。

Yídàn qìliúbiǎo de shùzhí xiǎoyú 3 MPa, jiù yào gēnghuàn qìpíng.
一旦气流表的数值小于 3 MPa，就要更换气瓶。

Rúguǒ hànfèng shang yǒu yàopí, jiù yào yòng gāngsīshuā qīnglǐ.
1 如果焊缝上有药皮，就要用钢丝刷清理。

____

Rúguǒ hànfèng shang yǒu huīchén, jiù yào yòng qīngjiébù cāshì.
2 如果焊缝上有灰尘，就要用清洁布擦拭。

____

Rúguǒ hànfèng shang yǒu āotūchù, jiù yào yòng dǎmójī dǎmó.
3 如果焊缝上有凹凸处，就要用打磨机打磨。

____

Rúguǒ hànfèng shang yǒu hànliú, jiù yào yòng qiāozhāchuí qiāopíng,
4 如果焊缝上有焊瘤，就要用敲渣锤敲平。

____

汉字书写 Writing Chinese Characters

yě 也 也 也

也 也 也 也 也

tā 他 他 他 他 他

他 他 他 他 他

tā 她 她 她 她 她 她

她 她 她 她 她

dì 地 地 地 地 地 地

地 地 地 地 地

文化拓展 Culture Insight

袁隆平

袁隆平，1930 年出生，中国著名的农学家，被誉为“杂交水稻之父”。他成功地培育出了世界上第一个高产的杂交水稻品种，这一品种被称为“超级稻”，并于 1973 年开始在中国大面积推广。袁隆平也因此于 2019 年获得“共和国勋章”。

随着世界人口的增长，人们对食品的需求越来越高。杂交水稻在许多国家，尤其是中国等亚非国家得到了大力推广。目前，杂交水稻已累计推广到印度、印度尼西亚、越南、菲律宾、美国、巴西等 70 多个国家，国外年种植面积近 800 万公顷。

Yuan Longping

Yuan Longping, born in 1930, is a famous Chinese agronomist and known as the "Father of Hybrid Rice". He successfully cultivated the world's first high-yielding hybrid rice variety, which was known as "super rice" and began to be widely popularized in China starting 1973. Yuan Longping was therefore awarded the "Medal of the Republic" in 2019.

With the growth of the world's population, there is an increasing demand for food, and hybrid rice has been popularized in many countries, especially in Asian and African countries such as China. At present, hybrid rice has been popularized in more than 70 countries, including India, Indonesia, Vietnam, the Philippines, the United States, and Brazil, with an annual planting area abroad of nearly 8 million hectares.

小结 Summary

词语 Words

朗读下列词语。Read the following words.

二保焊	二保焊机	焊丝	送丝机	气流表
气瓶	通信电缆	枪缆	务必	一旦……，就……

语法 Grammar

熟读句子。Read the following sentences.

1. 焊接前，务必注意气流表的数值。
2. 检测平面度时，高度尺务必贴紧平台。
3. 一旦气流表的数值小于 3 MPa，就要更换气瓶。
3. 一旦焊缝上有药皮，就要用钢丝刷清理。

课文理解 Text Comprehension

回答问题。Answer the questions.

1. 准备二保焊有几步？

____

2. 当气流表的数值小于 3 MPa 时，要做什么？

____

Èrbǎohàn de cāozuò

第30课 二保焊的操作

Lesson 30 Operating CO_2 Welding

复习 Revision

认读词语。**Recognize the words.**

气流表

气瓶

送丝机

焊丝

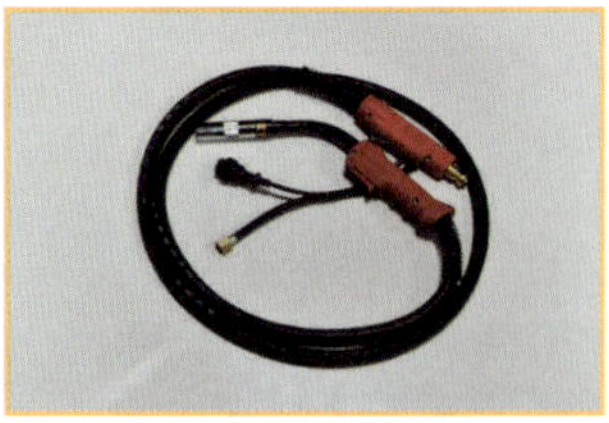

二保焊枪

通信电缆

热身 Warm-up

选择正确的图片。**Choose the right pictures.**

A

B
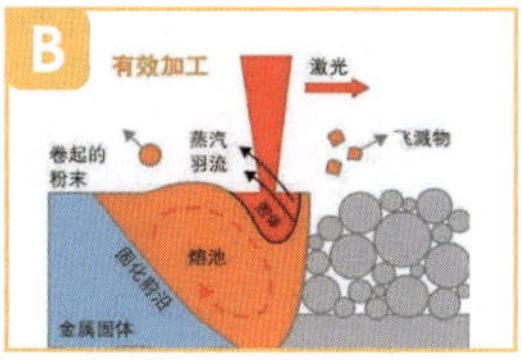

C

D
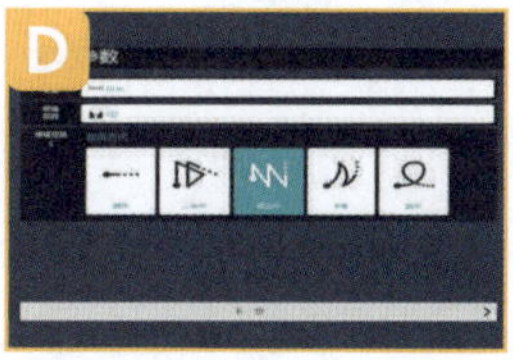

❶ 熔池 (róngchí) molten pool ( )　❷ 角焊缝 (jiǎohànfèng) fillet weld ( )

❸ 锯齿摆弧法 (jùchǐ bǎihúfǎ) sawtooth oscillation method ( )

❹ 咬边 (yǎobiān) undercutting ( )

学习生词 Words and Expressions 30-01

1	调节	tiáojié	*v.*	to adjust
2	参数	cānshù	*n.*	parameter
3	扣动	kòudòng	*v.*	to press
4	摆动	bǎidòng	*v.*	to swing
5	锯齿摆弧法	jùchǐ bǎihúfǎ	*phr.*	sawtooth oscillation method
6	角焊缝	jiǎohànfèng	*n.*	fillet weld
7	始终	shǐzhōng	*adv.*	always
8	角度	jiǎodù	*n.*	angle

9	电弧	diànhú	*n.*	electric arc
10	长度	chángdù	*n.*	length
11	速度	sùdù	*n.*	speed
12	熔池	róngchí	*n.*	molten pool
13	温度	wēndù	*n.*	temperature
14	咬边	yǎobiān	*n.*	undercutting

词语练习 Word Exercises

1. 判断图片与词语是否相符。**Judge whether the pictures match the words.**

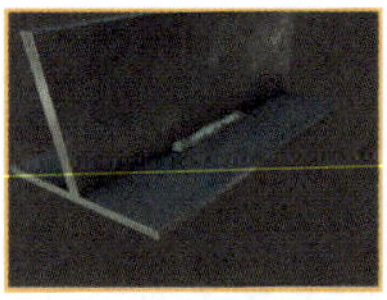

角焊缝 (　　)

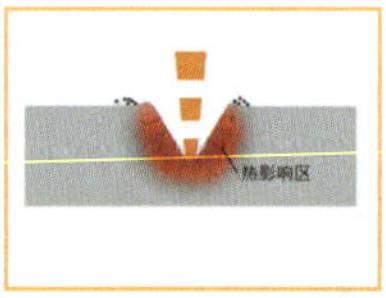

熔池 (　　)

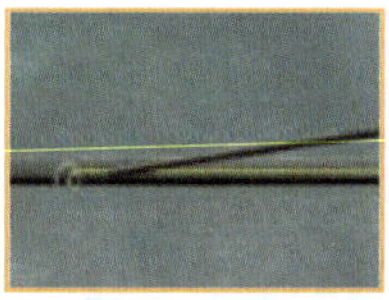

锯齿摆弧法 (　　)

咬边 (　　)

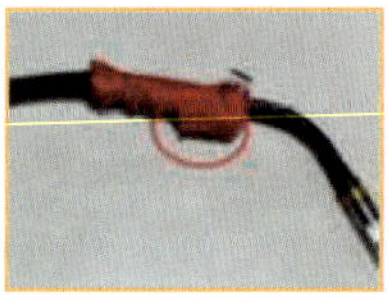

焊枪按钮 (　　)

2. 词语连线。**Word Matching.**

tiáojié 调节	ànniǔ 按钮
kòudòng 扣动	cānshù 参数
bǎochí 保持	hànqiāng 焊枪
bǎidòng 摆动	sùdù 速度

学习课文 Text 30-02

Èrbǎohàn de cāozuò
二保焊的操作

Tiáojié èrbǎohànjī hé sòngsījī de cānshù, kòudòng
调节 二保焊机 和 送丝机 的 参数，扣动
èrbǎohànqiāng de ànniǔ qǐhú.
二保焊枪 的 按钮 起弧。

Bǎidòng hànqiāng, yòng jùchǐ bǎihúfǎ hànjiē jiǎohànfèng.
摆动 焊枪，用锯齿摆弧法 焊接 角焊缝。

Hànjiē shí, yīnggāi shǐzhōng bǎochí héshì de hànjiē jiǎodù、
焊接时，应该 始终 保持合适的焊接角度、
diànhú chángdù hé hànjiē sùdù, bìngqiě yào zhùyì róngchí wēndù,
电弧长度和焊接速度，并且要注意熔池温度，
búyào chūxiàn yǎobiān.
不要出现 咬边。

Hànjiē hòu, bùjǐn yào qīnglǐ hànfèng, hái yào duì hànfèng
焊接后，不仅要清理焊缝，还要对焊缝
zhìliàng jìnxíng jiǎncè.
质量进行检测。

Operating CO_2 Welding

Adjust the parameters of the CO_2 welding machine and wire feeder, and press the button of the CO_2 welding torch to start the arc.

Swing the welding torch and weld the fillet weld using the sawtooth oscillation method.

When welding, always maintain the proper welding angle, arc length and welding speed, and pay attention to the temperature of the molten pool to avoid undercutting.

After welding, it is not only necessary to clean the welding seam, but also to check the quality of the welding seam.

课文练习 Text Exercises

1. 选择合适的词语。Choose the appropriate words to fill in the blanks.

1. 焊接时，应该保持合适的焊接（A. 角度　B. 长度）、电弧（A. 长度　B. 速度）和焊接（A. 速度　B. 温度）。
2. 扣动（A. 探头　B. 按钮）开始焊接。
3. 调节焊机和送丝机的参数（A. 前　B. 后），摆动焊枪起弧。
4. 焊接时，应该注意熔池的（A. 温度　B. 角度）。

2. 选择合适的词语填空。**Choose the appropriate words to fill in the blanks.**

A. 起弧　B. 始终　C. 咬边　D. 参数　E. 角焊缝

1 焊接前，先调节二保焊机和送丝机的________，再扣动二保焊枪的按钮________。摆动焊枪，用锯齿摆弧法焊接________。

2 焊接时，应该________保持合适的焊接角度、电弧长度和焊接速度，并且要注意熔池温度，不要出现________。

学习语法 Grammar

语法点 1 Grammar Point 1

副词：始终　The Adverb: 始终

表示从开始到结束的整个过程持续不变。

"始终" means that the entire process remains unchanged from beginning to end.

1 Hànjiē shí, yīnggāi shǐzhōng bǎochí héshì de hànjiē jiǎodù、 diànhú chángdù hé hànjiē sùdù.
焊接时，应该始终保持合适的焊接角度、电弧长度和焊接速度。
When welding, always maintain the proper welding angle, arc length and welding speed.

2 Zài chējiān gōngzuò shí, yào shǐzhōng dàihǎo ānquánmào.
在车间工作时，要始终戴好安全帽。
When working in the workshop, always wear a safety cap/helmet.

3 Hànjiē shí, yào shǐzhōng dàihǎo hànjiē miànzhào.
焊接时，要始终戴好焊接面罩。
When welding, always wear a welding mask.

语法点 1 练习　Exercise on Grammar Point 1

用“始终”改写下列句子，并朗读出来。**Rewrite the following sentences with “始终” and read them aloud.**

例如：

Hànjiē shí yīnggāi bǎochí héshì de hànjiē jiǎodù、 diànhú chángdù hé hànjiē sùdù.
焊接时，应该保持合适的焊接角度、电弧长度和焊接速度。

Hànjiē shí yīnggāi shǐzhōng bǎochí héshì de hànjiē jiǎodù、 diànhú chángdù hé hànjiē sùdù.
焊接时，应该始终保持合适的焊接角度、电弧长度和焊接速度。

1. Zài chējiān gōngzuò shí, yào dàihǎo ānquánmào.
在车间工作时，要戴好安全帽。

____

2. Hànjiē shí, yào dàihǎo hànjiē miànzhào.
焊接时，要戴好焊接面罩。

____

3. Jīchuáng jiāgōng shí, yào dàihǎo fánghù yǎnjìng.
机床加工时，要戴好防护眼镜。

____

4. Huàxiàn shí, gōngjiàn yào tiējǐn fāngxiāng.
划线时，工件要贴紧方箱。

____

语法点 2 Grammar Point 2

递进复句：不仅……，还……

Progressive Compound Sentence: 不仅……，还……

表示进一步申述说明，后一分句的意思比前一分句的意思更进一层。

"不仅……，还……" indicates further explanation, with the meaning of the second clause going a step further than that of the first.

1. Hànjiē hòu, bùjǐn yào qīnglǐ hànfèng, hái yào duì hànfèng zhìliàng jìnxíng jiǎncè.
焊接后，不仅要清理焊缝，还要对焊缝质量进行检测。
After welding, it is not only necessary to clean the welding seam, but also to check the quality of the welding seam.

2. Hànjiē hòu, bùjǐn yào jiǎnchá hànfèng, hái yào jiǎnchá rèyǐngxiǎng qūyù.
焊接后，不仅要检查焊缝，还要检查热影响区域。
After welding, not only the welding seam should be inspected, but also the heat affected area.

3. Cāozuò jīchuáng shí, bùjǐn yào chuānhǎo gōngzuòfú, hái yào zājǐn lǐngkǒu、xiùkǒu.
操作机床时，不仅要穿好工作服，还要扎紧领口、袖口。
When operating the machine tool, not only do you need to wear working clothes, but you also need to tighten the neckband and cuffs.

语法点 2 练习 Exercise on Grammar Point 2

用"不仅……，还……"改写下列句子，并朗读出来。**Rewrite the following sentences with "不仅……，还……" and read them aloud.**

例如：

Hànjiē hòu, yào qīnglǐ hànfèng. Hànjiē hòu, yào duì hànfèng zhìliàng jìnxíng jiǎncè.
①焊接后，要清理焊缝 ②焊接后，要对焊缝质量进行检测。

Hànjiē hòu, bùjǐn yào qīnglǐ hànfèng, hái yào duì hànfèng zhìliàng jìnxíng jiǎncè.
焊接后，不仅要清理焊缝，还要对焊缝质量进行检测。

1. Hànjiē hòu, yào jiǎnchá hànfèng. Hànjiē hòu, yào jiǎnchá rèyǐngxiǎng qūyù.
①焊接后，要检查焊缝。②焊接后，要检查热影响区域

____

Cāozuò jīchuáng shí, yào chuānhǎo gōngzuòfú. Cāozuò jīchuáng shí, yào zājǐn lǐngkǒu、xiùkǒu.

2 ①操作 机床 时，要 穿好 工作服。②操作 机床 时，要扎紧 领口、袖口。

Zuànkǒng shí, yào yìbiān zuàn, yìbiān páixiè. Zuànkǒng shí, yào yòng shuāzi qīnglǐ qiēxiè.

3 ①钻孔 时，要一边钻，一边排屑。② 钻孔 时，要 用 刷子清理 切屑。

Jiékè huì gàn qiángōng. Jiékè huì gàn hàngōng.

4 杰克会 干 钳工。②杰克会 干 焊工。

汉字书写 Writing Chinese Characters

shuǐ 水 水 水 水

水	水	水	水	水						

bīng 冰 冰 冰 冰 冰 冰

冰	冰	冰	冰	冰						

quán 泉 泉 泉 泉 泉 泉 泉 泉 泉

泉	泉	泉	泉	泉						

bèng 泵 泵 泵 泵 泵 泵 泵 泵 泵

泵	泵	泵	泵	泵						

职业拓展 Career Insight

精益化生产

精益化生产是由麻省理工学院提出的、适用于现代制造业的一种生产方式。它是一种先进的管理理念，以满足客户需求为目标，强调全员参与和持续改进，通过优化流程和精益求精，实现标准化作业。

精益化生产的本质就是及时制造，消灭故障，消除一切浪费，向零缺陷、零库存进军。据了解，企业推行精益化生产后，新产品的研发周期可以缩短一半，同时可减少一半的人力资源投入，并在此基础上大幅度提升产品合格率。

Lean Production

Lean production is a production method proposed by MIT, designed for modern manufacturing. It is an advanced management philosophy that aims to meet customer needs, emphasizes full participation and continuous improvement, and achieves standardized operations through process optimization and commitment to excellence.

The essence of lean production is timely manufacturing, eliminating faults and waste, and advancing towards zero defects and zero inventory. According to available information, after implementing lean production, enterprises can shorten the R&D cycle of new products by half, reduce human resource investment by half, and significantly improve product pass rate on this basis.

小结 Summary

词语 Words

朗读下列词语。**Read the following words.**

调节	扣动	参数	温度	角焊缝
角度	电弧	咬边	始终	不仅……，还……

语法 Grammar

熟读句子。**Read the following sentences.**

1. 焊接时，应该始终保持合适的焊接角度、电弧长度和焊接速度。
2. 在车间工作时，要始终戴好安全帽。
3. 焊接后，不仅要清理焊缝，还要对焊缝质量进行检测。
4. 焊接后，不仅要检查焊缝，还要检查热影响区域。

课文理解 Text Comprehension

回答问题。**Answer the questions.**

1. 二保焊操作前要做什么？
2. 二保焊操作时要注意什么？（用“始终”造句回答）
3. 二保焊的操作完成后要干什么？（用“不仅……，还……”造句回答）